T0288654

Chan and Gill have put into our hands a compelling work on the benefits of, and skills involved in, topical preaching. Anyone who loves preaching or wants to be better equipped to preach should read this book. I can't wait to use it to train preachers in Europe.

—**Cristian Barbosu,** Harvest Church of Arad, Romania

We need preachers who bring the bread of life to hungry people in a way that is true, biblical, winsome, and ultimately life-giving. Chan and Gill equip us with tools for this crucial task as they offer insight on how to proclaim Christ to a needy world. May we catch their vision.

—**Daryl Bay,** Hope Community Church, Nelson, New Zealand

For some, topical preaching is a black hole: needed, but who knows how to get in there and get through it well? This book effectively unpacks what is required homiletically, theologically, pastorally, and exegetically with an eye on the cultural requirements that make communication work. This is a book I have longed to have. Every preacher should step into the pulpit confidently with its wisdom in hand.

—**Darrell L. Bock,** Dallas Theological Seminary

Chan and Gill have made an incredible contribution to the study of preaching by providing a work that is fresh and faithful. With robust realism and penetrating insight, the authors provide a convincing case for the how and the why of topical preaching. Not only will I use this book with my preaching team at church, it will become a staple in my homiletics classes.

—**Bernie Cueto,** Palm Beach Atlantic University

I said I didn't believe in topical preaching. But the truth is, I didn't know how to do it while staying true to my convictions about preaching. At last, Chan and Gill have taught me how to construct topical sermons that are culturally and pastorally sensitive, scriptural, theological, and centered on Christ. This is the book that has been missing from the evangelical preacher's library. I am thankful it is no longer missing from mine.

—**Alison Gerber,** preacher; pastor; contributor to *Preaching Today*

For Chan and Gill, topical preaching in a complex world isn't as difficult as one might think. This helpful book provides markers for preachers to follow as they prepare to preach sermons that address—and need to address—issues facing congregations, the church, and wider society today and in the future.

—**Scott M. Gibson,** George W. Truett Theological Seminary

Chan and Gill have gifted the church and the academy with an outstanding resource that answers the many questions that loom large about topical preaching. This is the best homiletics book on the topic, bar none. Read it and respond to its wisdom for yourself and for the sake of your congregation.

—**Matthew D. Kim,** Gordon-Conwell Theological Seminary

Faithfully handling God's Word while addressing a topic well takes real skill. This great practical book unravels all the aspects involved and gives workable strategies for approaching each. The resources here are invaluable, and I'll be using them again and again.

—**Karen Morris,** Australian Fellowship of Evangelical Students

Chan and Gill winningly stretch our minds and perspectives regarding topical preaching. In doing so, they strengthen and expand our understanding of preaching and our call to contextualize and connect God's enduring truths with the current concerns of the world.

—**Rev. Laura Murray,** author, *Pray As You Are*

I will keep this book within arm's reach in my study. While pursuing 100 percent truth and 100 percent relevance, Gill and Chan remind us that topical preaching is worthwhile, timely, and needed to introduce the love and grace of Jesus to the world today. This is a stellar work that will have lasting impact.

—**Clay Scroggins,** author, *How to Lead When You're Not in Charge*

TOPICAL PREACHING IN A COMPLEX WORLD

HOW TO PROCLAIM TRUTH AND RELEVANCE AT THE SAME TIME

SAM CHAN AND MALCOLM GILL

ZONDERVAN
ACADEMIC

ZONDERVAN ACADEMIC

Topical Preaching in a Complex World
Copyright © 2021 by Sam Chan and Malcolm Gill

Requests for information should be addressed to:
Zondervan, *3900 Sparks Dr. SE, Grand Rapids, Michigan 49546*

Zondervan titles may be purchased in bulk for educational, business, fundraising, or sales promotional use. For information, please email SpecialMarkets@Zondervan.com.

ISBN 978-0-310-10887-0 (hardcover)

ISBN 978-0-310-10890-0 (softcover)

ISBN 978-0-310-10888-7 (ebook)

ISBN 978-0-310-13904-1 (audio)

All Scripture quotations, unless otherwise indicated, are taken from The Holy Bible, New International Version®, NIV®. Copyright © 1973, 1978, 1984, 2011 by Biblica, Inc.® Used by permission of Zondervan. All rights reserved worldwide. www.Zondervan.com. The "NIV" and "New International Version" are trademarks registered in the United States Patent and Trademark Office by Biblica, Inc.®

Any internet addresses (websites, blogs, etc.) and telephone numbers in this book are offered as a resource. They are not intended in any way to be or imply an endorsement by Zondervan, nor does Zondervan vouch for the content of these sites and numbers for the life of this book.

All rights reserved. No part of this publication may be reproduced, stored in a retrieval system, or transmitted in any form or by any means—electronic, mechanical, photocopy, recording, or any other—except for brief quotations in printed reviews, without the prior permission of the publisher.

Cover design: LUCAS Art & Design, Jenison, MI
Cover image: John Lucas
Interior design: Kait Lamphere

Printed in the United States of America

21 22 23 24 25 26 27 28 29 30 31 /LSC/ 15 14 13 12 11 10 9 8 7 6 5 4 3 2 1

From Sam:
To my wife, Stephanie,
who gives me the freedom to explore
(and who let me buy a motorbike)

To my boys Toby, Cooper, and Jonty,
who embrace chaos and fun
(and who occasionally do the laundry)

To my parents, Winnie (1939–2021) and Joseph,
who were my biggest fans, coming to
hear every sermon I preached
(and who reluctantly let me play rugby)

From Malcolm:
Para Tamara,
mi esposa, mi amor, mi corazón

CONTENTS

FOREWORD

Sometimes people try too hard to make their point. Take for instance rapper Shad Moss, aka Bow Wow, who unintentionally started a viral movement on social media after he posted a picture of a private jet implying that was the way he traveled. When someone posted a picture of him sitting on a commercial jet later the same day, people hammered Bow Wow for trying too hard to look successful. It led to a Twitter and Instagram trend called the #bowwowchallenge, where people posted two side-by-side pictures: one making their real life look more glamorous than it is and a second showing the reality of their situation. For example, someone might post a selfie from their relaxing beach vacation next to a zoomed-out picture showing they were actually lying on the sidewalk in front of an advertisement for some exotic location. The #bowwowchallenge was fun, but harmless.

When we try too hard, it often leads to unintended consequences. Followers of Jesus are known for loving their Bibles and affirming sound, biblical preaching. But in our attempts to stand on the Word and stand up for preaching, sometimes we try too hard.

Today we see preachers arguing that expository preaching verse by verse through books is *the* way to preach. To be fair, it is the primary way I preach, and I think it's the best way over time. But like the deceptive photos from the #bowwowchallenge, we fool ourselves and others if we claim it is the only way to preach God's Word faithfully.

Other valuable methods have been used by godly preachers throughout church history and in the Bible.

Sam Chan and Malcolm Gill push back against the notion that the only way to preach is verse by verse through books. While affirming biblical preaching in general and expository preaching in particular, the authors argue humbly yet winsomely that there are other ways to preach the Word of God faithfully.

Chan and Gill demonstrate how the renowned preachers of Christian history often did not measure up to current expository preaching standards. They are right when they say, "We need to think of our methods as siblings rather than combatants." Rather than viewing various preaching styles as right or wrong, they call the preacher to understand these methods as different ways to exercise cross-cultural wisdom.

John Stott shed light on our preaching task in the title of his book *Between Two Worlds.* As preachers of God's Word, we must bridge the worlds of Scripture and contemporary culture. When we speak of the biblical world to the neglect of today's context, we speak truth that may not communicate. When we speak to our context without a clear grounding in the Word, we communicate well, but without the necessary truth. Preaching must do both, and Chan and Gill help us to see ways to do this.

They write, "To preach well, we need to work on our exegesis of not only the Holy Scriptures but also the world in which we live. In preaching, we publicly engage with people as we seek to integrate the timeless truth of God's grace in Jesus into the everyday situations of our lives."

I'm convinced there are several ways to preach that can be faithful to the text of Scripture. These include verse-by-verse, thematic, narrative, and topical sermons. Chan and Gill give particular attention to what some would call a preaching oxymoron: the topical sermon that is also faithful to the biblical text. While this is one of the most highly contested, ridiculed, and derided preaching formats, Chan and Gill show that this sermon style can convey the message of Scripture.

In addition, Chan and Gill assert that we must consider a variety of factors as we approach the preaching task. One of these would certainly be the authority of Scripture. God has given us a sure and true Word. But there are other factors. We must think globally today: if we were preaching to the Pokot in East Africa or to the Quechua people in the highlands of Peru, how would we best communicate the Word of God?

We often hear people say, "Just preach the Word." And while we should certainly do that, the thoughtful preacher who is on mission and seeks to communicate the Word well also asks questions like, "How can I connect the Word with real people in ways that ultimately change hearts?"

This leads to another factor that is particularly important when communicating with an unreached culture or with a biblically illiterate culture in America. We have to start with an understanding of our culture's starting point as we proclaim the Word. Typically, in preaching we start with, "The Bible says . . ." That's obviously important. But at the same time, we also ought to ask ourselves, "Why is this message important and how does it relate to my audience?" Then we can prompt hearers to ask themselves, "What am I going to do with what the Bible says about it?"

The Bible is relevant to every culture; we don't need to "make" the Bible relevant. Our challenge is to help people see how Scripture is relevant and then let the Bible set the agenda. But in doing so, we have to figure out how people learn and how we can communicate with them in biblical and transformative ways.

This is where Chan and Gill significantly help the preacher. Their content walks through ways to communicate the Word of God effectively with different models. While some have made following a form of expository preaching a baseline for orthodoxy, Chan and Gill illuminate alternate approaches as viable expressions of faithful preaching. And—citing renowned preachers from the New Testament and history—they make their case well. They demonstrate how topical preaching focused on fidelity to Scripture develops a biblical worldview and helps listeners apply Scripture to their daily lives.

But they do more than this: Chan and Gill help the preacher see how to preach the same Word of God to an audience of both believers and unbelievers. They help with cultural exegesis that is guided by biblical exegesis. They show how to turn any topical sermon toward Jesus and his work. This is a momentous task that many preachers do not know how to tackle.

If you are convinced that verse-by-verse, book-by-book exposition is the only way to preach, read this book with an open mind. You will find help in your preaching even if you aren't convinced by the authors' argument regarding topical preaching. If you are compelled as a preacher to communicate the Word of God faithfully to this time and your place, read it and find help not only to communicate contextually but also to do so biblically. If you are a novice preacher, read this book to learn helpful ways to communicate the Word of God faithfully and helpfully.

In *Power through Prayer*, E. M. Bounds wrote, "Preaching is God's great institution for the planting and maturing of spiritual life. When properly executed, its benefits are untold; when wrongly executed, no evil can exceed its damaging results." Chan and Gill show the preacher how to properly implement biblical preaching in our world today.

—Ed Stetzer

ACKNOWLEDGMENTS

FROM SAM: When a butterfly flaps its wings in China, it sets up a sequence of events that eventually leads to a tornado in the USA. If this is true, then many butterflies have flapped their wings to make this book possible.

Joe Mock, my pastor at West Sydney Chinese Christian Church (WSCCC), is the first butterfly that flapped its wings. When I was a junior doctor, Joe bravely put me on his church's preaching roster. This began a lifelong journey for me to master the craft of preaching.

Next was my former youth-group leader, Lawrence Tan, who generously gave me a set of cassette tapes (remember them?) of Haddon Robinson speaking at a preaching conference at Sydney Missionary and Bible College (SMBC) in 1993. Haddon's talks fired me up to preach to both the heart and the mind.

It also fired me up to attend SMBC and learn preaching. It was at this college that my fellow students Morgan Powell and Darren Hindle wowed me with their preaching. They cleverly weaved so many illustrations into their sermons. They showed me the power of stories to win over the imagination.

My parents, Winnie and Joseph, then paid for my PhD studies at Trinity Evangelical Divinity School (TEDS) in Chicago so I could further explore both the theology and practice of preaching.

At TEDS, my PhD supervisor, fellow-Aussie Graham Cole, supervised my 80,000 word (yikes!) dissertation on speech-act theory and preaching, which gave me the theological warrant to try out different methods of preaching.

Later, back home in Australia, Aaron Koh, Andrew Wong, Christine Dillon, and John G modeled what creative preaching could look like.

But finally, in the most seemingly random event, I attended the wedding of Thomas and Kate Wang in Atlanta in 2004. At the reception I sat next to Sean and Charlene McGrew, whom I had never met and have never seen since. But in that brief moment, they told me that I simply must meet a guy called Malcolm Gill when I returned to Australia.

And so I did.

Malcolm Gill is a larger than life figure. Full of dad jokes. Cancer survivor. Trustworthy karaoke buddy. The whole world is only six degrees of separation from Malcom Gill. And now, by reading this book, you also are inexorably linked to Malcolm Gill.

FROM MALCOLM: During my ministry life, I have been privileged to serve alongside and learn from a stellar cast of men and women. These individuals have faithfully modeled to me both excellence of character and an unwavering commitment to the gospel. During the highs and lows of ministry life, these individuals have encouraged me to keep going.

Thanks to Kit Barker, Ian Maddock, Geoff Harper, Derek Brotherson, Rachel Ciano, Kirk Patston, Rob Smith, Pierre Thielemans, Tim Silberman, Andrew Koulyras, and Jono Geddes for laughing at my jokes and reminding me of the things that really matter. I honor the Second XI, and the Denver Seven. Remember the Alamo!

To Jono Dykes, LT Hopper, Chris Thomas, Roy Gomez, Paul Tripp, Craig Stalder, Matthais Loong, Damien Whitington, William Subash, Abraham Joseph, Chuck Swindoll, Greg Spires, Abe Meysenburg, Josh Reeve, Sonny Singh, Mark Tough, Bryan Chapell, Timothy Warren, Abe Kuruvilla, Stephen Trew, Kanishka Raffel, and Chris Allan: I thank God for the contribution each of you has made to my ministry and to my life. I am indebted to you.

To the *Lions, Lions, Lions* Whatsapp group—great banter, better blokes. Wee Timmy, Murphy boys, and Pastor Bay, I'm so proud of you guys. Having a small role in your ministry development has been one of the highlights of my ministry life.

A big thank-you to my American family. To Dave and Angela Greenwood, Bernie and Ana Cueto, Steve and Julie Sanchez: the Gills love and miss you all. A special thank-you to David and Marsha Hammock. Thanks for your generous support, encouragement, hospitality, and love shown to Tamara, me, and our kids. You're our favorite Texans.

To my parents, Eddy and Marlene: thanks for letting me travel the world as a twenty-year-old as I followed God's leading in my life. Dad, your jokes are still the best. Mum, your Downie stories are still unbelievable. To the Gómez family: you're the best in-laws I've ever had.

A special shout out to the team at Zondervan, who have worked hard with Sam and me in the process of writing this book. When travel restrictions ease, Sam and I would love to sit down with you and enjoy your company. Until then, we'll raise a frosty beverage in honor of you, Ryan Pazdur, Kyle Rohane, Josh Kessler, and Brian Phipps.

To my mate Sam Chan: when I was told by American friends (shout out to Sean and Charlene McGrew) that there was a Chinese version of me whom I should meet, I didn't know what to think. When we finally met, it became clear why they said this. Here was a guy who was shorter than average, with killer jokes and a flair for the ridiculous, and somebody who married up. Since our introduction, together we've performed live karaoke and stand-up comedy gigs, shared the platform at large youth events, hiked canyons in the Middle East, eaten Tex-Mex in North America, and now have written a book together. It's been fun, Dr. Chan. I can't wait for our next challenge!

Finally, to Tamara, Annabel, Adam, and Zara: you guys are the best. From Paris to Peru, Galápagos to the Gold Coast, Chicago to Cambridge, we've had quite the adventure. Though we're often way too loud, too busy, and too tired, I still love chasing llamas with you and looking for spoons.

INTRODUCTION
The Problem Every Preacher Will Face
SAM CHAN

A little more than a decade ago, I was asked by a Christian singles organization to speak at their end-of-year dinner. They chose me because I was an established Christian conference speaker. Although I was primarily an expository preacher, the organizers were confident I could also deliver a great after-dinner speech.

Several months before the dinner, the organizers talked to me in person. They wanted the after-dinner talk to address the topic of being a Christian single. But they didn't want me to present a biblical theology of singleness or preach an expository sermon from 1 Corinthians 7 or other "singleness" passages in the Bible. They were clear: they wanted a *topical* message.

I had only one problem: I didn't know how to do this. None of the standard books on preaching had anything on how to prepare topical sermons. Nor did any of the homiletics classes I had attended. Nor did any of the preaching conferences. Worse, in my theological tradition I had been taught to be suspicious of topical preaching; it demonstrated a lack of confidence in the Bible.

I simply had no idea how to prepare and deliver a topical talk. So when the night arrived, I preached an old three-point expository sermon I had preached many times before, and merely changed the ending to include some application on singleness.

At best I got some polite comments afterward. At worst people's looks indicated that my biblical talk had minimal connection with the advertised topic. They could not have been less fooled by my disingenuous work-around. I went home vowing never to repeat that poor performance. I felt like the unfaithful servant who had not adequately used the talents given to him. As a result, I have dedicated the past decade of my preaching ministry to mastering the art of topical preaching.

This book is a product of that journey. It exists because sooner or later you will be asked to preach a topical sermon. When that happens, we hope this book will equip you to do so.

CHAPTER 1

EMBRACING THE TOPICAL SERMON

Am I Even Allowed to Preach This Way?

MALCOLM GILL

Several years ago my wife and I attended a wedding reception for a lovely young couple. There was a bounty of delicious food, raucous laughter, impromptu dancing, and of course a love-smitten couple. It was a beautiful occasion. As the festivities drew to a close, it came time for the wedding speeches. As a minister who has officiated several weddings, I've heard a variety of interesting, moving, and emotional speeches, but the wedding speech on this day took me by surprise.

One of the groom's parents began their wedding speech with the following statement: "I thank God that my child was raised in a church committed to expository preaching." Not, "I thank God for bringing this couple together" or, "I thank God for this wonderful celebration" or even, "I thank God for answering our prayers and giving our son a wife." No, the first reason for thanksgiving on this day was expository preaching. That certainly did not come from the wedding speech playbook.

While I applaud the parent's gratefulness—after all, what preacher doesn't want to hear accolades to sermons—the emphasis on a specific style of preaching seemed a little over the top. In fairness, I think this exuberant parent was trying to communicate their thankfulness to God that their child had been shaped by the Scriptures in his upbringing. But what most people at the reception probably heard was this common sentiment in evangelicalism: expository preaching is what real Christians are all about.

Expository preaching has always been part of my spiritual growth. Like the young man at the wedding, I too grew up in a church committed to expository preaching. Also, like the groom's parent, I am grateful to God that for most of my life I've sat under the faithful week-by-week exposition of God's Word. Both my coauthor and I attended seminaries committed to training men and women to preach expository sermons.

For the past decade, I've taught the method of expository preaching to hundreds of men and women, many of whom are in preaching-related ministries. I regularly am invited to critique expository sermons and regularly consult those practicing expository preaching. It has been the bread and butter of my pulpit ministry. Let it be clear to the reader: I deeply value expository preaching.

I bet you're waiting for the *but*, and here it comes. I deeply value expository preaching, but it is not the only form of preaching that God uses and blesses. And in some circumstances and contexts, expository preaching may not be the best form of preaching to employ.

There, I've said it. While I believe in the value of the expository preaching style, I don't believe it is the only way to preach. Now, I imagine some of you, in sympathy with the parent at the wedding, may be tempted to close the book at this point. Some of you are likely shocked by the thought that expository preaching is not the only faithful approach to communicating God's Word. Some may be nervous, and rightly so, with the suggestion that there are alternate ways of preaching. And perhaps some of you are checking your receipt to see if you can return the book to the store for a refund. Please, hold on for just a minute and let me explain!

IS EXPOSITORY PREACHING THE ONLY FAITHFUL STYLE?

It may surprise you, but for many Christians the assertion that expository preaching is the only option is foreign. For many, particularly in the majority world, the practice of verse-by-verse, unit-by-unit, book-by-book preaching is quite unfamiliar. Often in these places, textual, topical, biographical, and evangelistic sermons are more common than what we might classify as expository.

Visit Peru, for example, and you will hear many sermons delivered in the form of a story. Such preaching explores biblical truth, but it does so in a form where truth is embedded within a narrative. In contrast, in India it is not uncommon to hear the truths of Scripture delivered through a parable, a wise allegory that invites the listener to reflect on scriptural ideas. In Iran, the sermon often involves ancient poetic overtones that resonate with the listener and at the same time convey biblical truth.

Within such cultures, proposition-based expository preaching is either foreign or deemed to be less useful in cultural engagement. It may be viewed positively, but it is certainly not viewed as an either-or issue. Expository preaching is one of several good ways of proclaiming biblical truth to God's people.

For many in Western evangelicalism, however, expository preaching is not simply one method of communication; it is the right and only approach one should take. While there is something of a sliding scale regarding the forcefulness with which people hold this conviction, for many expository preaching is a nonnegotiable issue. Such people, of which you may be one, suggest for a variety of good reasons that expository preaching is helpful and should be given pride of place in the pulpit. On this I am sympathetic. Again, I believe that the consistent preaching of passages and books within Scripture in an orderly manner has great merit.[1]

In this book, we are not demeaning traditional expository preaching, nor do we believe it is irrelevant to contemporary practice. Rather we are arguing that preachers should not muddy the water by failing to differentiate between what is Christian dogma and what is merely best cultural practice. Let us not confuse what is mandated in Scripture with what is simply Christian wisdom.

To avoid such confusion, we must, even in considering our methods of preaching, carefully distinguish between substance and style, content and form, issues of orthodoxy and issues of orthopraxy. I suspect that some within evangelical circles have come to understand the method of preaching as a gauge of spiritual convention. For many it is the benchmark of whether one values Scripture, believes the gospel, and is spiritually mature. However, such conclusions go well beyond the evidence of Scripture and certainly against the flow of much of church history.

What Is a Sermon?

What is a sermon? And what is a sermon's purpose? The word sermon comes from the Latin *sermo*, which means "continuous speech or discourse." The term is not mentioned in the Scriptures, though there are several examples of extended speeches that we would consider to be sermonic. Jesus, for example, delivers an extended discourse recorded in Matthew 5–7 which we commonly refer to as the Sermon on the Mount. In Acts, we find similar lengthy speeches by people like Peter, Stephen, and Paul. A basic understanding of a sermon is that it is an extended speech.

What distinguishes a sermon from any other monologue, however, is the sermon's purpose. What the sermon aims to do is expressed in part in the New Testament. What we call a sermon, the New Testament refers to as a "word of exhortation" (Acts 13:15; Heb. 13:22). The sermon is an exhortation—a message spoken to urge and encourage someone to some type of response.

SIBLINGS, NOT COMPETITORS

Choosing between expository and topical preaching has often been presented as an either-or decision. Who hasn't heard the quip "I once preached a topical sermon, and then I promptly repented of it"? Such statements, often accompanied with the muffled laughter usually reserved for a bad dad joke, insinuate that any preaching style outside of expository should be avoided. Normally, in such thinking, expository preaching is portrayed as representing faithfulness and truth, while topical preaching is caricatured as human-centered and biblically suspect. Expository preaching is presented as valuing Scripture, whereas topical preaching is depicted as driven by human interest.

Such portrayals are unhelpful. Rather than viewing the styles of preaching as competitors, it would be more helpful to consider them as siblings in the same family.

As all parents know, it is not advisable to show favoritism to your children. I have three children. To avoid the charge of favoritism, I often address my eldest child, Annabel, as "my favorite firstborn," my middle child, Adam, as "my favorite son," and my youngest, Zara, as "my favorite baby girl." They all want to be favorite, so I rely on categories unique to each of them. If I compare one child with another, it will end in disappointment, anger, and tears—and that just from their mother!

The reason parents are advised not to compare children is because children by nature are unique. My children have their own personalities, their own music preferences, their own hobbies, and their own friends. They are all children, but they are different. And different does not mean wrong; it simply means different. I don't expect or even want them to be the same, because they're not. Each one enriches my life through his or her different yet equally valuable presence.

In considering preaching, we need to think of our methods as siblings rather than combatants. We should not ask whether we should preach either expository or topical sermons. Rather we should ask, "Does this context or event most call for an expository or topical approach?

What Can We Learn about Preaching from Church History?

If you and I were to look back over history, we would discover that most Christians in the past preached quite differently than we do today. Take Jonathan Edwards's famous sermon "Sinners in the Hands of an Angry God," delivered in 1741.

The sermon was based on a phrase found in Deuteronomy 32:35: "In due time their foot will slip." Edwards took this phrase and connected it with a similar saying in Psalm 73:18–19 before launching into a ten-point theological treatise on God's judgment. Scattered throughout his sermon were at least sixteen sections of Scripture, among which were references to Proverbs, Ecclesiastes, Isaiah, Ezekiel, Luke, John, and Revelation.

Jonathan Edwards's famous sermon broke most of the rules taught in modern-day expository preaching classes. Edwards read a single text and then bounced all over the place. Though his thoughts were thoroughly orthodox and his theology sound, he made almost no reference to the historical context or cultural milieu of the original audience, nor did he mention the original languages. Edwards didn't even specify what verses he referenced! As far as sermon evaluations go, Mr. Edwards would fare quite poorly in most of today's homiletics courses.

The reality is, of course, that God famously used that sermon to bring many people to himself. He used Edwards in his time, through Edwards's style of preaching. The same reflection could be made of sermons delivered by John Wesley, George Whitefield, Charles Spurgeon, and even Billy Graham. Regarding Billy Graham, it has been observed, "Graham was not a great preacher, if by great we mean eloquent. He knew it, and almost everyone else did, too, including his wife. 'Homiletically,' said W. E. Sangster, a leading cleric in England, 'his sermons leave almost everything to be desired.' Graham admitted that he was a champion rambler, with as many as seventeen points in a single sermon. He told one biographer that the subject and the words of his first sermon were 'mercifully lost to memory.'"[2] Few would question the impact of Billy Graham's gospel preaching, yet the manner of his approach, like that of Jonathan Edwards, would no doubt cause many contemporary homileticians to balk. Neither Graham nor Edwards fits neatly into modern mainstream approaches to preaching.

A survey of preaching throughout history reveals that God has used many styles of preaching and preachers to communicate his truth. God, it seems, has not felt obligated to speak only through our expository method of preaching. If we were to compare the preaching of Edwards or Graham with that of other figures in church history, such as Irenaeus, Basil the Great, or John Knox, we would find that each preaching style is markedly different from the others. Culture, historical context, and pastoral purpose all played a part in how and what they preached. The same is true for us today. We are all shaped, even in our preaching style, by the era in which we live.

If church history teaches us anything, it reminds us that there has never been one uniform way to preach. It should caution us about being too rigid or dogmatic regarding our methodology of preaching, whatever that may be.

Would this audience or situation benefit most from a textual, evangelistic, or biographical sermon?"

Which form of communication to employ, as almost all cross-cultural missionaries can testify, is most often an issue of wisdom rather than a moral decision of right or wrong. Pitting approaches of communication against each other can be couched in terms of suitability, cultural appropriateness, and even effectiveness, but we should be wary about declaring with certainty the moral or theological superiority of one method over another. A method of communication is not something to repent over, but perhaps an overzealous commitment to only one style, whatever that is, may call for a dose of caution. So let's reflect on why we should consider adding topical sermons to our toolbox.

WHY SHOULD WE PREACH TOPICAL SERMONS?

Shortly after my wife and I married, we read the popular book *The Five Love Languages* by Gary Chapman.[3] The premise of the book is that we each best respond to one of five different expressions of love: words of affirmation, quality time, receiving gifts, acts of service, and physical touch. What was insightful for me as I read the book is that each of us tends to express love the way that we best receive it.

For me, love is best expressed through words of affirmation. Like many others, I feel valued when a kind is word is directed my way. The problem is that I projected what I valued most onto my wife. I complimented her for almost everything. "These mashed potatos you prepared are fantastic!" "You are the best driver in your family!" "I don't know how you do it, but you are such a good salsa dancer."

While these accolades were all genuine, especially about the dancing, and Tamara politely thanked me, my words never seemed to hit the mark. That was, I discovered, because her love languages are acts of service and receiving gifts. Better than a kind word for my wife is taking out the trash or buying her something nice. Words are good, but not best.

Likewise, when we were first married, Tamara bought me excessive amounts of clothes. I appreciated her gifts, but after she bought me a fifth pair of shoes, I started to wonder what was going on. While I attributed her gifts to my ailing fashion sense, Tamara, I discovered, bought me new shoes and shirts every other week to demonstrate her love for me.

Over the years, I have discovered that what is true of expressing love to another in marriage is also true of Christian growth and maturity. Many of us tend to reflect the values and practices that have been meaningful to us, particularly in our formative years. For many of us, that means a certain way of learning or reading the Bible or praying. In our desire to disciple others, we often simply perpetuate what was helpful to us. While this is not wrong and is often wise, many of us have wondered why people don't respond the way that we may have in the past. The answer, at least in part, could be that we have failed to recognize that others learn and grow in a way that is different from us.

Topical Preaching Recognizes We Are Diverse Learners

When it comes to the way we grow as disciples of Christ, we should not assume that we all mature and learn in an identical way. While our Christian confession is fixed to theological truth, our Christian witness and practice are as diverse as we are.

As people, we are not uniform; we are by nature distinct. Our cultural background, biblical literacy, experience within the Christian community, and formal education all feed into the way in which we learn and develop as disciples of Jesus. Therefore if we are to preach to a variety of audiences, we must seek to work within the learning frameworks that are most helpful to those we seek to reach.

In his ministry, the apostle Paul recognized the diversity of learning styles. Think about the way he addressed the topic of salvation with different audiences. Fred Sanders observes,

> When the jailer in Philippi asked him [Paul], "What must I do to be saved?" he did not hem or haw, mumble or ramble. He did not stop to search his memory, pondering which passages of Scripture or trajectories of argument might be relevant to this question. He did not correct the jailer by saying, "It would be better if you asked me, 'What has God done to save me?'" He did not take out a piece of chalk and diagram the history of salvation on the walls of the prison,

or talk about predestination, or explore the spiritual dynamics of the jailer's quest for meaning. He said, "Believe in the Lord Jesus, and you will be saved" (Acts 16:31). On the other hand, when writing to the Ephesian church, to whom he had declared "the whole counsel of God" (Acts 20:27), he did not just keep repeating "Believe in the Lord Jesus" over and over, as if he had nothing more to say. For them, he described the eternal purposes of God the Father in choosing us to receive redemption through the blood of his beloved Son and to be sealed with the Holy Spirit of promise (Eph. 1:3–14).[4]

While the topic of salvation was the central issue to both audiences, the way Paul addressed it was, at least in part, shaped by his audience's knowledge, context, and background.

For the unbelieving Philippian jailer, the focus of the message was a concise, direct call to respond to Jesus. For the Ephesian church, the topic of salvation was posited as a pastoral encouragement by way of the longest Greek sentence in the New Testament. Same topic, different audience, different purpose, different style.

By learning to preach topical sermons, you recognize and value that people learn differently. While many people appreciate the logic and flow of regular and consistent proposition-based analyses of passages, as demonstrated in expository preaching, many others feel far more at home in contexts where truths are more implicit and are embedded in images or concepts rather than explicit statements.

In mainstream culture, we continue to teach and preach using styles that we are most familiar with. Often these mirror the methods of learning we received growing up. We reflect and echo the norms and styles we are accustomed to and have known all of our lives. The challenge, however, is that those we now preach to are growing up in different educational contexts where they have experienced new and diverse approaches to learning. Their learning styles are not better or worse than those of previous generations, but they are often different.

Topical preaching recognizes that we might need to take a slightly different route than the expository one to arrive at truth. When I was a child at school, my exams were almost always an assessment of my ability to memorize information and then reproduce it on paper. In recent years, there has been a slight but significant shift in focus, where now exams often present real-life problems and scenarios that students, sometimes collaboratively, must seek to solve. Students are still interested in facts, but there is more emphasis on integration and problem solving.

In expository preaching we typically start with the facts. We walk through a passage verse by verse and explain the details. We confer information and, hopefully, work toward the theological thrust of the passage. Then we demonstrate the relevance of that to our world, often in the concluding, application section of the sermon. In topical preaching we simply reverse the order. We start with the real-world, existential issue or topic and then seek to shed light on the issue by providing responsible biblical insight.

Both approaches are interested in truth. Both seek to apply God's wisdom to life. The difference lies in the path to such truth. Expository preaching starts with biblical wisdom and then seeks to apply its relevance, and topical preaching starts with an issue of relevance and then seeks to find what the Bible says about it. (See fig. 1.)

Figure 1

EXPOSITORY PREACHING

Biblical Wisdom
What does the Bible say in this passage? ➡️ *Relevance*
How does this apply to areas of everyday life?

TOPICAL PREACHING

Relevance
A topic of everyday life ➡️ *Biblical Wisdom*
How does the Bible inform the way I should think about this topic?

Is There a Right Way to Preach?

When I was in my midtwenties, I backpacked across Europe with two of my friends. In preparation for our trip, we each committed to reading up on European art, particularly from the Renaissance period. This study proved valuable, as we were then able to enjoy the countless exhibits with a semi-informed perspective on the assorted techniques and styles that characterized the various artworks.

One of the interesting aspects of our art exploration was that each of us was drawn to different features. While I was intrigued by period sculptures, one of my friends enjoyed architectural designs, and my other friend found pleasure in the realism of oil paintings. All were wonderful expressions of the Renaissance period, but as enthusiasts, we gravitated to certain styles.

Sermons, like art, have human involvement and as a result contain an element of individuality. Some people enjoy sermons that focus on information, while others find preaching that connects with the emotions helpful. Still others engage best with narrative-style messages. Some of this is personality based, some is a learned appreciation, and some is simply preference.

In communicating truth, God, in his wisdom, saw fit to provide us with multiple ways of listening and learning. Among other things, within the Bible we have songs, poetry, proverbs, story, parable, apocalyptic, prophecy, and epistles. Some readers of the Bible are naturally drawn to the more artistic aspects of Scripture. For such people a poetic couplet, a wordplay, or a metaphor bring much delight. In contrast, others have a natural affinity for the logic and flow of an epistle. They find no greater joy than in unpacking a dense paragraph of the apostle Paul's subordinate clauses.

Thankfully, our creative God has spoken to us in a variety of forms. While the good news of Christ is the fixed center of the story, the means of pointing us to that story are wonderfully and stylistically diverse.

God's creative diversity can also be observed in the way he has chosen to speak through diverse human agency. Anyone who studies biblical Greek will quickly discover that Paul's Greek is different in style from John's, which is different from Luke's, which is different from Peter's. God has not chosen to speak uniformly through one style of writing or one type of human personality. Though God's voice is heard in every expression in the Scriptures, the means of his speaking are diverse.

In preaching, we should not expect every sermon to be the same in style, explanation, application, or delivery. By nature, we preach with our unique personalities to listeners with their own dispositions and learning preferences. While one can preach erroneous content, there is no right style in which to preach or deliver a particular passage.

God's creative intention is to use a variety of methods and messengers to deliver truth. In the past he has used everything from an emotional fisherman like Peter to the sophisticated artistry of the preacher of Hebrews. He has spoken through the weeping prophet Jeremiah and the poetic majesty of the psalmists. God has created us to be diverse, and this should be embraced rather than minimized.

While my friends and I had different preferences for Renaissance art, over the course of our European adventure, we came to admire all forms of art, even those we weren't inclined to. Sermons, like art, are diverse, and while some styles and content may not always move us the same way, over time we can learn to engage with and appreciate the varied ways God speaks through his Word and his messengers.

While many of us are most comfortable with learning facts and then seeking to find relevance, many within our culture are primarily asking questions of relevance. By persisting in only one approach to teaching, we may be missing an opportunity to reach out to such people with biblical truth.

Paul did not ask the Philippian jailer to rephrase his question, nor did he take the topic of salvation and turn it into a lesson on salvation history. Rather he addressed the Philippian jailer's immediate issue of relevance and brought to bear on it the good news message of Jesus. He met the person with the existential dilemma and responded by pointing him to Christ.

Topical preaching, like expository preaching, should be committed to biblical truth; it simply arrives there a different way. This style of preaching recognizes that for many within our world the best way to engage is not to begin with information they may or may not listen to but to begin with real-world issues they are wrestling with.[5]

After identifying and articulating the topic or issue, the topical preacher then seeks to share how the gospel of grace addresses it or feeds into our understanding of it. Topical preaching recognizes and values that people are diverse and offers another way for people to understand and appropriate the gospel.

Topical Preaching Embraces Diverse Cultural Expressions

The German theologian Helmut Thielicke observed, "The gospel must be preached afresh and told in new ways to every generation, since every generation has its own unique questions. The gospel must constantly be forwarded to a new address, because the recipient is repeatedly changing his place of residence."[6] Sermons change because our audiences change. How Jesus engaged with the religious leader Nicodemus in John 3 is different from how he spoke to a troubled Samaritan woman in John 4. How the apostle Paul shared the gospel with the devout Jewish community in the synagogue in Berea (Acts 17:10–12) was different from the way he addressed the religious pluralism of those in Athens (Acts 17:16–34). Jesus, Paul, and effective communicators of every age recognize that to be heard, you must first speak in a way to be understood.

"I Know a Man Who Owns a Snake"

Differences in learning styles became apparent to me while I was in seminary. During one lecture, a student asked the professor about the due date of an assignment. The student was asking a specific question and wanted a specific answer. Everything seemed straightforward until the professor responded.

Rather than offering a direct answer, the professor, who was from a non-Western country and context, said, "I know a man who owns a snake." He began telling us about the nature of the reptile and its relationship to the owner. I listened intently, wondering, *What is he talking about?* After a few minutes the story ended abruptly. I could tell from the faces of my classmates that I was not the only one dumbfounded by the response. I'm still not sure what he was talking about.

For my non-Western professor the answer to the question was embedded in the story. Most of us in the class, however, were hoping for something less vague: "Just tell me the due date!" We desired an explicit answer, but the professor offered up a story with an implicit response.

In preaching there will be some in your audience who resonate most with plain explanation, and others who feel most engaged with story. Both explicit and implicit reasoning have their place. The key is to know your audience.

And if you're wondering how the assignment turned out, I ended up missing the deadline.

We all know the story of the young king David, who, while walking on his roof in Jerusalem "in the spring, at the time when kings go off to war," saw the beautiful Bathsheba and lusted after her (2 Sam. 11:1–3). He then committed adultery with Bathsheba and had her husband, Uriah, murdered before taking her to be his wife.

Now, suppose you lived in David's day. How would you preach if David suddenly turned up in your congregation? The expository preacher within me says the most natural place to land would be to provide an exposition of the section of Exodus we commonly refer to as the Decalogue, or the Ten Commandments. Addressing the prohibition on adultery (Ex. 20:14) would be good. "You shall not murder" (v. 13) would be right on the money. "You shall not covet your neighbor's wife" (v. 17)—that would preach. One might imagine that any or all of these verses would be great ways to confront David with his sin. We might have suggested to Nathan the following homiletic outline.

I. You have sinned against God by committing adultery.
II. You have sinned against God by murdering.
III. You have sinned against God by coveting.
   Application: Repent!

Three simple propositions and an application.

But that is not what Nathan does when he confronts David. He tells a story. Not just any story—Nathan talks about a precious sheep and a seasoned shepherd. As we know, the narrative ends with a wicked man taking and killing the beloved ewe of a poor man. At this David cries out for justice against the offending sinner, to which Nathan famously responds, "You are the man!" (2 Sam. 12:7).

Though I don't think Nathan was seeking to establish a paradigm for preaching, there is something here we would do well to observe. Nathan used a form of communication that was most suitable for his audience. While he could have given a series of propositions, uttered a prophetic oracle, or even applied a proverb, instead he spoke through a story. He embedded his message in the vehicle of a narrative about a sheep as he engaged a shepherd.

In different cultures, people resonate with different styles of message. While this doesn't mean that within a particular culture there shouldn't be variety—we know David loved meditating on the Law—we should take seriously the audience to whom we are speaking and seek to recognize and value that they might come at truth differently than we do. Contextualizing both the message and the method we use to communicate it can often be the difference between an audience merely hearing your words and their truly listening.

Missionaries, over many generations, have long understood this. For most people serving in cross-cultural contexts, orientation to the field often involves extended time learning and listening to the locals before embarking on Word-based ministry. Missionaries seek to understand first and foremost a people's cultural norms to discover their worldview. They ask themselves, "How do these people think? What do they value? How do they learn? What should and shouldn't be said, and in what manner? How do they best process ideas?"

In an increasingly global and multicultural world, all Christian preachers would do well to learn from the cross-cultural missionary approach. We should all develop skills to listen to, evaluate, and reflect on the varied ways people engage. Much of Christian preaching today is irrelevant and boring, not because the Scriptures are boring but because the preacher has taken little interest in understanding the best way to communicate God's timeless truth.[7]

Topical preaching can be one way, among others, whereby the preacher can communicate biblical truth with cultural relevance and sensitivity. By beginning with a topic and then seeking to address that issue with the gospel, the topical preacher uses a known cultural grid to understand truth.

In topical sermons, preachers seek to identify, understand, and engage with the various struggles, dilemmas, and hot-button issues that everyday people wrestle with, by providing a biblical and theological response. At its best, topical preaching is not, as poorly caricatured by some, a form of human-centric, self-help sharing of ideas. Rather it simply provides biblical and theologically shaped insight into real issues by addressing them head on. While there can be a danger of forcing issues that the Bible doesn't deal with back on Scripture, this temptation exists with all styles of preaching. Effective topical preaching aims to connect with the realities of everyday life through an engagement with culture, not through a tacked-on, token application at the conclusion of a sermon.

While people in some cultures, particularly those in the affluent West, have been reared in a context in which truth is gleaned through explanation, examination, and proposition-based reductionisms, those in the majority world and increasingly those growing up in a postmodern culture resonate more with other ways of approaching truth.

Preachers would do well to consider employing topical preaching at times, as it provides a style that seeks to integrate biblical truth with day-to-day living. This will require listening to and learning from our culture, which in some respects requires more effort than simply exegeting a biblical text.

Topical Preaching Facilitates the Development of a Christian Worldview

Mia is a third-year university student. She has never missed a week of the Bible study group on campus. This year her group has been making its way through the book of 1 Peter section by section. Mia is excited about all that she's learning, and she particularly enjoys it when the leader gives insight into the historical and cultural background of the biblical text. She has even learned a Greek word or two along the way.

One day after Bible study, Mia runs into her good buddy Alexa, who is also a Christian. Noticing that her friend looks downcast, she asks, "Are you okay, Alexa?" Alexa replies, "Not really. With everything going on in the world—disease, war, and on a personal note, my parents' divorce—I'm feeling anxious, and I think I'm depressed. I know the Bible says we should have joy, but I'm not feeling it. Mia, you love the Lord. Maybe you can tell me what the Bible says about anxiety and depression."

Paul and Sarah are a Christian couple who have been married for twelve years. Though they married young, they are mature and have overcome a few relational hurdles. They seem from all outward signs to be doing okay.

Recently, however, they have experienced some tension, so they decide to seek marriage counseling. As they visit with their pastor, they raise a few issues. There are the normal challenges of communication, listening, and anger. Then, in the midst of the conversation, Paul puts his cards on the table. "Pastor, the real issue here is that God has not given us a child. We've been praying, but there has been no result. This is causing friction. The question we have been wrestling with is this: is it okay to seek IVF treatment to have a child? What does the Bible say?"

Jack is a thirty-five-year-old builder who is a Sunday school teacher in his church. Jack is also a twin. One day after work Jack notices that he has five missed calls on his cell phone, all from his mother. He immediately calls her to confirm that everything is all right. Sadly, she informs Jack that his twin brother has been killed in a tragic workplace accident. Jack, understandably, is devastated. He asks himself, *Why would God let this happen? Where was God when my brother needed him?*

Mia, Paul and Sarah, and Jack all love the Lord, love the Scriptures, and want to know what God thinks and how they should respond. The problem for them—and for all of us struggling with such things—is that the Bible doesn't directly address the issues they are facing. There are no verses in Scripture that mention IVF. There isn't a section of Scripture that outlines a comprehensive response to anxiety, depression, or unexpected death. Is God silent on these matters? Does he not care? What does it look like to have the mind of Christ regarding these issues?

Topical preaching recognizes that these and issues like them are real and significant and need to be addressed. Topical preaching aims to address real-life issues head-on by providing biblical insight into ways of thinking Christianly about all of life. While good expository preaching may provide snapshots of relevance that sometimes intersect with such issues, the value of topical preaching is that the goal is to directly address the questions people are asking. Topical preaching is not built around felt needs, as some falsely claim. Rather it is seeking to provide a Christ-centered paradigm in which to understand how to navigate our fallen world with all of its complexity.

In essence topical preaching is about helping people to develop a Christian worldview. It aims to facilitate the shaping of the Christian's mind by helping the person think through every aspect of life through a biblical, theological, gospel-shaped grid. It is this mental renewal that Paul has in mind when he writes in Romans 12:2, "Do not conform to the pattern of this world, but be transformed by the renewing of your mind. Then you will be able to test and approve what God's will is—his good, pleasing and perfect will."

As Christians, we need a renewing of the mind. In light of the work of Christ and our connectedness to him, we need to rewire the way that we think and act in every aspect of our lives. We want to think Christianly about topics like success, money, achievement, marriage, child-rearing, alcohol, sex, social media, and entertainment. Topical preaching gives the preacher the opportunity to address areas of importance to the listeners while offering divine insights into how they might think about those areas.

Topical Preaching Integrates Truth with Life

While I would love to preach to people intrigued by a chiastic structure, a subtle wordplay, or a historical insight, the reality is that when I get up to preach, I can safely assume my audience consists of a large number of people whose minds are preoccupied with real issues of life.

Some folks are wrestling with marriage and relational breakdowns, and others are burdened because they are being bullied in their workplace. Some are lonely and wondering whether anyone would miss them if they were gone, and others are anxious about whether they can pay the bills.

While other forms of preaching can acknowledge these realities, many preachers feel that the sermon is simply about the faithful communication of textual information. Preaching, however, is not primarily about teaching facts to produce smarter sinners. Rather preaching should aim to bring about transformation as the Spirit of God takes biblical truth and refashions the listener's mind to bring about conformity to Christ.

In the Great Commission, Jesus says, "Go and make disciples of all nations, baptizing them in the name of the Father and of the Son and of the Holy Spirit, and teaching them to obey everything I have commanded you. And surely I am with you always, to the very end of the age" (Matt. 28:19–20).

Notice what he does not say. The commission is not to simply "go and make disciples of all nations, . . . teaching them." No, it continues: ". . . to obey." The goal of preaching, as with the commission of Jesus, is to lead people to obedience. Life change. Conformity to Christ's image. Topical preaching seeks to identify how we might do that in all areas of life, whether or not they are directly mentioned in Scripture.

Far too much contemporary preaching focuses on theological content but fails to move listeners to integrate truth with life. The sermon should not provide a choice between content and obedience. It should address both. Topical preaching provides a helpful way of joining those two things, by providing a theological lens through which we can better see ourselves and the world in which we live.

WHY DO WE AVOID TOPICAL PREACHING?

Topical preaching, like every other form of preaching, has its short-comings and challenges. Because of various abuses of this type of preaching, some people have thrown out the baby with the bathwater. After hearing sermons in which preachers misapply a verse or section of Scripture to serve their own agenda, these people say, "See! You should never preach topical messages."

While the possibility exists of misapplying a text when wrestling with an issue not directly addressed in Scripture, the danger of misusing Scripture exists in every style of preaching. Fidelity to the meaning of the text is not governed by whether the structure of a sermon is inductive, deductive, semi-inductive, expository, biographical, narrative, or topical. Despite this there are two particular challenges to developing a topical message: first, many preachers don't know where to begin, and second, topical preaching requires a unique skill set.

We Don't Know Where to Begin

Over the past two decades, I've had the joy of preaching in a variety of contexts. While much of that preaching has been in churches I've served, I've also frequently preached as a guest in churches, conferences, and other settings. Whenever I'm invited to preach, I ask what they would like me to speak on. Usually, if they give me a section of Scripture or a book of the Bible, I breathe a big sigh of relief. These are things I've been trained for, and I feel comfortable preaching in this way.

Recently, however, I've noticed a cultural shift: rather than being directed to preach about specific books or sections of the Bible, increasingly I'm asked to address topics. "Can you do a series on tough questions?" people ask. "Can you speak on Christian hope?" "Can you address the Bible's teaching on gender and sexuality?" "Can you give a series of talks on heaven and hell?"

While some of these talks pair well with a specific portion of

Scripture, most topics don't naturally fit into the straightforward exegesis of a single unit of text. Topical preaching requires that the preacher think about the topic theologically. The topical preacher must think across the breadth of the Scriptures to determine how they inform us regarding the topic.

Some subjects are explicitly referenced. If I'm asked to speak on the Holy Spirit, who he is and what he does, I start by finding clear biblical references. Other topics, however, are never mentioned in Scripture. Social media is not directly addressed in the pages of the Bible, so I need to look through an interpretive lens to discover how to think Christianly about that topic. The challenge in doing this well is that it requires a level of competence in systematic and biblical theology. The effective topical preacher demonstrates proficiency in extracting theologically nuanced ideas that relate to the issue at hand, but knowing which texts to reference and what theological ideas feed into our understanding of a topic can be challenging.

Another difference between topical and expository preaching is the amount of time spent in the texts. A common charge leveled at topical preachers is that they don't spend enough time in the text. Time, however, should not be the gauge of orthodoxy.

Topical preaching by nature is focused on theological concepts more than on providing the historical background of a passage. This does not mean, however, that it is less biblical. As one of preaching's senior statesmen, Bryan Chapell, observes,

Aspects of the development of the main idea of a topical sermon may come from how the subject has been addressed in history or present culture. Other aspects of the sermon's development may come from other biblical passages. None of these topical sermon characteristics mean that it is necessarily unbiblical or inferior to an expository message. There can be many legitimate reasons to explore a subject along lines other than those formed by a specific passage of Scripture. If for a portion of the sermon we wanted to explore present thinking about racism, elder care, or consumerism, there is nothing wrong with examining how attitudes have developed in our culture, even if those issues are not specifically mentioned in the biblical text. There is often great pastoral wisdom in proving why a subject needs to be addressed before showing how the Scriptures speak to it.

Topical sermons can be very biblical, even if they do not follow the structure of a biblical passage. The key to remaining biblical is making sure the subject is ultimately addressed according to principles drawn from Scripture.[8]

One of the challenges of preaching topical sermons well is being judicious in drawing out the right biblical and theological principles that relate to the topic. Knowing what lens is best to view the subject is not always easy.

Topical Preaching Requires a Unique Skill Set

If you're like me, then one of the temptations of your preaching ministry is to play it safe and preach the way you always have. If your preaching isn't broken, don't fix it, right? Well, while the bread and butter of my preaching has been to work through books of the Bible in an expository manner, my preaching has been enriched as I've branched out into other styles.

Over the past few years, I've attempted many styles of preaching. I have preached first-person narrative sermons in the voice of a biblical character. I have delivered biographical messages in which I focused on the life of someone in history, biblical and otherwise, and reflected on how they can point us to Jesus. I have spoken on topical issues and doctrinal matters, and I have used techniques of storytelling. In some sermons I've even encouraged listeners to get involved, by soliciting feedback on a topic or passage mid-sermon.

Many of these messages have taken me way out of my comfort zone. Sometimes it has been nerve-racking, but more often I have found it refreshing. I suspect this is true for my congregations as well.

While new sermon styles offer clear benefits to preachers and their audiences, they require of you some type of change. This can be tough. To become a topical preacher, you will need to further develop skills in reading the Scriptures theologically. You will need to listen to and evaluate your cultural context. You may need to mix up the way you preach, your sermon length, your style of illustration, and the scope of exegesis you undertake. It may feel unnatural and uncomfortable. These things, however, should not hinder you from exploring topical preaching. Most rewarding things in life involve preparation and challenge, and topical preaching is no different.

Brad the Crazy Kiwi

Brad is one of my friends in pastoral ministry. I call Brad the crazy Kiwi because he is from New Zealand and he is willing to try things most of us wouldn't. A few years ago Brad decided to preach a sermon at his church as a first-person narrative. He walked out onto the stage to deliver his sermon dressed in robes and preached the sermon as if he were Moses. At first he received a few shocked looks and some muffled laughter. Some probably wondered if this was some kind of dare, while others concluded their pastor needed a vacation. But after the initial shock most listeners engaged with the sermon in a way they never had before. Brad the crazy Kiwi took a creative risk.

After the sermon Brad received quite a response. From that time onward middle-aged men of the church would approach him every few months to ask, "Can you preach another one of those dress-up sermons? They're fantastic!"

Many of us might not be as brave—or crazy—as Brad, but I applaud people like him who venture outside of their comfort zones to try something new to better communicate with others. When was the last time you took a risk in your preaching style?

TOPICAL PREACHING IS NOT A SIN, IT'S AN OPPORTUNITY

As preachers, we need to constantly revisit and reevaluate the world and our place in it as our cultures ebb and flow. To preach well, we need to work on our exegesis of not only the Holy Scriptures but also the world in which we live. In preaching, we publicly engage with people as we seek to integrate the timeless truth of God's grace in Jesus into the everyday situations of our lives.

Topical preaching is one of several preaching styles that aim to facilitate this integration by helping us view life through the lens of the gospel. Rather than perpetuating the myth that topical sermons should be avoided—or even repented of—we can and should see them as one tool of many in the preacher's toolbox which can be used to communicate the wonderful news of Jesus. Topical preaching gives the preacher another avenue by which to engage listeners with the theological truth of the gospel.

CHAPTER 2

HOW TO APPROACH A TOPIC

What Is My Interpretive Lens?

SAM CHAN

I regularly attend a Chinese church in Sydney, Australia. The Chinese Christian culture can be very traditional, formal, and hierarchical. The older generation expects honor from the younger generation. Titles are important. People must do things according to the rules. When you preach a sermon, the church expects you to wear a suit and tie.

But I was once asked to preach at a church in one of the beach suburbs of Sydney. Here the Anglo Christian culture is the opposite of the culture of my Chinese church. It is contemporary, relaxed, and egalitarian. People call each other by their first names. When you preach a sermon, the church would laugh if you wore a suit and tie.

So I dressed down by wearing a business shirt, pants, and leather shoes. Definitely no suit and tie. But when I turned up at this Anglo church, their minister looked at me with a horrified expression. He was in a T-shirt, shorts, and flip-flops. Compared with him, I was still terrifyingly overdressed.

But what's the problem with that? In my Chinese church it's better to err on the safe side by overdressing. To that culture a suit and tie represent respect, dignity, and honor. To wear a T-shirt would be disrespectful and arrogant. It would show that the preacher is not a team player.

But in this Anglo church at the beach, I came across as holier-than-thou, arrogant, and self-righteous. Who did I think I was? I was being disrespectful! A T-shirt would have shown me to be humble and one of the people.

Different cultures have different interpretive lenses. Cultures use these lenses to interpret the same "text"—in this case a business shirt—resulting in opposite meanings. One culture will oppose the business shirt—it's disrespectful! The other culture will affirm this same shirt—it's respectful!

In the same way that cultures have different ways of interpreting the same text, preachers also have different ways of interpreting the same topic. For example, if we have to preach on the topic of the internet, one preacher will oppose it—the internet is evil! But another preacher will affirm it—the internet is a gift from God! Preachers come to a topic with an interpretive lens; we can either oppose our topic or affirm it. But which one should it be?

THE CULTURE WARS

I grew up in a family with Christian parents whose interpretive lens filtered everything through the culture wars. We had to turn off the TV whenever a rock music video interrupted our cartoons. We never went to the movies. I never went to school dances. My parents' underlying philosophy must have been that such things were of the world and therefore (at best) irrelevant to or (at worst) incompatible with a Christian lifestyle.

As a child, I heard many Christian speakers use a culture wars model to speak on topics such as rock and roll. Their template was something like this: "The world says *this* about rock and roll, but the Bible says *this* instead." You can substitute many other topics for rock and roll, such as finances, sports, careers, dating, and fashion.

Should a Christian Be Worldly?

How worldly should a Christian be? Greg Clarke explains it this way:

On the one hand, Christians have little in common with the world. Although God's world was once "good" (Genesis 1), it was corrupted by the effects of sin (Genesis 3). Thus, this world is destined for destruction (2 Peter 3:10). God's ways and the world's ways are *discontinuous*.

As a result, Christians should stay separate from the world. For example, Paul makes *worldly wisdom* the foil of *godly wisdom* (1 Cor. 1:20–25; 2 Cor. 1:12). Christians should not seek the world's wisdom, which is foolishness in disguise. Christians should instead seek Christ, who is the true wisdom from God. John goes farther. The world, which is darkness and evil, is in active opposition to Christ and his followers (John 3:19; 15:18–19). Christians are not to love the world; they must choose to love either the Father or the world (1 John 2:15–16). "Don't conform to the world" is the Christian motto (Rom. 12:2).

On the other hand, in Wisdom Literature, Christ is personified as *worldly wisdom*. This wisdom is part of the fabric of God's creation; the ways of the world are the ways of God. We become wise by observing and conforming to God's truth, beauty, and goodness in this world (Proverbs 8; Ps. 24:1).

In the New Testament, God's ways are still *continuous* with the world's ways. For example, Paul still sees God's creation as good, to be welcomed and not rejected (1 Tim. 4:4). God has not abandoned this world. It is part of God's program for redemption. God is reconciling the world to himself (2 Cor. 5:19). This world will one day be redeemed (Rom. 8:21).

In the Gospels, Jesus often teaches in parables. The entire

premise of the parables is that there must be continuity between the ways of the world and God's ways. Otherwise the analogy would break down.

John takes it farther. God loves the world (John 3:16). God affirms the world in the incarnation and resurrection: Christ, the Logos, became flesh and dwelt in this world (John 1:14). After Christ's resurrection, he is still embodied, keeping his scars and eating a physical meal with his disciples (John 20:27; 21:10–14). Ultimately, the kingdom of the world will become the kingdom of our Lord (Rev. 11:15). There is a stunning continuity between the world's ways and God's ways.

Thus, in the Bible, there is both *discontinuity* and *continuity* between a Christian and their world. There will always be elements of this world that a Christian must oppose, rebuke, condemn, judge, and separate from. But there will also be elements that a Christian can learn from, approve, affirm, and embrace.[1]

At the same time, my Christian culture was affirming of "high culture." It was welcoming of classical music, choirs, and chess. But at some point I started to wonder, what was the difference between the morals of Beethoven and the Beatles? Tchaikovsky and Tarantino? Shakespeare and Stan Lee? Kasparov and KISS?

It seemed to me that Christians had a somewhat arbitrary interpretive lens when it came to cultural topics. The same Christian culture that opposed the media, movies, and Madonna was happy to affirm microwave ovens, motorcars, and Mozart. Somehow my Christian culture was both combative and complementary, with no clear guidelines for when to be one and not the other. But what if there's a more informed way? In this chapter we will describe our choice of interpretive lenses and explain how we can use these lenses in a more deliberate and nuanced manner.

THE T-SPECTRUM

Whenever we think about a topic, we choose from a spectrum of approaches describing how Christ views the topic, which I call the T-Spectrum.[2] This spectrum, ranging from T1 to T4, describes four possible approaches for preachers as they speak about a topic.

T1 approach: Christ opposes your topic.
T2 approach: Christ replaces your topic.
T3 approach: Christ fulfills your topic.
T4 approach: Christ affirms your topic.

The T1 and T2 approaches assume that God's ways are discontinuous with the topic. In contrast the T3 and T4 approaches assume that God's ways are continuous with the topic. Theologically, we can see how there is room for all four approaches. Our doctrines of sin and universal human depravity tell us that something in every topic will oppose, defy, suppress, and run away from God's truth. There will always be a place for T1 and T2 approaches. But our doctrines of common grace, general revelation, and the image of God also tell us that something in every topic will express God's truth, goodness, and beauty. There will also be a place for T3 and T4 approaches.

We can see models of each approach in the Bible. T1 is what Jesus did when he went through the temple with a whip (John 2:13–17). It's hard to be more oppositional than what Jesus did on that day! The money changers needed to stop what they were doing, repent, and follow Jesus, the true temple of God.

T2 is what Jesus did when he told the rich young ruler to leave behind his riches and follow him (Luke 18:22). Jesus undermined the rich man's view of wealth. The man thought he was secure and destined for eternal life. But his wealth was an obstacle to his entry to the kingdom of God.

The T-Spectrum

	T1	T2	T3	T4
The Place of Christ	Christ opposes your topic.	Christ replaces your topic.	Christ fulfills your topic.	Christ affirms your topic.
The Message	"This topic is evil, and you must reject it to follow Christ."	"This topic is a false god, and you should replace it with Christ."	"This topic is heading in the right direction, but it's Christ that you're looking for."	"This topic belongs under the headship of Christ."
The Preacher's Aim	The preacher speaks against the topic.	The preacher undermines the topic.	The preacher repurposes the topic.	The preacher places the topic under the headship of Christ.
The Audience	People who adhere to this topic are guilty of transgressing God's laws.	People who adhere to this topic are guilty of idolatry.	People who adhere to this topic are desiring Jesus but in a broken way.	People, redeemed by Christ, enjoy the topic under Christ's headship.
Application	"You must repent and submit to Christ instead."	"You must replace this topic with Christ in your life."	"Christ fulfills the God-given, right desire you were looking to satisfy in this topic."	"Worship Jesus and enjoy this topic."

	T1	T2	T3	T4
Model	Jesus clearing the temple with a whip	Jesus speaking to the rich young ruler	Jesus speaking to the Samaritan woman; Paul speaking to the Athenians	Jesus speaking to the leper
Example in the Bible: Money	"No one can serve two masters. . . . You cannot serve both God and money" (Matt. 6:24).	"You still lack one thing. Sell everything you have and give to the poor, and you will have treasure in heaven. Then come, follow me" (Luke 18:22).	"Zacchaeus stood up and said to the Lord, 'Look, Lord! Here and now I give half of my possessions to the poor'" (Luke 19:8).	"The man who had received five bags of gold brought the other five. 'Master,' he said, 'you entrusted me with five bags of gold. See, I have gained five more'" (Matt. 25:20).
Salvation—Historical Stage	The fall	The fall	Creation	Redemption and consummation
Wisdom Literature Metaphor	"Fools," "mockers," "simple," "sluggard" (Prov. 1:22, 32; 6:6, 9)	"Meaningless, a chasing after the wind" (Eccl. 1:14)	"Eternity in the human heart" (Eccl. 3:11)	"Fear of the LORD" (Prov. 1:7; Eccl. 3:14)

T3 is Jesus telling the Samaritan woman at the well about living water (John 4:13–14). Jesus promised to fulfill the woman's innermost longing. The woman came looking for water, but only Jesus could satisfy her deeper thirst. Paul's speech at Athens is another example of T3. Instead of opposing the Athenians' idol worship, Paul repurposed it as their religious longing for the Unknown God: Christ (Acts 17:22–23). They came to worship idols, but they should have been worshiping Jesus.

T4 is Jesus speaking to the man healed with leprosy (Luke 17:11–19). Ten men had begged to be healed. Jesus gave them what they wanted by healing them. But only one man, a Samaritan, came back to thank Jesus. The Samaritan placed himself under the redeeming headship of Jesus, and Jesus affirmed his healing. While healing is a good thing to ask for, it should properly be enjoyed in a saved relationship with Jesus, which only the Samaritan got to experience.

It's not difficult to imagine how any of these four approaches would be biblical and valid ways of addressing any of the following topics: money, work, sex, success, security, sports, fashion, validation, or leisure.

The T-Spectrum of Topical Sermons on Money

Let's take the topic of money as an example. From the T-Spectrum, we can choose a model to use for our sermon.

A T1 sermon would say that Jesus opposes our wealth. We store up treasures either on earth or in heaven (Matt. 6:19–21). We can serve only one master: either God or money (Matt. 6:24). Our message would be that our love of money is wrong and will lead to all kinds of evil (1 Tim. 6:10). People need to repent of their love of money and submit to the rule of Jesus instead.

A T2 sermon would say that Jesus ought to replace money in our hearts. Money has become a false god that we worship. Money has displaced Jesus, assuming his rightful place in our lives. Our message would be like that of Jesus to the rich young ruler: give up your money and follow Jesus instead (Luke 18:22). Stop trusting in money and be "rich toward God" (Luke 12:21).

A T3 sermon would say that Jesus fulfills our longing for money. Money and the ability to enjoy it are good gifts from God (Eccl. 5:19). Being poor leads to its own temptations (Prov. 30:9). But if we elevate money to become our security or status, then it will sadly disappoint (Eccl. 5:10). Worse, it will destroy us in our endless quest (Eccl. 5:13–14). But if we belong to Jesus, then Jesus gives us the security and status that we are longing for (Heb. 13:5–6). Jesus frees us from whatever hold money has on us. An example is Zacchaeus, who is able to give away his money, unlike the rich young ruler (Luke 19:8).

A T4 sermon would say that Jesus affirms our money. Jesus is our Lord and Savior, and we serve him. All we have belongs to him (Ps. 24:1). We are therefore stewards of our wealth, which comes from God in the first place. Money, as God's gracious gift, allows us to be self-sufficient and not a burden on others (2 Thess. 3:8). It allows us to maximize our opportunities to further God's kingdom (Matt. 25:20). We can also use our wealth to be generous to others as Jesus was once generous to us (2 Cor. 8:9).

The T-Spectrum of Topical Sermons on Work

Let's take the topic of work as another example. A T1 sermon would say that Jesus opposes our work. Work becomes an expression of our human sinfulness—an outlet for all forms of evil and rebellion against God (Ps. 28:4; Isa. 29:15; Rev. 9:20–21). Work oppresses the poor and robs people of basic justice (Amos 8:5–6; James 2:6–7). God will condemn and judge work such as this (Zeph. 1:11; Rev. 18:9–24). If this is what your work has become, then you need to repent and submit to Jesus (Luke 19:8–10).

A T2 sermon would say that Jesus replaces our work. Work is a false god. Work has displaced Jesus, assuming his rightful place in our lives. Our work distracts us from Jesus (Luke 10:38–42). Work breeds a blasphemous arrogance in our lives, as if we were autonomous and in control (James 4:13–17). Work allows us to store up for ourselves and live as if there were no God (Luke 12:21). We need to stop worshiping our work and trust in God instead. We should replace our devotion to earthly work with a devotion to the work of the Lord, which is never in vain (1 Cor. 15:58).

A T3 sermon would say that Jesus fulfills our longing for work. We have been created by God for work (Gen. 2:15; Prov. 12:11; 22:29). We image our creator when we work. Work is a good gift from God to enjoy (Eccl. 2:24; 3:13, 22). But our work is also doomed to be frustrating (Gen. 3:17–19; Eccl. 2:17). It is a constant reminder of our sin against God. By itself work cannot fulfill our cries for transcendence, community, purpose, hope, and meaning (Eccl. 3:11). Only Jesus can fulfill our hearts' deepest longings. If we have Jesus, then this frees us from whatever hold work has on us. We can once again use our work to support ourselves and not become a burden on others and to be generous to those less fortunate (1 Thess. 4:11–12; 2 Thess. 3:7–10; 2 Cor. 8:9). But our work doesn't have to become our identity and purpose. We already have all these things in Jesus (Eph. 1:3–23).

A T4 sermon would say that Jesus affirms our work. Jesus is our Lord and Savior. We have been called by Jesus to work (1 Cor. 7:21–24). Work is our vocation—a calling! Ultimately, we work for Jesus and not for our earthly bosses or for ourselves (Col. 3:24; Eph. 6:5–8). In effect Jesus undoes the frustrations of the Genesis 3 curses, as expressed in Ecclesiastes, because Jesus sees everything and will make sure we get what we deserve for our work (Eph. 6:8). Our work is incredibly purposeful when it is done for Jesus. We make the most of every opportunity, knowing that we are stewards of our work and that our work belongs under the headship of Jesus (Matt. 25:20). It is somehow part of his plan for the universe (Eph. 1:9–10). Our present work anticipates the future work we will do in the new heaven and new earth (Amos 9:13–15).

Biblical Theology and the T-Spectrum

Biblical theology traces themes diachronically across the Bible, placing them in their distinct salvation-historical stages and then showing how the theme ultimately leads to Jesus.

An obvious example is the biblical theme "Temple." At creation God dwells with Adam and Eve in the garden of Eden. In this sense the garden itself is the temple. After the fall God dwells with his people in the tabernacle and subsequently in the temple. But in both places an elaborate set of rituals, sacrifices, and priests is necessary in order to meet God there. At redemption the incarnate Jesus becomes the temple, with God's people also becoming the temple. At the consummation there is no need for a physical temple, because God dwells with his people in the new heaven and the new earth (Rev. 21:22).

When we research a topical sermon, we can similarly trace how our topic fits according to biblical theology into each salvation-historical stage. Let's research the topic "Sex and Marriage." At creation, sex and marriage are God's good design for Adam and Eve (Gen. 1:27–28; 2:18–25). After the fall, sex and marriage are prone to conflict, dysfunction, and violence (Gen. 3:15). At redemption, sex and marriage are images of Christ's sacrificial love for the church. Moreover, God's people are now free to enjoy and model the original good design of sex and marriage (Eph. 5:22–33). At the consummation, sex and marriage are images of God dwelling with his people forever in the new heaven and new earth (Matt. 22:30; Rev. 21:1–4).

Biblical theology also teaches us to give a nuanced and balanced treatment of our topic. At present we are in the now-and-not-yet stage of salvation history. We enjoy Christ's redeeming work, but we look forward to a future redemption. Thus we always look back to the original goodness of creation. Yet we live in a sinfully broken world, where God's creation falls short of its ideal. We also enjoy the headship of Jesus, under which we live redeemed lives that come close to God's ideal. And we still look forward to the not-yet kingdom, where our lives will be free of sin and frustration.

Models of Redemption and Topical Preaching

At creation, the first salvation-historical stage, God declared that everything he created was good. Thus every aspect of creation—nature, work, leisure, sex and marriage, human culture, entertainment, education, sports, arts, language—is inherently good (Genesis 1–2).

But how much of God's creation and human culture can we still affirm as God's redeemed people? How discontinuous or continuous is God's creation with God's future redeemed creation, the new heaven and new earth?

On the one hand, there is discontinuity. God's creation became corrupted after humans sinned at the fall (Genesis 3). At redemption Jesus came to save us from creation. He saved us from the chaos of nature, the darkness of demons, the sufferings of disease, and the foreverness of death (Luke 8:22–56). At consummation this earth will be destroyed (2 Peter 3:10). As a result, we are foreigners and exiles, merely passing through this present creation (1 Peter 2:11–12). As the classic hymn says, "This world is not my home." Our longing is for a future home discontinuous from our present home.

But on the other hand, there is also continuity. Although God's creation has been corrupted, even after the fall humans remain in the image of God (Gen. 9:6; James 3:9). At redemption Jesus comes to save us as creation. He becomes and remains incarnate—with our nature, with a body, immersed in culture, speaking a human language, eating our food (John 1:14). He turns water into wine (John 2:1–11). He calls us back to creational norms (Matt. 19:4–6). At consummation this earth will not be destroyed; it will be liberated (Rom. 8:21). As the classic children's Sunday school song says, "If I were a butterfly, I'd thank you, Lord, for giving me wings." Presumably, God is not going to abandon the butterfly in the new creation!

> The significance for us is this: A T1 or T2 sermon will see Christ's work primarily as Christ saving us *from* creation. It will see discontinuity between the world and the Christian life. As a result, it will have an oppositional and adversarial message: "The world says *this*, but God says *this* instead."
>
> But a T3 or T4 sermon will see Christ's work primarily as Christ saving us *as* creation. It will see continuity between the world and the Christian life. As a result, it will have an affirmational message: "Look at what God is telling us from his world."

When we employ the T-Spectrum, each stage of salvation history becomes useful. A T1 or T2 sermon looks mainly at the fall. We research the effects of sin on our topic. For example, sin has made sex and marriage expressions of human evil (T1) and idolatry (T2).

A T3 sermon looks mainly at creation. We see the original goodness of sex and marriage. But we acknowledge that by themselves they fall short. There is no redemption from our fallen human condition without the redeeming work of Jesus. Sex and marriage can never save us. We need Jesus for that.

A T4 sermon looks mainly at redemption and consummation. When everything is placed under the redeeming headship of Jesus, it can be enjoyed in its rightful place in God's universe. Sex and marriage foreshadow the person and work of Christ. Plus, under Jesus, sex and marriage can be our calling and our worship to God.

Wisdom Literature and the T-Spectrum

The Bible's wisdom literature is a very sophisticated genre. At the risk of oversimplifying, while the salvation-historical sections of the Bible concentrate on telling us how to be saved, the wisdom sections tell us how to be wise.

Should I answer a fool or not (Prov. 26:4–5)? Is this a time to keep or to throw away (Eccl. 3:6)? How long is too long to stay as a guest before they've had too much of me (Prov. 25:16–17)? The wisdom sections don't so much tell us the right thing to do or the true thing to believe as tell us to search for what is most apt—the wise thing to do. The Wisdom Literature is a fruitful source for our topical sermons because it is highly nuanced. It juggles the tensions between God's creation ideal, a fallen world, universal human longings, and a future hope.

When we research a topic, the Wisdom Literature gives us multiple approaches. Let us research the topic of pleasure. The Wisdom Literature has a high view of pleasure. God delighted in his creation (Prov. 8:30–31). Playfulness and fun are part of God's creation (Ps. 104:26). God's creation—food, wine, oil—exists not just to sustain us but to please us (Ps. 104:15). Laughing and dancing are part of the rhythms of life (Eccl. 3:4).

But the Wisdom Literature also has a low view of pleasure. By themselves pleasures are empty, unsatisfying, and lonely—"meaningless, a chasing after the wind" (Eccl. 2:1–11; Prov. 17:1). Chasing pleasures will lead to ruin (Prov. 21:17). People can also look for pleasures in wicked and sinful schemes (Prov. 10:23).

According to the Wisdom Literature, a human's deepest longing is for eternity (Eccl. 3:10–11). Our most primal need is to fear the Lord (Prov. 1:7; Eccl. 3:14). We can't properly enjoy pleasures until we're in a proper relationship with God. But if we fear God, we will be in rhythm with God, his universe, and the people around us (Eccl. 12:13), and that will be the best place to enjoy the pleasures God has gifted us.

The Wisdom Literature concludes that pleasures are God's good gift for us to enjoy (Eccl. 2:24–26; 3:12–13). But unless we're in a proper relationship with God, we ask too much of them, hoping to find eternity in our pleasures (Eccl. 3:11). If we do this, we will end up empty, unsatisfied, and alone (Eccl. 2:1–11). If we begin with the fear of the Lord, then we can experience pleasures simply as a good gift to enjoy, fully knowing that our cries for eternity will one day be answered in God (Eccl. 3:14; 12:1–14).

Using the Wisdom Literature as a Template for Topical Sermons

I have found the Wisdom Literature to be a rich, fruitful, and nuanced source of material for most topics I preach on. The Wisdom Literature gives us this useful template for preaching topical sermons:

1. This topic is a good gift from a good God to enjoy.
2. But by itself this topic can never satisfy; it is meaningless!
3. Worse, we can use this topic in foolish (sinful) ways.
4. This is because God has placed eternity in our hearts.
5. But if we fear God, we can enjoy a relationship with God and a way of life that works.
6. This frees us up to enjoy our topic for what it is: a good gift from a good God to enjoy.

Let's say we've been asked to preach to college students on the topic of study. The Wisdom Literature gives us the following template.

1. Study is a good gift from a good God to enjoy (Prov. 23:12).
   - Study is God's way of making us wise.
2. But by itself, study can never satisfy; it is meaningless (Eccl. 1:12–18; 2:12–16).
   - Study is burdensome.
   - The wise die the same death as the fool.
3. Worse, we can use study in foolish (sinful) ways (Prov. 21:24).
   - Study turns us into proud, arrogant, self-righteous mockers.

4. This is because God has placed eternity in our hearts
   (Eccl. 3:11).
   - We have a God-given, legitimate existential cry for
     meaning, purpose, and hope.
   - But only God can fulfill this God-given, legitimate
     existential cry.
5. So if we fear God, we can enjoy a relationship with God and
   a way of life that works (Eccl. 12:11–14).
   - We don't need to study to find our meaning, purpose,
     and hope.
   - Jesus gives us the meaning, purpose, and hope we're
     looking for.
   - God knows everything. This humbles us because we
     can't know everything, and it reassures us that we don't
     have to know everything.
   - Let Jesus become our wisdom.
6. This frees us up to enjoy our study simply for what it is:
   a good gift from a good God to enjoy (Eccl. 2:24–25; 3:22;
   5:18–20).
   - Appreciate, enjoy, and maximize the opportunities that
     God has given us to study (Matt. 25:14–30).

When we employ the T-Spectrum, we have a vast array of landing points in the Wisdom Literature. A T1 sermon preaches against the fool—and its variants, the mocker, the simpleton, the sluggard—in Proverbs, who looks for pleasure in sinful ways (Prov. 10:23; 18:2; 21:17).

A T2 sermon speaks about the emptiness of trying to live for pleasure, as an idol, without God in his rightful place in our lives (Eccl. 2:1–11). This is a recurring refrain of Ecclesiastes—how pleasures by themselves are unsatisfying, fleeting, ephemeral, transient, and unfruitful. They are "meaningless, a chasing after the wind; nothing was gained under the sun" (Eccl. 2:11).

A T3 sermon speaks about our cries for eternity (Eccl. 3:11), which can be fulfilled only by Jesus. If we expect to satisfy this deepest human longing with food, wine, laughing, and singing, then we will be sorely disappointed. We may even destroy ourselves in trying. But once we've found Jesus, we can enjoy the pleasures of God's creation for what they are: a good gift from our God to enjoy.

A T4 sermon speaks about the fear of the Lord, which is the beginning of all wisdom (Prov. 1:7). If we begin here, then we will be in rhythm with God's creation (Proverbs 8). We will be the wise person who knows when it is most apt to weep or laugh, mourn or dance (Eccl. 3:4). When we enjoy the pleasures of God's creation, it is our act of gratitude and worship. We look back to Eden (Psalm 104) but at the same time long for the new heaven and new earth (Ps. 104:31–35; Eccl. 12:13–14). Perhaps it can even take us to Jesus, wisdom personified, who knew when it was apt to eat and drink, sing and dance, saying, "Wisdom is proved right by her deeds" (Matt. 11:19; Luke 7:34–35).

HOW TO USE THE T-SPECTRUM TO PREACH PERSUASIVELY

It's been useful to speak of T1, T2, T3, and T4 sermons as if they were mutually exclusive elements. But most topical sermons will combine T1, T2, T3, and T4 elements because each topic deserves a nuanced and balanced approach. This is the art of persuasive preaching.

To preach persuasively, a preacher must work through three logical movements.

1. **Resonance.** Here we construct the topic.
   - We say something that will resonate with our audience.
   - The aim is to get the audience saying, "Yes! Yes! Yes!" We want them thinking, *This preacher gets me. This preacher*

understands my world. This preacher has emotionally connected with my life.

- We do this by speaking the audience's worldview back to them.
- The audience feels affirmed, stable, and secure.
- A metaphor for this stage is a full glass of water, representing the audience's current worldview.

2. **Dissonance.** Here we deconstruct the topic.
   - We say something that will disequilibrate our audience.
   - The aim is to get the audience saying, "Huh? I've never thought of it that way before. I've got a problem."
   - We do this by showing either a deficiency in their worldview (they have a gap they can't account for) or a dissonance in their worldview (they're juggling conflicting ideas and can't have it both ways).
   - The audience feels deconstructed, disequilibrated, destabilized.
   - A metaphor for this stage is tipping the glass of water upside down and emptying it in front of their eyes. The emptied glass represents their deconstructed worldview.

3. **Gospel fulfillment.** Here we reconstruct the topic with a christological perspective.
   - We say something that will reconfigure the audience with the gospel.
   - The aim here is to get the audience saying, "I didn't know it, but I need Jesus to complete my worldview. It's Jesus I've been looking for all along!"
   - We do this by completing their worldview with Jesus.
   - The audience feels a longing to be fulfilled by Jesus.
   - A metaphor for this stage is filling up the glass with new water. Their worldview is now completed with the gospel.

Resonance, Dissonance, Gospel Fulfillment

Persuasive Sequence	1. Resonance	2. Dissonance	3. Gospel Fulfillment
What we do to the topic	construct	deconstruct	reconstruct
What we do to the audience	resonate with them	dissonate	reconfigure them with the gospel
The audience says	"Yes!"	"Huh?"	"I need Jesus!"
Our method	Speak their worldview back to them.	Demonstrate a deficiency or dissonance in their worldview.	Complete their worldview with Jesus.
The audience feels	affirmed, stable, secure	deconstructed, disequilibrated, destabilized	longing to be fulfilled by Jesus
Metaphor	We show them a cup filled with their worldview.	We empty the cup in front of their eyes.	We fill the cup with the gospel.

We can use a combination of T1, T2, T3, and T4 to achieve this resonance, dissonance, gospel-fulfillment sequence. But the way we do this will depend on our audience.

My church's youth pastor and I once sat down to write a talk on the topic of YOLO. YOLO is a bit dated now, but a few years ago it was a popular buzzword which stood for the phrase "You Only Live Once." The idea of YOLO is this: You only live once, so you'd better make the most of each day before you die. Do whatever makes you happy, and don't listen to what anyone else tells you to do.

YOLO is a great expression of Western individualism. The pursuit of pleasure trumps collective responsibility. Immediate rewards trump delayed rewards. Don't let anyone else tell you what to be; you do you! So how can we preach persuasively on the topic of YOLO?

47

Normally, you could achieve the resonance, dissonance, gospel-fulfillment sequence this way:

1. **Resonance.** Here we find something the audience agrees with about YOLO. For example, God has programmed pleasure into his creation (Ps. 104:26).
2. **Dissonance.** If all we do is pursue pleasure, we end up empty and unsatisfied (Eccl. 2:1–11).
3. **Gospel fulfillment.** Jesus fulfills our cry for eternity, so that we don't have to enjoy pleasures alone but can enjoy them in a relationship with God (Eccl. 3:11–14).

But my church is a Chinese church. Most of the high schoolers do not subscribe to Western individualism. They belong to an Asian culture of honor and shame, in which they do their best to honor their parents by studying hard to achieve high grades. They shun short-term pleasures (sports, leisure, parties) to pursue long-term career goals. It's the complete opposite to the culture of YOLO. A Chinese youth often believes that collective responsibility trumps the pursuit of pleasure. Delayed rewards trump immediate rewards.

In this culture the resonance, dissonance, gospel-fulfillment sequence is flipped around.

1. **Resonance.** Here we find something the audience agrees with about YOLO. For example, the pursuit of short-term pleasure is foolish and leads to ruin (Prov. 21:17).
2. **Dissonance.** God himself delights in his creation and wants you to do the same (Ps. 104:26; 1 Tim. 4:4–5). And what if our pursuit of long-term goals—career, wealth, status—is just as self-centered, self-destructive, and idolatrous as YOLO?
3. **Gospel fulfillment.** Jesus fulfills our cry for eternity, so that we can trust him with our status and security. God has our long-term goals in his hands (Matt. 6:19–34). YOLO is correct!

We have only one life to live for Christ, so let's do as much as we can in this life to serve him (Phil. 1:21).

Can you see what happened? We had to affirm YOLO to resonate with Western individualists (T4). Then we had to oppose YOLO to dissonate them (T1 and T2). Then we had to fulfill them with the gospel to show how they can enjoy pleasures in a proper relationship with Christ (T3).

But we had to oppose YOLO to resonate with Asian collectivists (T1 and T2). Then we had to affirm YOLO to dissonate them (T4). Then we had to fulfill them with the gospel to show how they can find true security and status (T3).

We had to flip T1 and T2 with T4. We're addressing the same topic—YOLO—but the two audiences have different interpretive lenses. As a result, we've had to mix up how we arrange the T1, T2, T3, and T4 elements to preach persuasively to them.

SAMPLE SERMON: "HOW TO SURVIVE THE DAILY GRIND"

At my work with City Bible Forum, I usually speak to city workers—a mix of believers and nonbelievers—on a topic that has been given to me. One time I was given the topic "How to Survive the Daily Grind."

I began the talk by defining the topic: "The daily grind is us doing the same thing over and over again every day. We wake up, eat breakfast, drive to work, park in the same spot, work at the same desk, order the same lunch from the same cafeteria, go home, eat the same dinner, watch the same show on TV, go to bed, and do it all over again the next day." From this I set up the question: "How do we survive this daily grind?"

Where did I go from here? I used the Wisdom Literature as a template for my sermon (see "Using the Wisdom Literature as a Template for Topical Sermons" earlier in this chapter). But I moved the elements around so my sermon would be more persuasive. First, I resonated with my audience. I agreed with them that the daily grind is a source of frustration. There is something mind numbing and soul destroying about doing the same thing every day. Worse, it doesn't feel like we're achieving anything. Like Sisyphus from Greek mythology, we do the same thing every day, only to have to do it all over again the next day. Our daily grind is "meaningless, a chasing after the wind" (Eccl. 2:11).

Second, I dissonated the audience. I suggested that humans require a daily routine. There is something reassuring in having things happen repeatedly and reliably. Moreover, what if our daily routine is a blessing from God? After all, it's a blessing to have the same job every day. It's a blessing to have a bus come at the same time every day. It's a blessing to have the same food in the same cafeteria every day. What if our daily grind isn't a curse but a blessing from God—a good gift to be thankful for?

Third, I fulfilled the audience with the gospel. I suggested that our daily routine is the music of God. Music requires rhythm, repetition, harmony, and melody—a *logos*! According to the ancient Greeks, *logos* (which we thinly translate into English as "word") is the unifying principle that binds the universe together. *Logos* is the "logic" of the universe; it is the rhythm, repetition, harmony, and melody by which the universe runs. If so, then this is what our daily routine is: it is the musical rhythm, repetition, harmony, and melody—the *logos!*—of the universe. And so there must be a composer: a *Logos* who became flesh. Music is best enjoyed if we know the composer. In the same way, our daily routine is best enjoyed in a worshipful relationship with our creator God, Jesus Christ.

So how can we survive our daily grind? By beginning with the fear of the Lord, which will put us in rhythm and harmony with the God who loves us. This way we can see the wonder and beauty in having things happen the same way every day. We can enjoy our daily routine as a good gift to thank God for.

CHAPTER 3

HOW TO PREACH TO TWO AUDIENCES

Is It Possible to Engage Believers and Nonbelievers?

MALCOLM GILL

I like golf, but I'm not that good at it. When I'm out on the links, it is rare for my game to come together. If the driver is working, my putting is off. If my short game is on fire, then my chipping is rubbish. I semi-regularly commit to improving my game but shortly thereafter determine to quit. Golf is enjoyable but immensely frustrating.

Because of my inconsistency in both form and commitment, I have in recent years discovered a helpful way to enjoy golf without disappointment: the driving range. The driving range is the perfect place for me to meet my golfing needs. I don't need to carry my clubs around, no one keeps score, it doesn't matter if I slice or shank my shots, and I can hit as many balls as I like without consequence. The driving range is fantastic.

Some time ago, I was down at the driving range belting balls as hard as I could, when I looked around and noticed the diversity of others participating. There was a teenage girl who could barely hit the ball off the tee. She was getting a lesson, but it didn't appear to be paying off. Next to her was a beefy tradesman in a bright-orange work vest. Looking as if he had come from a rough day at work, he was smashing the balls with anger. Farther down was a nicely dressed Asian businessman who was measured in his swing and cleanly hitting balls straight down the fairway. This was a motley crowd. Different ages, different careers, different cultures, but one common love (or frustration): golf.

While observing these golfers, out of the corner of my eye I noticed a golf cart making its way onto the driving range fairway. For a few bucks an hour, some poor college student had the unenviable job of gathering the scattered golf balls. Eighty yards from the golf tees, the young man steered and veered his way around, plucking balls off the ground to return them to the clubhouse. If you've ever been to a driving range, you know that when you see the golf ball collector guy on the fairway, there is only one thing to do. Your head, your heart, and your hands all shout to you, "Hit the golf cart!"

While some among you may think me a sinner, you know in your heart that this is the golfer's natural bent! As I watched my fellow golfers that day, I could see I was not alone in my desire. The teenage girl was trying just a bit harder to make contact in the direction of the cart. The tradesman was like a machine chugging out shots with the same aim. Even the measured business guy adjusted his stance, looked up, and started methodically delivering shots within the vicinity of the cart. The universal nature of golfers everywhere is to hit the moving golf cart.

In life, just as at the driving range, there are some things we all desire. As individuals, we all seek meaning and purpose in our existence. We all long for peace, love, and joy in our relationships. As communities, we all yearn for justice, safety, and financial stability. Regardless of our ethnicity, age, education level, and marital status, some elements of life we all share in common.

The Scriptures affirm the common realities of our human condition.

The Bible highlights that we all wrestle with the reality of death. It doesn't matter what century we live in or what family we are from; "people are destined to die" (Heb. 9:27).

Likewise, the Bible speaks to the truth that we all have a disposition to do wrong. The prophet Jeremiah says that our hearts are deceitful (Jer. 17:9), and this is shown in the decisions we make. Put up a "Wet paint: don't touch!" sign in the hallway, and the first thing a passerby thinks will be, *Is that really true?* All of us have a heart issue.

Topical preaching recognizes the common issues that every human wrestles with. Whether it is the search for personal significance and meaning in life, or facing the reality of pain, injustice, or death, topical preaching seeks to tackle head on the common existential cries of the human heart. Topical preaching, as with other forms of preaching, seeks to provide a biblical framework on how to navigate this broken world.

The Bible exposes the truth that all of us, regardless of culture or age, are affected by the results of living in a broken world. We are victims of our damaged world and contributors to its brokenness. We all suffer because of fractured interpersonal, political, and social relationships, and we all hope for a better day to come.

Given the reality of our human experience, one would think that preaching would be a simple, straightforward thing: identify each common need of humanity and address it. The problem with this, however, is that while we share things in common, we are still individuals.

All people are sinners, but folks in the audiences we address will be struggling with different aspects of sin. Some people will be wrestling with the guilt and shame of their own sin, whereas others will be suffering because of someone else's transgression against them.

In any given crowd, some individuals will be rejoicing because of a great week or an answer to prayer, but others sitting next to them will be grieving over the loss of a loved one. A young couple may be rejoicing over their recent engagement while a single person wrestles with the pain of loneliness. Though our deepest needs are the same, our daily challenges are not.

Given this tension of similarity and dissimilarity, questions naturally arise for a preacher. How does one preach meaningfully to different groups in the same audience? How do you preach in such a way that all people can engage and interact with the truth of Scripture, no matter their individual issues? How do you preach a sermon to God's people when some folks in your congregation have not yet embraced Jesus as Lord? Is it possible to address both audiences in one sermon?

THE CHALLENGE AND OPPORTUNITY OF PREACHING TO A MIXED AUDIENCE

Pastor Daryl arises early on Sunday morning eager to share God's Word. Having worked hard during the week exegeting the text, thinking through the theological ideas behind the text, and then considering the contemporary implications for his audience, Daryl feels ready to go. As he steps up into the pulpit, he prays that God will speak through his Holy Spirit and that people will respond in repentance and faith as they submit to the Lord Jesus.

At the same time, Vijay feels a sense of shame as he prepares to listen to Pastor Daryl. He just can't seem to shake his addiction to pornography. As much as he tries, he always seems to fail. This week was no different. He feels woefully inadequate to be at church. *God*, he prays, *I'm so ashamed to be here. Please forgive me.*

Vanessa sits in her regular seat and is keen to hear from God. A faithful Bible study leader in the church, Vanessa loves to take notes when Pastor Daryl preaches. She has pen in hand, her Bible is open, and she is ready to listen. Today in particular, Vanessa wants to hear from the Lord. Unbeknownst to the others in church, Vanessa has been wrestling with depression, and this Sunday she feels particularly low. *God*, she prays, *speak to me and let me know you're present. I feel so sad right now.*

Timmy is a middle-aged bricklayer who loves to play rugby. Recently a friend of his, named Jonty, invited him to consider the claims of Christianity. Uninterested, Timmy dismissed Jonty as a religious fundamentalist. Later that night, however, he couldn't shake off his conversation with his enthusiastic friend. Finally, he grabbed his phone and googled to find a church in his area, where he could learn more about Jesus. He discovered the church where Pastor Daryl preaches and decided to attend.

Arriving early, Timmy sits in the back and waits for the service to begin. Though he doesn't have any faith background, he is now genuinely curious to learn what this is all about. As he watches Pastor Daryl get ready to speak, he prays, *God, if you really exist, then show me.*

All over the world, in different contexts and languages, people like Vijay, Vanessa, and Timmy are joining in gatherings to listen to sermons. Some of these individuals come with hearts that are broken, others with tears of joy. Some struggle with mental health, others with addiction. Some attend with resolute faith and joy, while others harbor skepticism and doubt. Even among those who haven't embraced Jesus as Lord, some are open and curious about Christianity, while others are apathetic or even antagonistic to Jesus and his claims. The challenge for Pastor Daryl is that he can't tell where the hearts of the people in his audience lie.

No doubt, the pastor would love to be able to identify the needs of his audience. If there were a section of the church designated for doubters, he would want to address the people sitting there. If there were a seating area for those wrestling with their marriage or for people who desire to be married, the pastor would want to make sure his message connected with people sitting in those seats. If a group were identified as discouraged, the preacher would love to know this.

Of course, neither Pastor Daryl nor any of us can accurately gauge the spiritual condition of each person's heart. Preachers are challenged to put God's truth before people in a clear and engaging manner, trusting God to do his good work in their lives. Preaching to the deep needs of people isn't easy, because only God knows their hearts.

Though it is challenging to preach to a diverse group of needy people, preaching also affords the preacher a great opportunity. God has promised that the proclamation of his Word will achieve his purposes, and his promise stands regardless of the spiritual makeup of an audience. Isaiah 55:9–11 records the declaration of the Lord.

> "As the heavens are higher than the earth,
>> so are my ways higher than your ways
>> and my thoughts than your thoughts.
> As the rain and the snow
>> come down from heaven,
> and do not return to it
>> without watering the earth
> and making it bud and flourish,
>> so that it yields seed for the sower and bread for the eater,
> so is my word that goes out from my mouth:
>> It will not return to me empty,
> but will accomplish what I desire
>> and achieve the purpose for which I sent it."

The astonishing privilege of preachers is that God speaks his Word through them. Regardless of the audience or context, God has promised that his Word will not return empty. This should empower preachers with confidence to proclaim in any setting. When God's Word is presented to his people, God speaks. When God's Word is presented to unbelievers, God speaks. When Pastor Daryl preaches, he might not know the precise heart issues of Vijay, Vanessa, or Timmy, but he can rest assured that God will speak. What a great opportunity and privilege.

There are two goals for a sermon when a preacher faces both the opportunity and the challenge of addressing an audience of believers and unbelievers. The sermon should aim to edify the people of God, and it should aim to evangelize the lost.

THE SERMON SHOULD EDIFY GOD'S PEOPLE

What comes to mind when you hear the word sermon? Perhaps you visualize a preacher offering an explanation of a passage from the Bible. They read the passage, then seek to enlighten your understanding of how the passage fits together and what it means.

Alternately, perhaps you see the sermon more as a formal, structured teaching on an area of doctrine. The preacher is interested in explanation of the Bible, but the emphasis is on the ideas or theology of the Scriptures and what Christians should believe.

Or you might perceive the sermon as a kind of pep talk to inspire believers. The preacher delivers a stirring homily designed to help the audience navigate another week of life.

What is a sermon? As we mentioned in chapter 1, what we commonly refer to as a sermon, the New Testament refers to as a "word of exhortation" (Acts 13:15; Heb. 13:22). The sermon is primarily an exhortation: it is a spoken discourse given to urge and encourage the listener to some type of response. Let's examine this a little more closely.

The Sermon as a Word of Exhortation

In Acts 13, Luke recounts the traveling work of Paul and his ministry colleagues. They arrive at Pisidian Antioch, and we read, "On the Sabbath they entered the synagogue and sat down. After the reading from the Law and the Prophets, the leaders of the synagogue sent word to them, saying, 'Brothers, if you have a word of exhortation for the people, please speak'" (vv. 14–15). The Scriptures are read, and an invitation is given to speak a word of exhortation. What follows in verses 16–41 is Paul's sermon to those in the synagogue.

A close inspection of Paul's word of exhortation reveals striking similarity with what we consider to be a sermon. His message is urgent, it is focused, and it aims to move the listener with a call to respond to his truth claims.

As we reflect on Paul's word of exhortation, we can observe several components of his message that are helpful for us to consider in our preaching.

1. Paul addresses the audience as "fellow Israelites," implying a shared commonality (Acts 13:16).
2. The word of exhortation comes after the reading of the Scriptures (v. 15).
3. When Paul delivers his word of exhortation, he incorporates biblical quotations in his message. He includes, among others, references and allusions to Psalms 2 and 16, Isaiah 55, and Habakkuk 1.
4. Paul develops a biblical theology by demonstrating the unfolding of salvation history related to Israel and his audience. He moves from the exodus (Acts 13:17) to the judges (v. 20) to the appointment of King David (v. 22) to Jesus (v. 23).
5. Paul's word of exhortation centers on a major topic: the "message of salvation" (v. 26).
6. Paul's word of exhortation has a christological focus, with Jesus' redemptive acts of death and resurrection as the high point of the message (vv. 26–39).
7. The message concludes with a pastoral application: respond appropriately (v. 40).

The word of exhortation given by Paul is thus characterized as a message that incorporates Scripture passages into a biblical theology that focuses on the topic of salvation found in Jesus Christ, which has application for the audience.

Hebrews as a Word of Exhortation

Although the word of exhortation delivered by Paul to those in Pisidian Antioch is relatively short, there is much we can glean from it about the edifying purpose of preaching. An even longer word of exhortation that helps us understand the nature of a sermon is the book of Hebrews (Heb. 13:22).

This book mirrors the characteristics of the Acts 13 sermon. The author weaves in a variety of Scripture references and explains the significance of Jesus in relation to those passages before providing a pastoral application to the listeners. In addition, the preacher of Hebrews embeds a series of effective rhetorical devices in the message, including alliteration, catchwords, repetition, and nuanced structures. Many of these stylistic features are present in pulpits today.

Concerning the preaching style of the word of exhortation in Hebrews, New Testament scholar John Dickson comments,

> So far as I can tell, the closest example in the Bible to a real exposition of biblical passages is found in the extended reflection, explanation, and Christological application of Old Testament texts in this wonderful New Testament book. The author doesn't just offer "proof texts"; he cites passages, makes observations about them, and then discusses their meaning for Christians. The most sustained examples are his treatment of Psalm 95 in Hebrews 3–4 and of Jeremiah 31 in Hebrews 8–10, but the whole letter is structured around biblical quotations and reflections. Even if it isn't exposition in the manner taught in preaching classes in evangelical colleges and seminaries today, it is close.[1]

The preacher of Hebrews, like Paul, quotes a variety of biblical passages and integrates them to provide theological ideas that form the foundation of the sermon. Also, like Paul, the author of Hebrews is immensely pastoral and concerned about the spiritual welfare of the audience. While providing biblical content and theological information, the author regularly pauses and illustrates and applies the text to both preacher and listeners.

Like Paul in the sermon of Acts 13, the author of Hebrews is not interested in merely transferring information to produce smarter sinners; rather the preacher wants to exhort the audience to life change on the basis of Christ's sufficiency.

Although the sermon of Hebrews and the preaching ministry of Paul in Acts 13 are not given to us primarily as paradigms for homiletics, we can learn much from them regarding the shape a sermon should take. The effective sermon should exhort its hearers; it should provide encouragement, comfort, and assurance. Sermons may involve teaching, explanation, and inspiration, but they should provide more than that. A modern-day sermon, like those in the New Testament, should aspire to give the people of God scriptural confidence that Christ is sufficient.

Preaching Exhorts to Edify

The preaching of the Word is the chief means through which God exhorts and encourages his people. But what is the goal of that encouragement? Paul reveals the aim of his proclamation ministry when he writes, "[Jesus] is the one we proclaim, admonishing and teaching everyone with all wisdom, so that we may present everyone fully mature in Christ" (Col. 1:28).

The goal of preaching Christ is maturity. In our proclamation ministry the goal is not simply to feed information or encourage; it is to preach in such a way that people can see the reality of their identity in Christ and out of that respond to God in obedience and faith. The sermon is not a one-off event. It is a contributing factor to the overall growth and maturity of God's people. The sermon provides edification.

The word edify is not particularly common in our daily vernacular. Behind the term's meaning is the idea of building up something or someone. Just as we may refer to a building as an edifice, so the Scriptures often liken God's people to a structure being built up. We read,

- "Just as you received Christ Jesus as Lord, continue to live your lives in him, rooted and *built up* in him, strengthened in the

faith as you were taught, and overflowing with thankfulness"
(Col. 2:6–7, emphasis mine).

• "Encourage one another and *build* each other *up*, just as in fact
  you are doing" (1 Thess. 5:11, emphasis mine).

• "You, dear friends, by *building* yourselves *up* in your most holy
  faith and praying in the Holy Spirit . . ." (Jude 20, emphasis mine).

• "In [Christ] the whole building is joined together and rises
  to become a holy temple in the Lord. And in him you too are
  being *built* together to become a dwelling in which God lives by
  his Spirit" (Eph. 2:21–22, emphasis mine).

The sermon is one of the tools God uses to build up his people. As we
preach, God strengthens us. As we respond to the preached Word, God
knocks off the rough edges, both individually and collectively, so that
we become his temple, his presence in the world.

The edification of God's people via the sermon involves a variety
of aspects. In his well-known charge to his protégé, Timothy, Paul says,
"Preach the word; be prepared in season and out of season; correct,
rebuke and encourage—with great patience and careful instruction"
(2 Tim. 4:2). The preaching to which Paul is calling Timothy requires
preparation. The phrase "in season and out of season" demonstrates the
willingness required regarding time. He's telling Timothy to be ready
every moment. Paul then gives three subsequent imperatives that define
what is involved in preaching the Word: "correct, rebuke and encourage."

When I sensed God's leading to full-time vocational Christian
ministry, I did not once think, *I can't wait to get into a preaching ministry of correcting and rebuking!* No, I'm not a man of confrontation,
nor do I enjoy addressing the shortcomings of other people. So Paul's
exhortation is quite shocking to me. Here's the thing, however. God
knows we all have areas in our lives that only he can correct. If you and
I are to work on God's edifice, the church, we must take seriously our
role to preach. This will mean, at times, chipping away at our spiritual
blind spots and those of our audience. Why? Because this is God's work.

Paul also tells Timothy the manner of our public edifying through the sermon. We are to do so with "great patience and careful instruction." As those building up God's people, we should preach with perseverance, knowing we are all works in progress. Just as a builder is careful with his tools and timber, so also preachers must remember that our job requires discipline and a meticulous attitude toward our sacred task.

The edification process, of course, is a divine work that God accomplishes through his Word. Prior to his command to Timothy to "preach the word," Paul highlights the nature of the Word. He says, "All Scripture is God-breathed and is useful for teaching, rebuking, correcting and training in righteousness, so that the servant of God may be thoroughly equipped for every good work" (2 Tim. 3:16–17). The messages we preach to God's people are born not of the preacher's intellect or communication capacity but of the God-breathed Scriptures.

The job of the preacher is not to make the Scriptures relevant. The Scriptures are relevant whether the preacher is or isn't. The role of the sermon is to build up listeners by helping integrate the truths of the inspired Word of God into all areas of their lives. Such a sermon helps make "the servant of God . . . thoroughly equipped for every good work."

Remember the Big Picture

I have taught homiletics for twenty years, and one of the consistent struggles I have observed in preaching in both the classroom and the church is the tendency to so focus on a particular hermeneutic or homiletic model that the preacher forgets the bigger purpose of why they are preaching at all. Even seasoned preachers can sometimes forget that preaching is about facilitating the growth of God's people into maturity in Christ.

As we've observed, preaching should aim to provide a word of exhortation to the people of God that is scriptural, theological, and centered on Christ, with the goal of facilitating the edification of God's people so they are equipped for every good work. But as we'll see, that's not the only goal of preaching.

THE SERMON SHOULD EVANGELIZE THE LOST

I love performing weddings. Call me a romantic, but I love the big day as the bride walks down the aisle to marry the man of her dreams. Family and friends gather for celebration. Vows and rings are exchanged. I love the emotion, the joy, and people getting along. The world is all as it should be. Weddings are fantastic.

As an ordained minister, I've been involved in my fair share of weddings over the years. I've had the privilege not only to attend weddings but also to officiate many of them. In most of these ceremonies, I've also had the responsibility of delivering the wedding sermon. It is a beautiful and significant moment when a couple's first act as newlyweds is to listen to God speak to them through his Word. But preaching at a wedding can be challenging.

Perhaps the most challenging dynamic of the wedding sermon is the audience. Though you are addressing a couple, a larger audience is listening in. Your sermon is not only to the husband and wife but to their many guests as well. Within the crowd are many types of listeners. Some are indifferent to the speaker and the message, while others are receptive. Some are antagonistic toward the preacher and message, while others are curious and polite.

Normally, at a wedding you find those who know and love Jesus, as well as those who darken the door of a church only for weddings and funerals. As I converse with people after the service, it often becomes apparent which folks aren't accustomed to listening to sermons. I usually pick this up by how they refer to me and my message. "Nice speech today, Father." "Good talk, Reverend!" "Thanks for your address, Minister—or is it Pastor?" While I do my best to put them at ease, their responses always remind me how foreign the context and content of the sermon must be for non-Christians.

What Is Going On Here?

During my Bible college days, I enrolled in a unit on church planting. As I looked at the course syllabus on the first day of class, I was intrigued to discover an unusual assignment. We were to attend a place of worship to observe its style and glean information about how it felt to be a visitor. But the place of worship we were to visit was not a church, it was a Jewish synagogue.

A few of my fellow students and I organized our visit and were surprisingly nervous on the day of our attendance. As we entered the front of the house of worship, we clearly stood out as different. We were nicely dressed, but our clothes were a little different from those of the other attendees. We had no prayer shawls, nor did we have the traditional kippah (head covering). A gentleman pointed us to a box where we grabbed kippahs, and then we were directed to our seats. Although everyone in our group was male, we were asked not to sit in the male section and were sent into what felt like the cheap seats near the corner. We felt like outsiders.

The service began with some prayers and an introduction. We felt a little self-conscious as we sensed the eyes of regulars bearing down on us. Whether our insecurities were real or unfounded, we felt awkward. During a part of the service that was performed in Hebrew, we felt lost. At times people would suddenly stand, so we joined in. Then they would sit, and we'd follow. Next they stood and turned to face the wall, chanting what seemed to be a prayer. We were bewildered. Finally, a kind elderly lady in front of us turned and quietly explained that we were facing toward Jerusalem as prayers were being offered. Not long after the prayers, the service ended, and we returned the kippahs and left.

After our visit the professor explained the nature of the

assignment. "I want you to write down how you felt as an outsider coming into an unfamiliar place with foreign practices. Then think about how somebody as an outsider to our Christian faith might feel entering your worship service." As we reflected on our experience, we all noted how we felt lost, embarrassed, and insecure because we didn't know what we were meant to do or say.

The professor wanted us to experience how people may feel when they enter our churches. He wanted us to put ourselves in the shoes of a visitor. He wanted us to remember the feeling of awkwardness, disorientation, and confusion. His point was not missed by those of us still reeling from our experience. While a guest might not always feel comfortable in our services, we should do our best to make sure our services and sermons are at least intelligible to them.

As we go about our sermon preparation, we should consider that there will be unbelievers in our audience. Not only is this true at weddings, but in most preaching contexts we should assume that sprinkled among the people of God are those who have not embraced Jesus as Lord.

Preach the Gospel with Regularity

When Jesus preached, he recognized that some people in his audience would respond favorably to his message of good news, and others would not. To illustrate this, he told a parable that likened the kingdom of God to a farmer who "went out to sow his seed" (Mark 4:3). As you'll recall from the parable, the farmer scattered seed all over the place, but out of the four soils the seeds fell on, only one produced the kind of harvest the farmer desired. The point of the parable is that wherever the gospel of the kingdom is preached, people will respond in diverse ways to it.

How Did You Know?

A few years ago our church was preaching a topical series on basic Christian doctrine. When it was my turn to preach, I was given the subject of atonement. I prayed and prepared during the week and on Sunday morning delivered the message. As I started the sermon, people seemed engaged. Some had their Bibles open, and others were taking notes. Some congregants looked pensive, while one or two looked quite tired.

Out of the corner my eye, I noticed one lady I'd never seen at our church before. The lady caught my eye because a few minutes into the sermon, I noticed she was mildly distressed. While it wasn't distracting to others, I could she was sobbing. I was barely into the first point of my sermon, so I wondered what was going on.

I concluded my sermon and returned to my seat in the audience. As the last song was being sung, I noticed the visitor moving quickly toward the exit. I wanted to touch base with her, so I met her as she was exiting. After introducing myself, I asked, "Is everything okay?" She responded, "How did you know?" *How did I know what?* I wondered.

She repeated, "How did you know?" After I told her that I didn't know what she was asking, she said, "Today is the five-year anniversary of my mother's death. She loved the Lord, and her prayer was that I would follow him. Yet since her death I've not attended any church. Because it is the anniversary of her death, I decided to visit."

She continued, "I came not expecting anything today, but as you preached, it was as if God was speaking just to me. He was reminding me of everything my mother ever taught me. Today God assured me that I'm not forgotten and that he cares. I asked, 'How did you know?' because it seemed like you were aware of this special day and my need to hear this message."

Of course, I was unaware of this lady's needs. I was in the dark regarding her heartbreak, I didn't know her mother, and I had no idea this was her first church service in five years. Thankfully, God was fully aware. God knows the hearts of people and what they need to hear. Our task as preacher is to put God's Word out there and trust him to do his work. God knows, he hears, and he speaks. That is why he, not the preacher, gets all the credit.

As someone from a nonagricultural background, I've often wondered, *If the farmer knew which kind of soil would produce a healthy harvest, why would he waste time scattering seed on the three useless soils? Why go to the effort of sowing in areas where he wouldn't achieve what he hoped for?* The answer, of course, is that the ancient farmer didn't know which soil would be productive. Neither do you or I know the hearts of those to whom we preach.

The job of the preacher is not to be a soil examiner or a spiritual fruit inspector; rather it is to put God's Word before people. The power of the gospel lies not in preachers but in the message they are preaching. Therefore, with regularity and confidence in God's power, we need to embed in our sermons the gospel message of hope.

Preach the Gospel with Intentionality

When I was fifteen years old, I attended a Christian camp, where I committed my life to Christ. I wish I could say I went to the camp with aspirations of wanting to know God and his Son, the Lord Jesus. In reality, however, I was at camp for one reason: to chase Christian girls! Much to my surprise, while I was there, my attention was drawn to the gospel message.

I recall vividly the evangelist Graham Ashby sharing with clarity, conviction, and simplicity the nature of the gospel. He spoke of our inadequacy and sin, Christ's all-sufficient death on our behalf, and God's vindication of Christ's work in his resurrection. He then called on those who wished to respond to God's offer of forgiveness to pray a prayer of repentance. Before the prayer, he asked us to do something simple. He invited those of us willing to pray to raise our hands to indicate we wanted to do this.

I was willing. I was convicted by the gospel message. This message was for me. God was speaking to me right then and there. Yes, I wanted to pray the prayer, but I also wanted to impress a girl who was sitting in my row, so there was no way I was raising a hand. What would she think if I did? Would she think less of me? In my pride, I kept my hands firmly in my pockets.

Fortunately for me, however, the evangelist still led the prayer, and though I didn't respond physically by raising a hand or going forward, I did respond in repentance and faith and echoed his prayer. Even in my repentance there was still pride. Thank goodness for God's grace! He is still working on that area in me.

Neither Graham nor anyone else that day knew what God had done in my heart. The preacher, the youth leaders, and the young lady next to me were unaware that God in his kindness had moved me from the kingdom of darkness into the kingdom of his dearly beloved Son. God knew, but no one else did at that stage. It would be years until I would reach out to Graham and let him know that as a youth I had responded to the gospel under his preaching.

Regardless of what you think of the visible means of responding—raising a hand, going forward during an altar call, filling out a card—the main thing to remember is that God wants us to give people an opportunity to respond to him in repentance and faith. In Romans we are assured that "everyone who calls on the name of the Lord will be saved" (Rom. 10:13).

While all of us would give a hearty amen to this, how do we facilitate it? The means of calling on the name of the Lord is elaborated in the following verses, which read, "How, then, can they call on the one they have not believed in? And how can they believe in the one of whom they have not heard? And how can they hear without someone preaching to them? . . . Faith comes from hearing the message, and the message is heard through the word about Christ" (Rom. 10:14, 17). While preaching is not the only avenue by which people call on the name of the Lord, it is one of the most significant ways God brings people to himself. People need to hear the gospel in order to respond. But do you and I believe this?

Over the past few years I have noticed a trend among churches to move away from providing any direct path to respond to God's call in a message. People will talk around the good news but never clearly explain how we embrace the good news. There are many evangelical churches that believe the gospel and speak of its importance but never explicitly call people to respond to it in the sermon. At such churches there is often an invitation to speak with the pastor after the sermon or to sign up for a course to investigate the claims of Jesus. These are good things, but I suspect that we often miss opportunities for people to call on the name of the Lord because we don't invite them to do so in our sermons. This is to our loss.

In our preaching we should be sowing the seed of the gospel in faith, trusting God to do what only he can do. I am not suggesting we sing "Just as I Am" every Sunday or pray "the sinner's prayer" on a weekly basis, but we would do well to remember to regularly provide our audience with opportunities for appropriate responses to the good news.

People are often ready to respond to the good news but don't know how. Use the sermon to facilitate avenues of response. Even if the focus of a sermon is the building up of God's people through edification, we should regularly articulate the message of salvation to those who have yet to respond. In your sermons seek to evangelize the lost.

TWO AUDIENCES, ONE NEED

When thinking through the two major purposes of preaching—edification and evangelization—we might initially conclude that those purposes are disparate. After all, how can we effectively build up God's people and at the same time invite others into the hope that is found in Christ?

When we dig a little deeper, however, we discover that the needs for edification and evangelism both stem from one common need. Neither the believer who needs to be built up nor the unbeliever who needs to be forgiven can live the way God intends through their own efforts, yet both parties intuitively believe they can.

The Bible is clear that we all have a sinful disposition and seek to live apart from God. The Scriptures say, "There is no one righteous, not even one; there is no one who understands; there is no one who seeks God. All have turned away, they have together become worthless; there is no one who does good, not even one" (Rom. 3:10–12). In approaching life, our natural bent, whether we are Christian or not, is to trust in ourselves and our own wisdom. Self-sufficiency and self-satisfaction are deep in our DNA. By nature, we are all broken and in need of God's grace, yet we strive in our own efforts to change ourselves.

Though outwardly believers may appear to have their act together in following God, they need his grace just as much as the broken rebels who have not yet bowed their knee to the Lord Jesus. We all have the false belief that we can solve our own problems and live independently from God. In his book *Preaching*, Tim Keller observes, "There are massive external differences between irreligious people, who may loudly denounce and subvert traditional moral norms, and very moral, religious, Bible-believing people who rely on their ethical goodness for their standing with God. Yet Paul says both are functioning as their own spiritual saviors, revealing that the internal differences are slight."[2] The problem we all have is that we try to find our adequacy in our own efforts rather than in the merit provided by Christ. Whether we are believers or unbelievers, we all have the same disposition to trust our own wisdom and effort rather than trusting God.

Believers Are Inadequate to Change Themselves

We believers often mistakenly assume that we start the Christian life by faith, but then our spiritual growth and sanctification become dependent on our own efforts. A failure to acknowledge this can lead to disastrous results in the pulpit. We may preach grace to enter the Christian life, but then we preach law to continue it. Bryan Chapell comments,

> Although such preaching is intended for good, its exclusive focus on getting divine blessings or approval through human works carries the message, "Doing enough of these things will get you right with God and your neighbor." By making human efforts alone the measure and the cause of godliness, listeners become subject to the simultaneous assaults of theological legalism and liberalism—which despite their perceived opposition on our social/political scales are theological twins, making one's relationship with God dependent on human goodness. True Christianity cannot be found on any scale that makes our relationship with God dependent on what we do rather than on faith in what Christ has done.[3]

If we are not wise, our preaching can easily slip into legalism, whereby we give Christians a list of things to do. We should provide exhortation that moves people toward obedience, but we must always couch this as a response to God's grace, not as a means of acquiring God's blessing. Why do we need to be so careful? Because even as believers, our natural disposition is to trust in ourselves, not in God.

Unbelievers Are Inadequate to Change Themselves

The message of the gospel is the same for all people everywhere. We are all sinners in need of a Savior. We are totally inadequate before God, and there is nothing we can do to merit a right standing before him. The good news message of the gospel, however, is that God, through Christ, has provided a way for us to have a relationship with him. Because of Jesus' sufficient sacrifice for our sins and his resurrection from the dead, God now offers forgiveness to all who in humble repentance and faith trust in his provision of Christ.

Though this message is familiar to us, most of us forget how counterintuitive it is. Most of us, from our youngest days, grow up trusting in our own efforts. Want to get somewhere in life? Work hard. You're at school; get the best grades you can. Get into college, study well, and earn that degree. Land that job. Work for that promotion. See that house? Put in the effort and it can be yours.

From infancy we are told we can achieve and earn if we just do enough. Yet this doesn't work in the economy of God. In the Scriptures we are told that "no one will be declared righteous in God's sight by the works of the law" (Rom. 3:20). No amount of striving can ever bring us into a right relationship with God.

To effectively preach the good news of Christ, we must begin by communicating humanity's need for redemption. We must not only help unbelievers see their failure to meet God's standard but also aid them in understanding the glorious work of God in providing Jesus. In our preaching we show people the wonderful, transforming grace of God. Why? Because just as with believers, unbelievers' natural bent is to look in futility to themselves for salvation rather than to the Lord.

TWO AUDIENCES, ONE SOLUTION

Believers and unbelievers share one common problem, and the solution to that problem is the same. The antidote to our sin problem is not ourselves but the grace of God shown to us in the Lord Jesus Christ. This is the compelling message every audience needs to hear.

Grace moves our attention from ourselves and our own feeble efforts to the God who meets our deepest needs. Grace-oriented messages focus on the majestic love, mercy, and kindness of God shown to us in Christ. Our motivation for loving and serving God is not to be driven by legalism or by the vain hope of winning God's favor. Rather God's astonishing love and mercy should motivate us to respond in gratitude to his call for obedience. We don't obey God to win acceptance by him; we respond out of deep thanksgiving since we already are accepted by him because of Christ's work.

How does this play out in a sermon? How can the one solution of God's grace in Christ exhort believers while evangelizing the lost?

Since the redemptive work of Christ is central to both the believer and the unbeliever, the gospel must be found in the sermon. This is not to say every message needs to look a certain way or have a particular structure. But every sermon, topical or otherwise, should have a distinct gospel orientation.

When we exhort believers through a sermon, our starting point must be the work of Christ. To borrow the language of Herman Ridderbos, it is crucial that we present the divine "indicative" before we call for the resultant "imperative." When we preach the truths of the gospel, the divine indicative, we provide the compelling motivation for the imperatives to change. Chapell explains:

> It is the aim of God to renew the affections of believers so that their hearts will most desire him and his ways. The desires of new creatures in Christ Jesus can be rightly nourished only by the truths of grace. When preachers nourish these affections with love for God, new affections drive out the desires of the world and thereby strengthen the will to serve God rightly and well. In addition, when rich apprehension of Christ's love makes the fulfillment of God's will our greatest delight, then his glory becomes our greatest pleasure and compulsion.[4]

We preach the wonders of God's character and his redemptive work in order to move the affections of the listener. In our sermons we aim to consistently expose our audience to the wonder of the gospel. The gospel exhorts the believer to live in holiness driven by thanksgiving, while it also evangelizes the unbeliever by showing the adequacy of Christ despite our failures. In our sermons there are multiple ways we evangelize through sharing gospel-based exhortation.

Show Them the Gospel Is Better Than They Imagine

When we edify believers with the truth of the gospel, we enlarge their vision. Take the biblical doctrine of hope. If I were exhorting believers on the hope that is found in the gospel, I would speak to the reality of resurrection beyond the grave. I would explain that because of Jesus' resurrection, believers can experience hope in the midst of death and loss. I would highlight how the promise of the redemption of the body brings solace to the believer wrestling with mental health issues or cancer. The doctrine of eternal security for those in Christ offers the believer peace in a world of chaos, and strength amid turmoil. By preaching these elements of God's grace and the assuredness of the promises secured in Christ, we can bring great encouragement to the children of God.

As unbelievers listen to those promises and hear of the assurance based on Christ, they will naturally experience an evangelistic thrust to the sermon. The exhortations are given to edify the believer, but they also evangelize the unbeliever by pushing them to reflect on the significant issues of assurance, death, and the afterlife. The truth comforts one group while challenging the other.

While there are no guarantees that the exhortation to believers will motivate the unbeliever to respond to Christ, the gospel orientation of the sermon should be comprehensible to the unregenerate listener and should challenge them to think about their eternal future.

Show Them the Gospel Is Believable

One of the wonders of exploring the big picture, or metanarrative, of the Bible is that it shows the tremendous unity and logic of the Scriptures. Over the past few decades of teaching and preaching the Bible, I am constantly surprised at the new things I discover about God and his world. I am often blown away by the Scriptures as I gain new insights into who God is and what he has done.

In my preaching I want to edify people by pointing them to the reliability, soundness, and sensibility of the gospel message. In sharing with them the depth of the gospel's beauty and wonder, I want to help my audience see how reasonable and right God's judgments are and how sound their hope is. Preaching the gospel helps you to "be prepared to give an answer to everyone who asks you to give the reason for the hope that you have" (1 Peter 3:15). When we show how the gospel makes sense, we foster in our people confidence not only to share their faith but to stand assured in their commitment.

In edifying believers with the logic, depth, beauty, and soundness of the gospel, we challenge those outside of Christ to consider the good news message. A person may refuse to submit themselves to the lordship of Christ, but they should not do so on the basis that the gospel is nonsensical or unreliable. While we edify believers, we also seek to evangelize the unbelievers in our audience by showing them the coherency and reason behind the gospel.

Show Them the Gospel Is Wise

A few years ago I was on a plane, sitting next to a man of a different faith. While our plane was preparing for takeoff, my neighbor and I exchanged a few pleasantries. I shared with him about my family and mentioned that I had been married for fifteen years. He was surprised by that and half-jokingly asked how I'd stayed married so long. Without batting an eye, I said, "It's because we try to have a Christ-centered marriage." My newfound friend was intrigued. "A what?" he asked. I explained to him that my marriage was based on the principle of Jesus' sacrificial love for the church. Jesus had laid down his life for the church, and now I was charged to love my wife in the same manner.

I also explained how the gospel shaped the way we learned to forgive each other in our marriage. I quoted Colossians 3:13: "Bear with each other and forgive one another if any of you has a grievance against someone. Forgive as the Lord forgave you." I told him we didn't hold on to bitterness or grudges because we sought to mirror God's forgiveness, which keeps no record of wrongs.

As I spoke, the gentlemen politely nodded his head in affirmation. By sharing a biblical truth with this man, I helped him understand with a little more clarity how forgiveness works in the Christian faith. Although he didn't embrace it, he was exposed to the wisdom of the gospel.

The gospel is God's provision of wisdom to navigate our lives. In 2 Timothy 3:15, Paul explains that the Scriptures "are able to make you *wise* for salvation through faith in Christ Jesus" (emphasis mine). When we teach the Scriptures, we expose people to the mind of God. Whether we are addressing the topics of wealth, sex, family, or justice, God has revealed in the gospel a wisdom about how to live. As we preach to the affairs of our day, we do so through the lens of gospel wisdom. As we follow the lead of the gospel and walk in step with the Holy Spirit, we are conformed to the image of Christ. We experience life the way God so wisely designed us to live. The gospel edifies us by showing us the paths of wisdom and life.

Show Them the Gospel Is Practical

Somebody once told me, "There are many things in life you can do by yourself, but being a Christian is not one of them." He was right. You and I don't live as isolated individuals but exist as part of communities within God's larger world. The gospel message recognizes this. Central to the gospel is the reality that we are called not only to love God but to love our neighbors as ourselves. The gospel provides us with the motivation to do this. The apostle John writes, "This is how God showed his love among us: He sent his one and only Son into the world that we might live through him. This is love: not that we loved God, but that he loved us and sent his Son as an atoning sacrifice for our sins. Dear friends, since God so loved us, we also ought to love one another" (1 John 4:9–11). We love others not because we have to or because it wins us brownie points with God or because he will love us more if we do. No, our love for others is born of a response to God's love for us.

When I exhort people on the practical outcomes of the gospel, I want to make clear why we do what we do. If I simply preach, "Give money to the poor, support the marginalized, forgive your enemy, and be compassionate to those who are hurting," I am merely giving instructions that any group could give. If I don't provide the motivation for the commands, I can give the impression that the Christian faith is just about law. If, however, I ground those same commands in the gospel, I provide the compelling reasons for our actions.

- Because God has been generous to us (2 Cor. 8:9), we are generous to others.
- Because God sought us when we were far away (Eph. 2:13), we support the marginalized.
- Because God in Christ has forgiven us (Col. 3:13), we forgive others.
- Because God is compassionate to us (Ps. 103:13), we show compassion to others.

In exhorting the people of God, we edify them by demonstrating the practical nature of the gospel. We help them see the natural outcomes of a proper response to the love of God shown to us in Christ. We also evangelize the lost by showing them how the gospel is born not out of doing things to be made right with God but out of a response to God's kindness. We expose them to the power of grace, not merit, as the motivation behind Christian obedience.

THE ULTIMATE SOLUTION TO OUR VARIED NEEDS

As Pastor Daryl rises to preach on Sunday morning, he asks that the Holy Spirit speak to the hearts of the gathered people as the Word is preached. Though not aware of the spiritual condition of each member of his audience, the pastor is confident of one thing: the greatest need of his listeners is the gospel.

Yes, Vijay, Vanessa, and Timmy have different struggles, but the ultimate solution to their challenges is not to be found in a sermon called "Three Ways to Change" or "How to Be a Faithful Friend." Instead the solution will be found in anchoring their lives to Christ. Though congregations are always mixed, Christ is the solution to the people's deepest needs. That is always the case with every sermon and every audience.

CHAPTER 4

HOW TO ADDRESS A TOPIC THEOLOGICALLY

What Does God Want to Say about This Topic?

SAM CHAN

Danica always enjoyed public speaking. When she was in high school, she was a member of the debate team. In her church community Danica was everybody's first choice as MC for worship services, birthdays, and weddings.

Soon Danica felt the call to go into pastoral ministry. She enrolled in a seminary and excelled at Greek, Hebrew, exegesis, and yes, homiletics. She especially loved the precision of expository preaching. By preaching on a clearly defined passage, such as Romans 3, she could tell you what Paul had to say about justification. Or by preaching on Hebrews 8, she could tell you what the writer of Hebrews had to say about the new covenant. Or by preaching on Ephesians 6:10–17, she could tell you what Paul had to say about the armor of God.

Danica appreciated the almost scientific precision and the elegant simplicity of expository preaching. It was easy to work out what to say—it was right there in front of her in the Bible passage. It was easy to verify her facts—she could check a few commentaries by respected scholars. And it was easy to establish trust with her audience—they could simply refer to their Bibles and check up on what Danica was saying.

One day Michelle, a friend at church, approached Danica. Michelle ran a think tank at her workplace, and they often invited experts and gifted speakers to address a variety of topics. Next month's topic was disruption, which was especially relevant because many workers were unsure about how frequent changes in technology would affect their jobs.

Michelle invited three speakers: an IT expert from Silicon Valley would speak on where to expect disruption, a venture capitalist from Wall Street would speak on the financial implications of disruption, and Danica was asked to address a Christian perspective on disruption.

Danica was flattered and excited. What a great opportunity to speak to a large, receptive crowd about the Christian worldview. But she was also frightened by the idea. Where was the Bible passage on disruption? What commentary could she go to? She couldn't look up *disruption* in her concordance. How would she know what to say?

TOPICAL PREACHING IS A THEOLOGICAL TASK

One big challenge involved with topical preaching is knowing what to say. Some topics may be easy to address. There are Bible passages that discuss things like money, prayer, and faith. But for other topics it's not so easy to think of Bible passages. How do we know what the Bible has to say about computer games, start-up companies, or retirement? These words don't exist in the Bible. Word studies, concordances, and commentaries are of little to no help.

This is when we realize that the role of topical preaching is a theological task. For expository preaching, we mainly use the methods of biblical exegesis—word studies, concordances, commentaries, biblical theology. But for topical preaching, we use the methods of systematic theology—the study of ideas, the use of supplemental sources in addition to the Bible, and the study of extrabiblical words. Expository preachers are skilled in Greek, Hebrew, and exegesis. But if we want to preach topically, we need to use the additional methods of systematic theology.

Imagine preaching on the topic of the Trinity. As Christians, we believe in the doctrine of the Trinity, which asserts that God exists as three-in-one: there is one God, but this Godhead exists as three separate persons—Father, Spirit, and Son—and each person is fully of the essence of God. We believe it because it's "biblical."

But no passage in the Bible asserts this doctrine in a straightforward way. Instead the doctrine is an implication of various passages in the Bible. Moreover, we've used extrabiblical words to describe the doctrine of the Trinity. We use words like *person, Godhead,* and *three-in-one* because we believe they precisely describe biblical truths. We have to employ philosophy to give us technical terms such as *person* and *essence.* We also rely on and interact with writings from extrabiblical people—Athanasius, Augustine, Basil, Barth—as well as councils and creeds. From these many sources, we synthesize or systematize a coherent and compelling argument for the Trinity.

This is what we have to do when we preach topically. We must speak on a topic that might not be expressed plainly in the Bible. Yet we try to discover what the Bible implies about the topic, using nonbiblical words and employing a wide variety of sources in addition to the Bible in order to come up with a systematized, coherent, and compelling argument on our topic.

The job of an exegete is to ask, "What is Paul saying in Romans 3?" or, "What is the author of Hebrews saying in Hebrews 8?" It is a descriptive task: what is the biblical writer saying? The job of a church historian is to ask, "What is Augustine saying about the Trinity?" or, "What is Barth saying about justification?" It is also a descriptive task: what did people in the history of the church say? But the job of a theologian is to ask, "What does God say about this topic?" Of course, we can't get our answer exactly right, because we are limited by our human finiteness and fallenness. But we do the best we can.

Exegesis and Systematic Theology

The debate about the relationship between expository preaching and topical preaching is, at its core, a debate about the relationship between exegesis and systematic theology.[1] The tools of grammatico-historical exegesis aim to describe and explain the text of the Bible, while the tools of systematic theology aim to prescribe ideas generated by the biblical text, though not using the exact same words of the Bible. The method of exegesis is to move inductively from the world of the text to the world of ideas, while the method of systematic theology is to move deductively from the world of ideas to the world of the text.

In a similar way, an expository sermon expounds a text of the Bible by using the tools of exegesis, while a topical sermon expounds an idea by using the tools of systematic theology. The method of expository preaching is to move inductively from the world of the text to the world of the hearer. The method of topical preaching is to move deductively from the world of the hearer to the world of the text.

We must see this relationship between exegesis and systematic theology as a symbiotic, dialectical, back-and-forth relationship rather than a dichotomous, either-or relationship. This is because we never truly come to the biblical text as a blank slate. We always approach the text with presuppositions: prior systems, grids, traditions, theologies, experiences, and interpretive lenses. We come to every text deductively as well as inductively.[2]

So we need to use what theologians call a dialogical or abductive approach to the text.[3] We come to the text acknowledging our presuppositions. We are honest about our biases and starting point, and then we have a back-and-forth dialogue in which the biblical text shapes our interpretive lens and our interpretive lens shapes our understanding of the text. It is simultaneously inductive and deductive.

This also happens in the world of preaching. No sermon is ever purely expository. No sermon is ever purely topical. Every sermon has elements of both in a back-and-forth dialogue. For example, every expository sermon must begin and end in the world of the hearer—this is the function of the introduction and application—and thus has some elements of topical preaching. If an expository sermon uses illustrations, it is also looking for conceptual overlap between the world of the hearer and the world of the Bible. Again, this is an element of topical preaching. And every topical sermon aims to communicate a biblical truth—even if it doesn't quote verses or use the exact words of the Bible—and thus has elements of expository preaching.

Both expository and topical sermons have these basic elements:

	Introduction	Bible's Message	Application
Location	The world of the hearer	The world of the Bible	The world of the hearer
Method	Uses the tools of systematic theology (and cultural exegesis)	Uses the tools of grammatico-historical exegesis (and cultural exegesis)	Uses the tools of systematic theology (and cultural exegesis)
Function	Demonstrates the relevance of the biblical message to the hearer	Demonstrates the meaning of the biblical text	Prescribes the relevance of the biblical message to the hearer

> The main difference between so-called expository and so-called topical sermons is the proportion and sequencing of these elements. A thirty-minute sermon at a Sunday church service to average, biblically literate church members might have a five-minute introduction, a twenty-minute Bible section, and a five-minute application. But a fifteen-minute Friday lunchtime talk at a cafeteria to office workers might have a four-minute introduction, a one-minute Bible section, and a ten-minute application.
>
> The difference between an expository and a topical sermon is one of pedagogy rather than theology, orthopraxy rather than orthodoxy, and form rather than content. This makes it even harder to believe that the difference between expository and topical sermons can become a line in the sand—or even a statement of faith—for some preaching schools, denominations, and churches.

We approximate what we think God would say about a particular topic, using a variety of sources, including special and general revelation, expressed in human language, analogies, symbols, and metaphors. It is ultimately a prescriptive task: what ought people to think and do about a topic?[4]

The job of a topical preacher is essentially the same as that of a theologian. We are given a topic, and we ask the question, "What does God say about this topic?"

This is why topical preaching can be frowned upon in sections of the Christian community. It is preposterous and dangerously ambitious to presume to know what God would say about extrabiblical topics such as stock market trading, fitness, or artificial intelligence. It is also open to spurious claims. How do we verify what the preacher is saying if there's no obvious Bible passage to consult? But we do this—attempt to know God's thoughts— all the time in theology! Yes, it is ambitious. Yes, it is open to abuses. But so is theology. And as with theology, the results of topical preaching, when done well, are highly rewarding.

HOW TO PREACH THEOLOGICALLY

Now that we understand our task of topical preaching to be like that of a systematic theologian, let's see what this looks like in six simple, concrete steps.

> Step 1: Define the topic.
> Step 2: Convert the topic into an issue.
> Step 3: Convert the issue into a question.
> Step 4: Research the answer.
> Step 5: Argue for a point.
> Step 6: Prepare a persuasive flow of ideas.

Let's expand on each step.

Step 1: Define the Topic

Let's say we've been given a topic to preach on. The first important step is to define the topic. We shouldn't redefine the topic to how we think it should be defined or how we want it to be defined. If we do so, the audience will feel like we pulled a bait and switch on them. Instead we need to define the topic as closely as possible to the way the term is ordinarily used in the context we're engaging with.[5]

Example: Disruption

Let's say we've been given the topic "Disruption," and we're speaking at a workplace think tank where the other speakers are from IT and

Wall Street. In this context *disruption* is a technical term. We are not free to redefine it to whatever we want the term to mean. The audience is turning up expecting to hear about disruption as they understand it.

The term *disruption* was coined by Clayton Christensen, a respected American business consultant, in his seminal book *The Innovator's Dilemma*.[6] It refers to how new companies or technologies make changes that eventually lead to the demise of established companies or technologies. The digital camera disrupted the film industry (Kodak). Online shopping (Amazon) has disrupted brick-and-mortar bookshops. Rideshare apps (Uber) have disrupted traditional taxi services. The term *disruption* is also defined by Peter Thiel, another key American entrepreneur and venture capitalist and a cofounder of PayPal, as a "contrarian truth" or a "counter narrative" that finds a better way to do things.[7]

Armed with this knowledge, we can begin writing the talk with the widely accepted definition of *disruption* as "a new, different, and better way of doing things."

Step 2: Convert the Topic into an Issue

We can't just talk about a topic. That leads to a nebulous, boring talk because it's not clear why it matters. Why is this talk important to the audience? If I were to get up now and say, "Today I'm going to talk about disruption," your eyes would glaze over. Your brain would check out. Zzzzzzzzzzzz. You have more immediate, interesting, and important things to worry about.

Our second step, then, is to convert our topic into an issue that needs to be addressed. How can I connect this topic to you at an emotional and existential level? What opportunities, threats, challenges, or crises are created by the topic? What excites you about this topic? What scares you? What saddens you? What problems need to be solved? If we can identify these things, then we can choose an issue that our audience wants us to address.

Answer the Questions People Are Asking

This is the job of theology: to answer the questions that people are asking. Ancient theologians, such as Augustine and Anselm, defined theology as "faith seeking understanding." We ask questions that our Christian faith then attempts to answer. Our questions set the agenda.

But different cultures ask different questions. Western theological books often begin with proofs for God's existence. This is because epistemology has long been the preoccupation of Western post-Enlightenment audiences. We begin with the questions that our culture is asking, which set the agenda for our theology.

But my missionary friends say that when they tried to teach Western theology in Africa, the audience was disinterested in proofs of God's existence. This is because their primary questions had to do with providence, not epistemology. Their main question was, "Why does God send lightning that kills my family and cattle?" Questions like that set the agenda for their particular theology.[8]

In Asia the audience might also be disinterested in Western theology. Their primary questions might have to do with discipleship and the supernatural. "How can I follow Jesus without dishonoring my parents?" or, "Do I go to the funeral of my parents if it includes idol worship?" or, "Can I eat in a restaurant that has an idol to a foreign god?"

The last time I looked, none of my Western theology books—Barth, Berkhof, Erickson, Grudem, Reymond—has a chapter telling me what to say to my Asian friends! There is no chapter on whether to attend the funerals of parents. There is no chapter on eating in Chinese restaurants where idols are prominently displayed. Yet these are the burning questions my Asian friends want answered.

This is because Western theology attempts to answer the questions asked by Westerners, not Asians.

Whether we've realized it or not, the job of theology has always been to answer the questions our audience is asking. Their questions have always set the agenda.

Example: Disruption

Let's return to our talk about disruption at the workplace think tank. Why are people turning up to listen to this discussion? What is their burning issue that needs to be addressed?

This is where we need to know our audience. If the workplace is a hub for start-up entrepreneurs, then our audience welcomes disruption. Disruption is an opportunity to get ahead, and people are looking for ways to disrupt. If this is our audience, their burning issue is that they hope to become the next major disruptor.

But if the workplace think tank is for people in established jobs, careers, and institutions, then our audience fears disruption. It threatens their income, livelihood, and future. Disruption is going to take away their jobs. They will find themselves in midlife, out of work, without the skills to get a new job in a disrupted industry. If this is our audience, their burning issue is that they hope never to be disrupted.

Step 3: Convert the Issue into a Question

We can't just talk about an issue. An issue is still abstract and leads to a mundane talk because we're still trying only to talk about something rather than address a problem. If I were to get up and say, "I'm going to talk about the exciting opportunities of disruption" or, "I'm going to talk about job security in the face of disruption," you would start looking at your watch. You would wish you were somewhere else. Your mind would drift to another place.

Our third step, then, is to convert our issue into a question that our audience wants answered, starting with one of these questioning words: who, what, where, when, why, or how. This is an art rather than a science. We play around with all the possible questions until we find one that feels just right. It's the question our audience really wants answered. It's the question that will keep our audience begging for more. It's the question that will keep our audience attentive for the next twenty to forty minutes of monologue. It's the gripping question our audience needs to have answered.

Example: Disruption

Returning to our talk about disruption, let's assume our audience is in established jobs, careers, and institutions. They fear disruption. They are the opposite of young, start-up entrepreneurs who welcome and seek disruption. For this audience disruption threatens everything they love: their income, livelihood, and future. If disruption comes along, our audience will be out of work, with limited prospects of finding new jobs in a disrupted industry.

Their issue is that disruption threatens to take away their current means of living. What question can I convert that to? Here I play around, using who, what, where, when, why, and how as my interrogative words.

- Who will be disrupted?
- What will disruption do to me?
- Where will disruption come from?
- When will I be disrupted?
- Why will I be disrupted?
- How can I survive disruption?

After reviewing these options, the how question feels like the best fit. We can tweak it into this question: How can I survive and thrive in disruption? This becomes the title of our talk: "Disruption: How to Survive and Thrive in an Ever-Changing World."

If we get this question right, then our audience will be sitting on the edge of their seats, leaning forward, begging to know what we're going to say next. But we can't just ask a gripping question. We also need an informed and nuanced answer.

Step 4: Research the Answer

If we did our previous step correctly, not only will our audience want to know the answer to our gripping question, but even we will want to know the answer! So our fourth step is to work out an answer to our question.

This is where our theological task begins. We are asking ourselves this question: What answer would God give to my audience?

It's time to put on our theologian hats. Our first main source of information will be special revelation, the Scriptures. What Bible passages directly or indirectly say something about our topic? What does the Wisdom Literature have to say? What does biblical theology say about our topic, especially how it develops through the stages of salvation history? Related to this, we can look at Christian sources, such as our Christian tradition, personal experiences, and Christian authors.

Our next main source of information will be general revelation. We can appeal to reason: what does logic, basic argument, and common sense say about this? Next we turn to non-Christian sources, especially informed voices that deserve to be heard: philosophers, op-ed writers, authors, TED speakers, NPR podcasters. If we're not aware of these sources, then our discussion will risk sounding naive and uninformed. And we can save ourselves a lot of work if smarter thinkers have already talked about our topic.

We can be generous to our non-Christian sources because our doctrine of general revelation says that all truth is God's truth: there must be some truth in every source, no matter how explicitly non-Christian. Our doctrine of common grace says that all goodness is God's goodness: there must be some goodness in every source, no matter how explicitly anti-Christian. Our doctrine of creation says that all beauty is God's beauty: there must be some beauty for us to appreciate in every source, no matter how depraved or broken. Our doctrine of wisdom says that all wisdom is God's wisdom: there must be some wisdom in all sources if they have properly observed the world around them. Our doctrine of the image of God says that every human reveals something about our God: there must be something divine in what they say, no matter how unfamiliar they are with the Christian God. Similarly, because every human heart cries out for eternity, then every source is an expression of the universal human longing for transcendence, purpose, meaning, and hope.

Yet our doctrine of sin says that every human source—Christian and non-Christian—is fallen. There must be some way of expressing human rebellion, suppression of the truth, brokenness, and the choice to run away from God.

Finally, because it is a Christian talk, we can ask how this topic might belong under the headship of Christ. We will say much more about this later, in chapter 8. But for now we can at least ask how this topic can be redeemed under Christ's loving and saving rule. What difference would one's knowing, loving, and worshiping Jesus make in regard to this topic?

This all adds up to make the point that when we research what to say about our topic, we can consult both Christian and non-Christian sources. When we do that, we ask these basic questions:

- What is true in our topic?
- What is good in our topic?
- What is beautiful in our topic?
- What is wise in our topic?
- What is divine in our topic? (What does it say about God?)
- What in our topic is the universal human cry for transcendence?
- What is sinful—fallen, broken, rebellious, truth-suppressing, evil—in our topic?

- What in our topic can be redeemed under the saving headship of Christ?

Example: Disruption

Let's go back to our example of a topical talk on disruption. If we research this topic, we may find the following information.

What is true in our topic?

According to Peter Thiel, the cofounder of PayPal, a disruptor finds a "contrarian truth," a truth that until now everybody has missed. It is essentially a "counter narrative," a different story from what everyone else is telling. But the essential element to disruption isn't that it disrupts merely for the sake of disrupting. A disruptor finds a better way of doing things.

Examples are easy to think of. Digital cameras have disrupted film cameras. Electronic messaging has disrupted snail mail. On-demand movies have disrupted video movie rentals.

A less obvious example is Rick Barry, who pioneered the underhand method for taking free throws in basketball. Conventional wisdom in basketball is to take free throws with an overhand technique. But Rick Barry found a better way. With his underhand method, Rick Barry had the highest free throw percentage (90 percent) in NBA history. It was so successful that even Wilt Chamberlain copied it and improved his free throw percentage from 40 percent to 60 percent.[9]

What is good and beautiful in our topic?

In the history of disruption, people have benefited from a new and better way of doing things. From the beginning of time, the discovery of fire and the invention of the wheel have made life better for us. Penicillin has saved many lives. The motorcar has made transportation available to the masses. Laparoscopic surgery has revolutionized medicine.

Before laparoscopic surgery an operation to remove a gall bladder was invasive, requiring many days in the hospital afterward to recover. But with laparoscopic surgery the gall bladder is removed with only a few small cuts, resulting in less pain and a short hospital stay. Humans benefit greatly from this improvement, and there is an elegant beauty to the new technique.

What is wise in our topic?

Wisdom literature in the Bible tells us that despite major changes in life, things still stay pretty much the same. There is nothing to be gained (Eccl. 1:3). Despite the conveniences from recent disruptions—smartphones, the internet, GPS navigation—we seem to be busier than ever before. Somehow, labor-saving devices have led to more work rather than less.

But the Wisdom Literature also says there is a time for everything. Sometimes we need to tear down, and sometimes we need to build up (Eccl. 3:3). In the natural rhythms of life, we need times of disruption as much as we need times of stability. Without disruption we grow complacent and stale. We see this in companies, like Kodak, that were pioneers in their field but stagnated and were eventually disrupted by newcomers. Disruption is both inevitable and necessary.

For this reason, Clayton Christensen, in his book *The Innovator's Dilemma*, advises companies to set up an off-site team whose job is to disrupt their own company. If you're going to be disrupted, it may as well come from yourself rather than someone else!

What is divine in our topic?

God is the original disruptor. When he created the universe, he brought something out of nothing. He created order from chaos. He made a universe that was good and beautiful.

God then created humans—in his image—to keep on disrupting. Adam and Eve were placed in the garden of Eden to disrupt. We were placed in God's creation to create goodness and beauty from the world around us.

In the Old Testament, God continued to disrupt. He uprooted Abraham from his hometown of Ur. He uprooted the Israelites from Egypt and transported them into Canaan. He chose a shepherd boy to become king of Israel. God's ways are not our ways. His salvation is described as a new song, a new creation, and a new heart.

In the New Testament, Jesus was also a disruptor. His teachings disrupted the established wisdom of the time. Jesus stormed through the temple with a whip. He established a new, different, and better way to be saved. The new wine would burst the old wineskins. The new covenant would disrupt the old covenant.

What in our topic is the universal human cry for transcendence?

We have seemingly conflicting human cries. On the one hand, disruption allows us to express our God-given desire to be creative, imaginative, and productive. We image our creator God when we design and engineer new and better ways of doing things.

On the other hand, we have the competing desire for stability and security. We like things to endure and stand the test of time. Our hearts cry out for eternity.

What is sinful—fallen, broken, rebellious, truth-suppressing, evil—in our topic?

We could argue that disruption by itself is a neutral event. But its consequences can be both beneficial and harmful. This is because of what philosophers call the "double power principle."[10] Whatever has the power to do good has the equal power to do harm. Fire has given us heat and cooked foods, but it has also burned people and homes. The invention of the wheel has given us motorcars, but it has also resulted in car accidents and fatalities. The invention of screen devices has blessed us with much convenience, but it has also addicted children to screens. Artificial intelligence (AI) has given us powerful algorithms that can interpret X-rays better than a human doctor can. But AI also threatens to take away our jobs and privacy.

Disruption is a neutral activity, but the motivation behind it can be well-intentioned or evil. When we try to invent new and better ways to do things, we might be motivated by compassion—we genuinely want to fix problems and improve the lives of others. Or we might be motivated by pride and insecurity—we want to make a name for ourselves. Or we might be motivated by a desire to harm.

Some of us fear disruption for good reasons—disruption means we will need to upskill and/or change jobs, or we will possibly lose our job. But often our fear of disruption comes from pride and insecurity—we have too much invested in the status quo. If we lose our job, we lose our name, fame, and reputation.

Plato illustrates our resistance to change with his famous allegory of the cave. In this allegory, people are chained inside a cave. They face the cave wall, with a flame behind them. They can't see the flame, but only the flickering shadows cast by the flame onto the wall. One prisoner breaks free and leaves the cave. This freed prisoner discovers a new and better world with sunshine, blue skies, trees, and animals. He rushes back inside the cave to tell the other prisoners, but they are threatened by this news and try to kill him.

In real life, Dr. Barry Marshall discovered that stomach ulcers are caused by bacteria and not acid. Conventional wisdom in medicine was to treat ulcers with antacids and sometimes surgery. Marshall disrupted the medical world by saying that ulcers should be treated with an antibiotic. But for many years no one believed him. Why? Because the medical community had too much invested in the status quo.

Similarly, Wilt Chamberlain eventually reverted to his overhand free throw technique, even though it was inferior. Why? Because the underhand method looks silly. It's called the granny technique. Wilt Chamberlain preferred looking cool and fitting in with conventional wisdom, even though it resulted in a poorer shooting percentage. As human beings, most of us prefer being wrong and fitting in over being right but not fitting in.

*What in our topic can be redeemed under
the saving headship of Christ?*

If disruption is inevitable and often necessary, how can we survive and thrive in a world of constant disruption? What difference will our knowing, loving, and worshiping Jesus make to us?

First, Jesus will give us the right motivation. In the end, disruption is a neutral event. It's what we do with it that makes it good or bad. Jesus teaches us to do unto others as we would want them to do unto us. But also it's who we are that matters most. In his sermon on the mount, Jesus told us to examine our hearts (Matt. 5:8, 28; 6:21). Why do we welcome or fear disruption? Is it out of jealousy, pride, fear, and insecurity? Or is it because of love, compassion, mercy, and justice?

Second, Jesus will give us the security we long for. Disruption threatens to take away our self-worth. We might lose our jobs. We might not have the skills. We might not be able to compete. But if Jesus gives us status, honor, dignity, and self-worth, then we don't need to find it elsewhere, like in our jobs, careers, or achievements. So if disruption takes away our jobs, we can mourn the loss of something we loved, but we will still have our status, honor, dignity, and self-worth.

Third, Jesus tells us to trust in him. Jesus taught that God will provide for our daily needs (Matt. 6:25–34). We can't control what disruption will do to our jobs, but we need to be okay with not being in control. We need to discover the peace from knowing that God is in control.

Fourth, Jesus disrupts us by telling us to seek the kingdom of God first. Jesus disrupts the conventional ways of the Western world, which tell us to chase our dreams and do whatever it takes to be happy. Jesus gives us a new and better way—to become part of a story bigger than our own. We can be part of God's story. One day his kingdom will come and disrupt everything. When that happens, we want to be part of this new and better way.

Step 5: Argue for a Point

We've researched an informed and nuanced answer to our gripping question. But we can't just unload this information onto our audience, or it will be an aimless ramble. It will be a data dump. It will be like reading engineering specifications to them or, worse, like reading bullet points on a PowerPoint slide. It will be a torrent of unorganized information that fails to say anything coherent.[11]

Our fifth step is to argue for a point. What exactly are we trying to say? Where is this talk going? What do we want the audience to do? To accomplish this, we ask ourselves, "After all our research in step 4, what is our one-sentence answer to the question we set up in step 3?"

Example: Disruption

In step 3 our question was, How can I survive and thrive in disruption? From step 4 our answer might be, Make sure my security is in Christ. If we're happy with this as our answer, then this becomes the whole point of our topical talk. We are ultimately trying to persuade our audience that they need to find their security in Christ. If we combine the question with the answer, then we also have our big idea for the topical talk: We survive and thrive in disruption by placing our security in Christ.

Step 6: Prepare a Persuasive Flow of Ideas

Now that we have a point to our talk, we need to work out how to get there. We have a destination but no journey. Step 6 is to prepare the talk that will persuasively get us to the point we're arguing for. Here I like to work through the logical movements we outlined in chapter 2.

1. **Resonance.** Say something our audience will agree with.
2. **Dissonance.** Say something that will disequilibrate our audience.

3. **Gospel fulfillment.** Say something that will point our audience toward the fulfillment only Jesus can provide.

Example: Disruption

If our audience is threatened by disruption, our sequence could go like this:

1. **Resonance.** Yes, disruption is a scary thing. It threatens to take away our jobs, careers, and livelihoods.
2. **Dissonance.** But disruption is an inevitable and necessary part of life. We need to know how to survive and thrive in this disruption.
3. **Gospel fulfillment.** But we need to find our security in Jesus. That way we won't be threatened by disruption and might be able to embrace disruption and thrive in it.

But let's say, for the sake of learning how to do this, that our audience is a group of young, start-up entrepreneurs who seek disruption. To be successful and pay the bills, this audience needs to find the next major disruption. Here our logical sequence will be the opposite.

1. **Resonance.** Yes, disruption is an inevitable and necessary part of life. It would be wonderful if we were the next new thing that disrupts an old way of doing things.
2. **Dissonance.** But not all disruption is good. Sometimes disruption has unintended consequences. Sometimes we do it for the wrong reasons—out of pride, selfish ambition, jealousy, and insecurity. If we do this, we end up bitter, empty, and lonely.
3. **Gospel fulfillment.** But we need to find our security in Jesus. If we're secure in Jesus, then we will disrupt for the right reasons, and we will survive and thrive whether or not we end up finding the next new thing.

The "Yes, But, But" Flow of a Talk

One helpful way of seeing whether our talk has an engaging and persuasive flow is to ask whether we can begin the talk's major transitions with the words yes, but, and but.

In our talk on disruption to those threatened by the topic, our talk should have this flow of ideas:

1. Yes, disruption is scary.
2. But disruption is inevitable and necessary.
3. But Jesus gives us a security that can't be disrupted.

Or if our talk on disruption is addressed to those who seek disruption, then our talk should have this flow of ideas:

1. Yes, disruption is inevitable and necessary.
2. But we can do disruption for the wrong reasons.
3. But if our security is in Jesus, then we will disrupt for the right reasons.

I call this the "yes, but, but" logical flow of a talk. If my talk's major transitions move sequentially through a "yes, but, but" grid, then I know it will most likely be engaging and persuasive.

SUMMARY OF THEOLOGICAL STEPS

Let's pull this all together now. From our six steps we now have:

1. Topic
2. Issue
3. Question

4. Answer
5. Point
6. Persuasive Flow

Each one of these has the following function in our talk.

Step	Function	The Listener's Question	Answer (from the Disruption Talk)
1. Topic	What?	"What are we talking about?"	"Disruption."
2. Issue	Why?	"Why is this important to me?"	"Because disruption threatens your job, career, livelihood."
3. Question	Want/Need	"Why do I want/ need to listen to this talk?"	"Because you want/ need to survive and thrive in disruption."
4. Answer	Solution	"What can I do?"	"Find your security in Jesus."
5. Point	Where?	"Where is this talk going?"	"The talk is going to argue that you should find your security in Jesus."
6. Persuasive Flow	How?	"How are you going to persuade me?"	"The talk will resonate with you, disequilibrate you, and point you toward fulfillment through the gospel."

Now when we write our talk:

1. Write the introduction so that it sets up our topic, issue, and question.
2. Write the body of the talk, following our persuasive flow of ideas.

3. At the end of the body, in what I call the bridge of the talk, clearly state the answer to our question. This is the big idea of the talk.

4. In the conclusion of the talk, give an application to the big idea.

We Are Opinion Writers

I enjoy reading the *New York Times*, especially the opinion pages. On these pages there are two categories of writers. First, there are the op-ed writers. They have a highly specialized knowledge of their topic; it's something they see and do every day. Usually, they have a PhD on this topic. They have written books. They have delivered TED Talks.

Second, there are the regular columnists—Jennifer Senior, Charles Blow, Frank Bruni, Maureen Dowd, David Brooks, Ross Douthat, Nicholas Kristof, Gail Collins. They write a column on a different topic each time, drawing from a generalized knowledge of the topics they cover, not a specialized knowledge. But they still give an informed, nuanced, and sophisticated discussion of each topic. To do this, they research widely from a variety of viewpoints. Then they systematize their information into a coherent, logical flow of ideas, with which they argue for a point.

This is what we're being asked to do when we preach on a topic. We are asked to become a *New York Times* columnist and give an informed and nuanced talk on something that we don't necessarily know much about. But unlike the *New York Times* columnist, we're not merely giving our own opinion. We're also trying to think, *What would God want to say about this topic?* We're trying to write an opinion piece on behalf of God!

Do I Need to Preach from a Bible Passage?

The first question I'm usually asked when I teach a seminar on topical preaching is, "Do I need a Bible passage?"

On face value this is a super simple question. A bit like, "What day is it today?" But once we dig deeper, it's actually a complex question in disguise, with a lot of hidden premises. It's the equivalent of asking, "Have you stopped hijacking planes?" There's no simple yes or no answer. (Perhaps you should talk to a lawyer before answering that question.)

I begin by saying, "Let's flip the question. How many verses does an expository sermon need?"

Let's say we're preaching from Romans 3. This is a great opportunity to expound the biblical truth of justification from the Bible passage. But how much of Romans 3 do we need?

Can I choose one verse—say, Romans 3:23? After all, there's enough biblical truth in that verse to fill a forty-minute sermon. Or do I choose a paragraph—say, Romans 3:21–26? Or do I choose the entire chapter?

It seems, even for an expository sermon, there's no right or wrong answer as to how few or many Bible verses to use.

This is because we are preaching biblical truth regardless of how many Bible verses we're using.

In the end the size of the Bible passage used in expository preaching is a decision based on wisdom. What best suits my sermon's context? What best suits my audience's expectation? What best suits the aim of my sermon?

It's the same, then, for topical preaching. Our aim is to preach biblical truth. But this won't depend on how many Bible verses are explicitly referenced.

So do I preach from a Bible passage or not? The answer is that, as with expository preaching, it's a decision based on wisdom. What best suits the expectations of my audience? What best suits the aim of my sermon? What is my context?

At a Sunday morning church service at 10:00 a.m., the organizers will ask me for a Bible passage. The audience will be expecting a Bible reading. Here it's wise to choose a Bible passage and refer to it in the sermon. But in contrast, when I give a ten-minute, TED-style talk at a pub at 8:00 p.m. to a mix of believers and nonbelievers, the organizers have given me a topic to talk on. They don't have time or space for a Bible reading. I can refer to verses in the Bible in my talk, but no one in the audience will have a Bible. Depending on context, I might not even refer to a specific verse. But I might say something like, "There's a story in the Bible in which Jesus talks to a religious leader . . ." or, "In the Christian tradition . . ." Because in the end it's still a biblical truth whether or not I explicitly reference a Bible verse to support it.

Hopefully, all of this put together will give us a theological discussion of our topic. But it won't just be information; it will address an issue that is close to our audience's heart. It will raise a question they want answered. Finally, it will persuasively flesh out an answer that will compel them to act.

SAMPLE SERMON: "HOW CAN WE SURVIVE AND THRIVE IN DISRUPTION?"

There was a large crowd of people helping themselves to coffee, other drinks, and snacks. These workplace think tanks were normally enjoyable, but this one was better than usual. All three speakers were highly knowledgeable and great communicators. The IT expert from Silicon Valley explained that the next disruption will most likely come from

China or India. The venture capitalist from Wall Street gave advice on where best to invest.

But most people were talking about the message given by the Christian speaker, Danica. Many of those who turned up were not Christians and had never heard a talk from the Christian perspective. They were surprised at how well Danica was able to connect with them emotionally and show the difference that Jesus makes.

Danica's introduction was a self-deprecating story about how she finally bought herself an iPhone. Now she was able to check messages, social media, and sports highlights on her phone. But her husband complained that she was always on her phone and they don't talk anymore. So Danica bought her husband an iPhone. Now they could talk! Problem solved.

Danica used this to set up the topic of disruption. She pointed out that innovation doesn't just disrupt marriages, it also disrupts people's jobs, careers, and livelihoods. Whole companies can be disrupted. Look at Kodak, Nokia, and Blockbuster. Danica then raised the question, "How can we survive and thrive in disruption?" At this point nobody was distracted. Nobody was checking their phones for messages. Nobody was looking out the window. People leaned forward, desperately wanting to know the answer to this question that touched them so deeply.

In the body of the talk, Danica proceeded to answer this question. First, she resonated with people's fear of disruption. It threatens the status quo that we already have so much invested in. Danica illustrated this with how she has a lot of the old German money, deutsche marks, stored in a shoebox, left over from the time she traveled to Germany as a college student. But these marks are now worthless because the European Union, with its euro currency, has disrupted everything. In the same way, disruption threatens to make valueless much of what gives us value: our career, work, status, income, and identity. Nobody wants to be that person in midlife without a job or the skills to find a new job. There's something shameful about not being valued anymore by our society.

Second, Danica showed how much of disruption is beneficial and necessary. Barry Marshall disrupted the medical community by showing that stomach ulcers can be treated with antibiotics. What once needed invasive surgery can now be cured with a tablet. But this change was resisted by the medical community because doctors had too much status and worth invested in the old status quo. History is littered with other examples of people resisting change out of fear and insecurity. Wilt Chamberlain resisted the underhand method of taking free throws, even though it was better, simply because it looked silly. Danica then shared Plato's analogy of the cave, in which people preferred being chained prisoners to being free to explore a new and better world outside the cave.

Third, addressing how to manage our fears and insecurities, Danica explained the difference Jesus can make. The Bible's story reveals that we have infinite worth. We are all created in the image of God. But more than this, if we love, worship, and follow Jesus, then Jesus declares us to be part of his family. We are worth so much to Jesus that he died for us and now lives for us. This means we don't have to fear disruption. Danica illustrated this with a fake wallet. Many of us travel with a fake wallet so that if we're robbed, we can hand over the fake wallet and keep our real wallet with money inside. We've been robbed, but we haven't been robbed of what's most valuable. In the same way, even if disruption threatens to rob us of our jobs, careers, and livelihoods, it can't ever rob us of the infinitely valuable fact that we are children loved by God.

Danica concluded with a story of how she once relied on the GPS map on her iPhone to travel around Hong Kong. At first the GPS map was helpful. It told her which bus to catch and which streets to walk. But then it couldn't find a signal, and Danica was helplessly lost. GPS is a disruptive technology, but it has its limits. This is true of all disruption. GPS can tell us which streets to walk, but it can't navigate the bigger questions of life: Who am I? Where is my value? Why am I here? Where am I going? For that we need Jesus, the original disruptor. He came to disrupt our lives. He came to take away our fears and insecurities. He came to give us a new and better way to find value—by dying for us, living for us, and bringing us into his family.

CHAPTER 5

HOW TO ADDRESS A TOPIC CULTURALLY

Why Do We Need to Preach with High Cultural Intelligence?

SAM CHAN

In many Asian cultures, when you eat at a restaurant with your friends, you never split the bill. One person offers to pay the bill for everyone. "I will pay!" But you should never let that person pay. You are supposed to fight them tooth and nail for the check. "I will pay!" "No, I will pay!" "I will pay!" "No, I will pay!" Back and forth it goes.[1]

In Anglo cultures, when you eat at a restaurant with your friends, you always split the bill. So if a person offers to pay the bill, you never fight them. If they're silly enough to pay for everyone, let them pay!

I am an Asian who grew up in Australia. That means I can choose when to be Asian and when to be Anglo. So when I go with my Asian friends to a restaurant and someone offers to pay the bill, I choose to be Anglo. I let them pay. I'm not going to fight them for the bill. Let their yes be yes!

What is the point of this story? It's to show that culture will always be part of who we are and what we do. Culture will determine what happens at that restaurant table. And culture will also determine what happens in a sermon.

KATE AND KAI

Imagine that we run a youth group that meets on Friday nights. One night Kate, a sixteen-year-old Asian American, walks in. She attends an elite private prep school. She plans to study hard, get good grades, and get into law school.

What do we say to Kate? We say, "Kate, you study too much. You have made study your idol. If you're serious about following Jesus, you need to take up a hobby. Enjoy some leisure. Go to the beach and enjoy God's creation. Even better, give up study altogether, go into full-time Christian ministry, and become a youth pastor!"

Later that night Kai walks in. Kai is a sixteen-year-old Californian surfer dude. He goes to the local high school. He plans to drop out of high school and take up a trade so he can spend the rest of his life surfing.

What do we say to Kai? We say, "Kai, you surf too much. You have made surfing your idol. If you're serious about following Jesus, you need to apply yourself in your studies. Use your God-given talents to get better grades. Go to college and get a degree. Even better, give that all up, go into full-time Christian ministry, and become a youth pastor!"

Can you see what we've done? We've asked Kate to become Kai and Kai to become Kate. And then, ultimately, we asked them to become us. We thought we were preaching the gospel to Kate and Kai, but we imposed our culture on them instead. Worse, we automatically attacked their culture because it was foreign to ours. Because it was unfamiliar to us, we assumed it was wrong.

How did this happen? We conflated our culture with the gospel, as if they were one and the same. How do we prevent this from happening? We need to recognize the role that culture plays in our preaching. Our problem is, how can we preach with high cultural intelligence (CQ) as well as emotional intelligence (EQ) and informational intelligence (IQ)?[2] To do this, we need to learn the art and skill of contextualization.

THE RELATIONSHIP BETWEEN CULTURE AND PREACHING

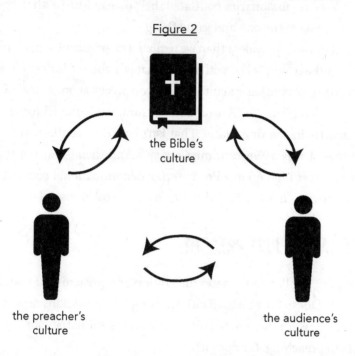

Figure 2

the Bible's culture

the preacher's culture

the audience's culture

Whenever we preach, there is an interplay between (1) our culture, (2) the Bible's culture, and (3) the audience's culture. (See fig. 2.) Usually, we're aware of the Bible's culture. That's why we have to translate the Bible's culture for our audience. The Bible's culture is not a straight one-to-one correlation with our culture or the audience's culture. We have to explain, "In those days, a shepherd did *this*," "In those days, a Samaritan meant *this*," and "In those days, a tax collector was like *this*." We're also typically aware of the audience's culture. Hopefully, we at least noticed that Kate and Kai come from different cultures.

But rarely are we aware of our own culture. We think we are a neutral, blank slate. Unlike Kate and Kai, we are devoid of any culture!

We often laugh at the well-meaning missionaries who made early attempts at bringing the gospel to other cultures. They didn't just bring the gospel; they also brought their Western culture and imposed it on the locals as if it were the gospel. They made them wear Western clothes, play Western musical instruments, and sing Western hymns. The Western missionaries conflated their own culture with the gospel, as if those were the one and same thing.

This is more prevalent than we realize. The president at my seminary once lightheartedly joked with me, "What is it about Chinese churches? They still make you wear a suit and tie if you preach at one of their Sunday services!" I replied, "Well, who do you think made the Chinese wear a suit and tie in the first place? That isn't exactly a traditional Chinese costume. It was a Western missionary!" And then, knowing that the president was high up in a Presbyterian denomination, I couldn't resist one more dig: "It was probably a Presbyterian missionary!"

WHY CAN'T I JUST PREACH?

Whenever I talk about contextualization and preaching, I usually see eyes roll. Doesn't contextualization belong in the missions department? It may be useful for cross-cultural, overseas ministry. But it doesn't apply to preaching. Or does it?

The seminary president I mentioned previously also said to me, "What's this contextualization stuff? All I know is that when I preach regularly"—by this he meant in English—"at a Chinese church, they understand me just fine!" He may have been partly joking, but only partly.

But we say this only because we don't notice our own culture, just like a fish doesn't notice the water around it and dog owners don't notice the dog smell in their living room. When I lived in the USA, well-meaning Americans would say to me, "Oh, I love your Australian accent!" Then they would ask me, "Do I have an accent to you?" They didn't think they had an accent. They couldn't hear it. They assumed their version of English was accentless. Everyone else in the world spoke with an accent except them.

What's more, many Americans told me they had a normal American accent. When I was in Missouri, someone told me the Missouri accent was the normal American accent. That's why they picked people from Missouri to be newsreaders. But when I was in Illinois, someone told me the Illinois accent was the normal one. That's why they picked people from Illinois to read the news. Wherever I went in the USA, people told me they had the normal American accent, and their state was the one from which newsreaders were chosen. (But I have to admit, I never once heard someone from Alabama claim this!)

More worryingly, some Americans told me they had the neutral English accent. I once met a guy from California who told me that the reason they made movies in Hollywood was because the Californian accent was neutral. Think about that. He was claiming that the whole world of English speakers—Irish, Scottish, English, Canadian, South African, Indian, Malaysian, Australian, Nigerian, Sri Lankan, Kenyan— all spoke with a distinct accent. But not Californians; they, of all people groups, had the neutral, blank-slate English accent. He could say this only because he was culturally unaware, ignorant of his own accent.

We do the same when we preach. If we're not aware of how our culture determines the way we give talks—form, content, genre, style, tone—then we are just as naive.

As a theologian, I have a little giggle when I see the titles of theology textbooks. If the textbook comes from Asia, we call it *Asian Theology*. If it comes from Africa, we call it *African Theology*. But if it comes from North America—like a Grudem, Erickson, or Reymond—then we simply call it *Theology*. Not *North American Theology*. Just *Theology*. As if it came out of Hollywood. It's the neutral, normative approach to theology, devoid of culture, context, or continent.

This is why we're never just preaching. There is no neutral, normative sermon that hovers above culture. Hollywood has an accent, and all preachers have a culture. If we're not aware of this, then we will impose on the audience our cultural norms as if they were the gospel truth.

To complicate this further, our audience also has a culture. Their culture will never overlap 100 percent with our culture. As a result, our preaching is automatically cross-cultural work. All forms of communication are cross-cultural. It's not just the missionaries who need to use the skills of contextualization; we all do.

WHAT IS CONTEXTUALIZATION?

We do three things when we preach: interpret the Bible's message, communicate that message, and apply it to our audience. But contextualization recognizes that preaching doesn't occur in a vacuum. As we've seen, culture is everywhere: the preacher, the Bible, and the audience all exist in cultures. As a result, culture shapes the task of preaching.

According to Jackson Wu, the task of contextualization needs to be broken down into:

1. **Exegetical contextualization:** recognizing the role our culture plays in our interpretation, communication, and application of the Bible's message.
2. **Cultural contextualization:** taking the Bible's message into our audience's culture and challenging them there.[3]

Now we'll dive into these two aspects of contextualization to see how they can and should affect our preaching.

1. Exegetical Contextualization
A. Our Culture and Interpretation

Our cultural lens helps us to see biblical ideas that other cultures may miss. But our culture also gives us blind spots that make us misunderstand or miss ideas in the Bible. An Asian American like Kate might come to the Bible with the lens of an Asian worldview. She will notice themes of shame and honor in the Bible. She will see "face" language that her Western counterparts will miss. Yet she might misunderstand her walk with God to be about duty, obligation, and perfectionism.

A Californian surfer dude like Kai might come to the Bible with the lens of Western individualism. He will notice the importance of the individual's personal decision to follow Jesus. But he might be blind to his corporate responsibilities as a member of Christ's body.

We all come to the Bible with cultural lenses, whether we realize it or not. In John 4, Jesus tells the Samaritan woman she has had five husbands, and the man she's presently with isn't even her husband. Most often I've seen people assume this means the woman is a sinner. She has broken God's law, because she has been serially unfaithful. She's an adulteress.

But in other cultures people might interpret the story to mean the woman has had five husbands who abandoned her, one by one. And the man she's presently with won't even dignify her by marrying her. She needs him for protection, but he uses her for sex and domestic work. She's been sinned against. She's broken.

There's not enough in the text to tell us which is the correct interpretation. Is she the sinner or the sinned against, the lawbreaker or the broken one? Our cultural traditions have shaped the way we interpret this familiar passage in the Bible. And we've probably been blind to alternative interpretations until now.[4]

B. Our Culture and Communication

Our culture determines how we prefer to communicate. Every culture has its own set of idioms, metaphors, symbols, stories, and forms of communication. But culture also causes us to misunderstand what is being communicated.

In the USA a common greeting is, "How are you doing?" But in Australia we say, "How are you *going*?" If you greet an American with, "How are you going?" they will usually reply, "By car." Another common USA greeting is, "What's up?" When Americans first greeted me this way, I took it as a literal question, not an idiomatic greeting. My confused reply was, "Er, the sky?"

An Asian American like Kate comes from what is called a high-context society, which is governed by a whole set of implicit, unspoken codes of conduct. High-context cultures prefer indirect communication—hint language. They are also event based rather than time based.[5] If Kate had brought her mother to hear the Friday night youth talk described previously, her mother would have found it too disrespectful, blunt, and informal. Worse, it would have been too brief at only fifteen minutes. If you were serious about Jesus, you would have gotten rid of the youth group games at the start and replaced them with a sixty-minute Bible talk.

A Californian dude like Kai comes from a low-context society, which is informal, direct, and casual. Low-context cultures prefer direct communication. A yes is a yes. A no simply means no. Kai would be unimpressed by your fifteen-minute talk. It was supposed to go for ten minutes, and you went five minutes too long. You had too much theory. There weren't enough funny stories. You took yourself too seriously. You should have had more games before the talk.

Kai might also be a concrete-relational learner, meaning he prefers stories over abstract ideas. If you don't tell him enough stories, then he thinks you're too snooty and don't live in his world. You're unrelatable. In comparison Kate might be an abstract-ideational learner. She loves bullet points, propositions, and explanations. If you tell too many stories, she gets frustrated. "Why don't you get to the point?"[6]

What about us? What are our cultural preferences for communication? I once taught preaching at a seminary where the principal and the preaching department insisted that a sermon must be expository and never topical, must have a single big idea from the text, and must be inductive and never deductive. Friends of mine once attended a denominational conference in which they were told that a sermon must be at least forty minutes long; otherwise they weren't serious enough about the Bible. I have been told that preaching must be linear, didactic, and propositional. I've also heard it said that we must never use illustrations or stories. I was once prohibited at my seminary from teaching storytelling as a method for preaching. Storytelling was for missionaries—who do cross-cultural work—but never for preachers. After all, preaching shouldn't have to worry about funny stuff like culture!

This is what happens when we fail to see the role culture plays in communication. If we think we are the ones without a culture, then we will absolutize things that are just our own cultural preferences. We will conflate our culture with biblical truths. We will end up confusing orthopraxy with orthodoxy, pedagogy with theology, and form with content. We will treat our cultural tradition as the privileged default starting point, as if any other cultural tradition were the eccentric anomaly.

C. Our Culture and Application

Culture shapes how we apply our sermon to our audience. This is another way of appropriating E. D. Hirsch's famous distinction between meaning and significance. Even if the text has a single meaning, there can be multiple significances for different audiences.

If the weather report says today will be fine, sunny, with blue skies and temperatures in the 70°F range, then the meaning of this weather report is that it will not rain today. But the significance will be different for different audiences. For the couple planning an outdoor wedding, the significance is that they don't have to worry about wet weather plans. For the farmer the significance is that the irrigation sprinklers will have to be turned on. For the painter the significance is that the decking can be painted today.

My PhD supervisor, Graham Cole, showed me how John the Baptist had different applications for his different audiences in Luke 3:10–14. To the crowd John's application was that they share food and clothing. To the tax collectors John's application was that they stop cheating. To the soldiers John's application was that they stop extorting money and accusing people falsely.

But if we think this is the only relationship between culture and application, then we're wrong. Because culture affects much more than this. A preacher's culture shapes how they think the talk should be applied.

Naive Realism versus Critical Realism

At this point we might be throwing our arms up in the air. "How can we ever get this right if we're so trapped in our own culture?" Well, don't despair. Just asking that question shows we're not 100 percent trapped. At least we've been able to critically distance ourselves from our culture to be able to ask that question.[7]

Here I find the epistemological distinction between naive realism and critical realism to be very helpful.[8] A naive realist believes there is objective reality and they have perfect objective knowledge of it. If they see a tree, then there really is a tree and they see this tree perfectly. They have a perfect image of that tree in their brain. If you don't see the tree in exactly the same way they do, then you are simply wrong. There can be only one way of seeing this tree.

Let's apply this to preaching. Let's say we're given the text of John 4. A naive realist will say there is an author-intended objective meaning to John 4 and they have perfect objective knowledge of it. From this they will produce a thirty-minute sermon with a single big idea from the text, three points, some illustrations, and an application.

But a naive realist will also believe their sermon is the perfect image of the text of John 4. If you also preach from John 4, then you must come up with the same sermon they did. If your sermon has a different big idea with a different set of points, different illustrations, and a different application, then your sermon is wrong. Because there is only one way to interpret, communicate, and apply this text.

My preaching professor used to teach a hermeneutical-homiletical template which he called "the preaching pyramid." All we had to do was apply his preaching pyramid to the text, and—voilà!—we were all supposed to end up with the same big idea, points, and application. We were even supposed to end up with the same dominant illustrating metaphor, which he called "the big picture." To this day I can remember his bewildered and frustrated expression when students—using the same template on the same text—came up with big pictures different from his.

In contrast a critical realist believes there is objective reality but we will necessarily have only an approximate, subjective representation of it. The tree exists objectively, but there is no single perfect image of it. After all, even to a photographer there exists multiple possible settings—which lens, which aperture setting, which shutter speed, which time of day? And a photograph isn't the only way to represent the tree. We can also "see" this tree through a variety of expressions—paintings, drawings, sculptures, poems, songs, videos, and digital art. There are also multiple mediums for each expression—clay or bronze sculpture, limerick or slam poetry, fifteen-second TikTok or five-minute YouTube video. And for each medium there are many possible styles—do we go with minimalism, impressionism, or cubism?

There might be one objective tree. But there is no single privileged, objective way to see this tree. Instead there exists a multitude of subjective representations. To a critical realist this is okay. It's through the multiple representations that we gain a better knowledge of the tree. We need the photo. We need the painting. We need the poem.

Will this release us into a world of idealism or subjectivism? No, because idealism and subjectivism are different. Idealism says there is no objective tree at all; subjectivism says we are totally trapped in our subjective worlds, with no access to the tree. To an idealist or subjectivist, we can say whatever we want: "You have your tree, and I have my tree." But critical realism says there is an objective tree, and we use this objective tree to critique our subjective representations of it. In the end, whether we use paint or crayon, we're still trying to draw *that* tree and not a hippopotamus!

Let's apply this to preaching. Let's say we're given the text of John 4. A critical realist will say there is an author-intended, objective meaning to John 4, but we don't have perfect, objective knowledge of it. Instead we have a variety of subjective representations. And we keep going back to the text of John 4 to critique our representations. It's through the multitude of approaches that we gain a better knowledge of the text.

If we are in a preaching class with ten students and we are all given the text of John 4, then we may very well end up with ten different sermons—ten different big ideas, ten different sets of points, ten different illustrations, and ten different applications. Moreover, there will be a variety of approaches. Some sermons will be didactic and propositional. Others will use storytelling. Some sermons will be logical and linear. Others will be circular. Some will be inductive. Others will be deductive. Some will be forty minutes long. Others will be only ten minutes. Some will be expository. But others will be topical. Some sermons might see things from an Asian perspective. Others might see them from an African perspective. Still others might see them from an Anglo perspective. And that's okay!

As preachers, we should be critical realists rather than naive realists. As a critical realist, I know I will never have the perfect snapshot representation of the truth. My version is not the one and only privileged way to portray it. Instead I need to continually listen to the community of interpreters, not just to my cultural community. We need an international community of interpreters: Africans, Asians, Australians. Together we can gain a better, closer, cumulative approximation of the truth.

Let's say Kate goes to her mother's Asian church on Sunday morning. The text for that morning is 1 Corinthians 6:19: "Your bodies are temples of the Holy Spirit." The Asian minister may apply this to Kate in this way: "You must not smoke." But let's say Kai goes with his dad to an Anglo church on that same Sunday. There the text is also 1 Corinthians 6:19. The Anglo minister might apply the text to Kai in this way: "You must not get a tattoo."

In my tradition in Sydney, the application for almost every talk was, "You must give up medicine, go to seminary, and become a full-time Christian minister." When I was in the USA, the application for almost every talk was, "Do morning devotions, support the work of missionaries, and tell your friends about Jesus." When I was in Siberia, the application for almost every talk was, "You must not drink alcohol."

These may all be valid and sound applications, but if we ignore the role our culture plays in arriving at them, then we again risk imposing our cultural traditions as universal binding norms. It will also blind us to how enculturated we are and stop us from exploring other valid and more nuanced applications.

2. Cultural Contextualization

According to Timothy Keller, the aim of cultural contextualization is both to enter and to challenge our audience's culture with our biblical message.[9] If we only enter a culture, then we have overadapted our message to fit the culture, but we have not challenged that culture with biblical norms. They are misinformed. We have not been necessarily offensive with the biblical norms. We have let them continue to do things they shouldn't do and have not asked them to give up what they need to give up. We have given them syncretism, in which they have been able to blend our biblical message with their culture. This is what missiologists call uncritical contextualization.

But if we only challenge that culture, then we have underadapted our message, because we have not yet entered that culture. They are underinformed. We have been unnecessarily offensive with non-biblical norms. We have asked them to give up things they don't have to give up. We have asked them to do things they don't have to do. We have given them legalism. This is what missiologists call colonialism or cultural imperialism. This is pharisaism. We have imposed our cultural norms on them as if they were biblical norms.

But the Goldilocks sweet spot is to both enter and challenge. If we do this, the audience is biblically informed. We have given them the contextualized biblical message. We have not imposed our cultural norms on them. Instead we have let them see what it looks like to follow Jesus in their culture. This is what missiologists call critical contextualization.

Let's look at a topic such as "Work" in Kate's Asian American culture. If we tell Kate she dishonors God whenever she gets poor grades on her exams, then we risk being guilty of syncretism. We have overadapted our preaching to her cultural norms. Work is now blended into her Asian views of duty, filial piety, and perfectionism. But the opposite would happen if we told Kate her work exists only so she can give away her money to missionaries or that she's at work only to tell her colleagues about Jesus, and otherwise she should give up her work and go into full-time Christian ministry, because that's the only work God is interested in. Here we are guilty of legalism. We have underadapted our preaching. We have imposed our cultural norms on Kate as if they were biblical norms.

Now let's look at the topic "Play" in a Californian surfing culture like Kai's. We can tell Kai that play is part of God's good creation and that God wants Kai to do whatever it takes to be happy. But if we do this, we risk being guilty of syncretism. Play is now blended into his Western views of autonomy, individualism, and independence. But the opposite would happen if we told Kai he can surf only if he's telling his surfing buddies about Jesus or training to be a counselor at Christian surf camps, because otherwise he should give up surfing and go into full-time Christian ministry. Here we are guilty of legalism and underadapting our message.

Often we think we should err on the safe side by not trying to contextualize at all, in case we overadapt and end up in syncretism. Better to underadapt and undercontextualize, just in case. But the opposite of syncretism isn't the pure Bible; it is legalism, colonialism, pharisaism, and cultural imperialism. That might be worse! Often in the New Testament, the opponents of Jesus were the Pharisees and legalists.

Syncretism, Legalism, and Undercontextualization

If I'm a legalist, it's because I'm also a syncretist without knowing it. Let's say I belong to a hierarchical Asian culture that equates wearing a suit and tie with respect. I might insist that we all must wear a suit and tie to worship God at our Sunday church service. I now have syncretism because I have conflated my Asian cultural norm with my Christian faith, as if they were the same—to wear a suit and tie on Sunday is to be a Christian.

But if I impose this cultural norm on other Christians as a biblical norm, then I am now guilty of legalism. I am making you do something the Bible is not asking you to do. None of us ever want to be legalists. We all tut-tut at the Pharisees in the New Testament. So why would I end up as a legalist myself? It's because, in my heart of hearts, I think I'm imposing a biblical norm, not a cultural norm. I can't see the difference. I can't see my own culture (like the fish in water), so I can't see my own syncretism.

If I can't see my own culture, then I will never see the need for contextualization. I will "just preach." I will think I'm giving a pure, neutral, culture-free sermon. But I can't see how much my preaching is a product of my culture. As a result, I will preach an undercontextualized sermon that risks being guilty of both syncretism (I'm preaching my culture and not the Bible) and legalism (I'm imposing my cultural norms on you).

WE WILL ALWAYS OVERADAPT AND UNDERADAPT

According to Timothy Keller, all our preaching will either overadapt or underadapt to a culture.[10] In Romans 8:14–17, Paul writes that if we have God's Spirit, then we will be adopted as God's children. We cry out, "*Abba*, Father!" But how do we explain the Aramaic term *abba* to contemporary people? If we tell Kai, our Californian surfer dude, that it means "old man," then we risk overadapting to his culture—in particular his egalitarian, casual approach to hierarchical relationships. At this point we have misinformed Kai. But if we leave *abba* untranslated, we risk underadapting to Kai's culture. Now *abba* is simply gobbledygook to Kai. It's meaningless. Kai is now underinformed by this biblical truth. He misses out on relating to God as his Father.

Let's say we try to tell the gospel to Kai. If we use only brokenness and healing as our metaphors for sin and salvation, then we risk overadapting our preaching to Kai's Western culture—in particular his loss of categories of guilt and retribution. Kai might blend our explanation of sin with his views of brokenness, turning sin into a sickness that can be healed by therapy, remorse, and self-help instead of an offense against a holy and wrathful God, which requires our repentance, Christ's atonement, and God's forgiveness. But if we focus only on guilt and forgiveness, then we risk underadapting our preaching to his culture. Kai will now be underinformed about the other metaphors of sin and salvation, such as shame and honor, brokenness and restoration, self-righteousness and exaltation, and falling short and reconciliation.

We can never get it exactly right, because we will forever have blind spots from our own culture. And we will never have perfect knowledge of another person's culture. But that shouldn't stop us from trying. Instead we need to keep consulting people of other cultures and allow them to collaborate with us and critique our preaching. We need an international community of preachers who can humbly learn from each other.

Adapting to a Culture

	Underadapt	Sweet Spot	Overadapt
Preacher	Doesn't enter (challenges only)	Enters and challenges	Doesn't challenge (enters only)
Audience	Can't understand (underinformed)	Understands (informed)	Doesn't understand (misinformed)
Application	You ask them to give up what they don't have to give up, and do what they don't have to do.	You ask them to give up what they have to give up, and do what they have to do.	You don't ask them to give up what they should give up, or do what they should do.
Offense of the gospel	Unnecessarily offensive	Necessarily offensive	Not necessarily offensive
Result	Legalism	Contextualized biblical truths	Syncretism
Category of contextualization (Hiebert)[11]	Colonialism, cultural imperialism	Critical contextualization	Uncritical contextualization

SO DO WE SPLIT THE BILL OR DON'T WE?

At the start of this chapter, we looked at the cultural minefield of splitting a bill at a restaurant. If my Asian friends offer to pay for the whole meal, I will be culturally tone-deaf if I don't at least pretend to fight them for the bill. But if my Anglo friends ask to split the bill, I will be culturally tone-deaf if I offer to pay for the whole thing. I will make them feel awkward. So how to know when to do what? It's not enough to know that culture exists and informs our actions. We also need to know how to read and interpret a particular culture. What does a culture believe about splitting a bill, and how should that inform the decisions I make when interacting with people from that culture? That will be the subject of our next chapter.

CHAPTER 6

HOW TO INTERPRET CULTURE

What Does It Look like to Preach with High Cultural Intelligence?

SAM CHAN

I subscribe to the *New Yorker* because it makes me feel culturally elite. The *New Yorker* is a highbrow magazine, famous for its articles, stories, poems, and especially its cartoons. If a writer can get a submission published by the *New Yorker*, that is often considered the pinnacle of success. In the opinion of many, there is no magazine more prestigious than that one.[1]

But here's my confession: I cannot read the *New Yorker*. The articles are way too long. The stories are impenetrable. I don't understand the poems. And—shock!—I don't get the cartoons; I find most of them bland and unfunny. Instead of reading the magazine, I simply let the issues pile up on my coffee table to impress people.

This is because I am a person of the sciences. In medical school I was taught how to read and interpret X-rays, EKGs, and FBCs. (I bet many writers for the *New Yorker* can't do that!) But no one taught me how to interpret a story or poem. What exactly am I supposed to do with a poem? I can tell you it has fourteen lines with an AABB rhyming scheme and that it's about a tree, but not much more than that.

We face the same challenge as preachers. We've been taught how to read and interpret the Bible. We even have fancy-named tools to do this, such as grammatico-historical exegesis. But many of us have not been taught how to read and interpret culture. How can we do this? What are our tools? That is what we're going to learn in this chapter.

WHAT IS CULTURE?

Kevin Vanhoozer explains that my culture is an interplay between my worldview and the texts my worldview produces.[2] (See fig. 3.) On the one hand, my worldview will produce texts, which express this worldview—movies, songs, poems, blogs, TV shows, fashion, paintings, sports, tattoos, cars, gardens, food, books, sculptures, traditions, rituals, symbols, and more. My worldview will also give me the lenses to interpret those texts. But on the other hand, my texts will shape and influence my worldview. There is a dynamic and dialectical relationship between my culture's worldview and my culture's texts.

The Need for Cultural Exegesis

It's not enough to preach information—a sermon with high IQ. We also need to preach with cultural intelligence—a sermon with high CQ. This is where recent works like Matthew Kim's *Preaching with Cultural Intelligence* have been so helpful.[3]

It's not enough to do biblical exegesis. We also need to do cultural exegesis. In the same way we read and interpret the Bible, we need to read and interpret culture—ours and the audience's.

Figure 3

Culture: A Dynamic Relationship between Worldview and Texts

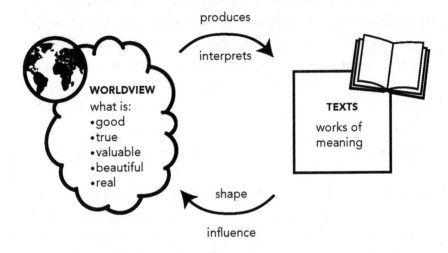

My worldview will have a system of beliefs when it comes to what is true, good, valuable, beautiful, and real. As an Asian Australian, I straddle both the Asian and Anglo worldviews. In my Asian worldview, study and good grades are valuable. If an Asian were to say to my parents, "Your son is very good. How can my son be like your son?" it would usually mean, "Your son got into medicine! How can my son also be studious and get into medicine?" As a result of my getting into medicine, my parents used to run a lot of parenting seminars in the Asian scene. In this Asian worldview, if your child gets into medicine at the University of Sydney, then you must have been a good parent.

But in the Anglo worldview, success in sports is highly prized. If an Anglo were to say to my Asian parents, "Wow, your son is very good at rugby!" this would mean nothing to my Asian parents. It's not prized at all. It's a threat to their value system. They might even react (as they probably did) by saying, "What? My son is good at rugby? He'll get hurt! He should be studying instead!" I remember many a high school rugby game after which my Asian dad expressed his disapproval. "Son, you played too hard today. You don't have to play so hard."

Can you see what's happened? The text was, "Your son is good at rugby!" Anglos, looking through their cultural lens, interpreted this as something good, valuable, and beautiful. But my parents, looking through their Asian cultural lens, interpreted this as something not good, not valuable, and not beautiful. It had no aesthetic value to them at all. It threatened what they thought was good, valuable, and beautiful: my studies.

When I taught in a seminary, I used to do an experiment. I said to my class, "I want you to imagine that we're not in a classroom right now. Instead we're all at the beach. The sun is shining. There's not a cloud in the sky. The water is cool, crisp, and crystal blue. The sand is soft and white. You take your shoes off. You walk into the water and get your feet wet."

Then I asked the class, "Who here is feeling relaxed right now?" Most of the class put up their hands. They were chilled, soothed, and relaxed just thinking about this.

But then I said to the class, "If you're Asian, you are probably super stressed right now. *What do you mean I'm in direct sunshine? Quick! Put up an umbrella. I don't want my skin to go brown. What do you mean I'm barefoot, standing in sand? Brush off the sand! I don't want to bring sand back into my car or my house. What do you mean my feet are wet? Eeeew! Now I'm going to catch a cold and die. Why did you bring me here? Can't we be indoors in a classroom?*"

What is beautiful for one culture is abominable in another. The same scenario—a beach—was interpreted through two different lenses, from two different worldviews.

To do another experiment, I asked my class, "If you were going for an important job interview, would you wear a plain white business shirt or a business shirt with color or perhaps a pattern?"

Most of the class chose a shirt with color or a pattern. Why? Because a plain white shirt would say they were dull, boring, and unadventurous. But a shirt with color or a pattern would say they were independent, entrepreneurial, and creative thinkers. These are highly desired traits in a worker. This would make it more likely for them to get a job.

But then I said to the class, "If you're Asian, you probably chose the plain white business shirt because it says you are humble. You're a team player. You don't want to stand out. If you choose a shirt with color or a pattern, it says you're a proud, arrogant upstart. There's an Asian proverb that says, 'The nail that sticks out gets hammered down!'"

Again, we had the same text—a plain white business shirt—but two cultures and two worldviews. The Western worldview values individualism, but the Asian worldview values collectivism. Each culture has a different interpretive lens and comes up with a different meaning.

HOW CAN WE INTERPRET A CULTURE?

Here are three simple ways of interpreting a culture, represented by three questions we should ask about it.

1. What Are Its Views?

We can choose from a variety of topics—God, humans, good and evil, death, reality, salvation—and see what a culture says about that topic. But these are quite abstract. I like how Kevin Vanhoozer chooses from a list of topics that are more concrete.

- beauty
- body
- children
- cities
- gardens
- gifts
- guilt and shame
- hope
- justice

- marriage
- sickness
- worship[4]

We can immediately see how this provides a window into most cultures. Let's take the topic of gardens. In my suburb, those of English heritage keep their gardens tidy. Those of Italian heritage often concrete their gardens because it's more practical. Those of Asian heritage often grow vegetables, which they try to sell.

Perhaps we can add other topics to Vanhoozer's list: bathrooms, body hair, coffee, eating out, gambling, hospitality, kitchens, motorcars, elderly people, shorts, sports, travel, vacations, work, and youth. All of these topics and more will give us insight into how cultures are distinct from one another.

2. What Are Its Themes?

Paul Hiebert suggests that we look at themes and their opposites, or counterthemes. Every culture belongs somewhere on a group of spectra between themes and counterthemes. (See fig. 4.)[5]

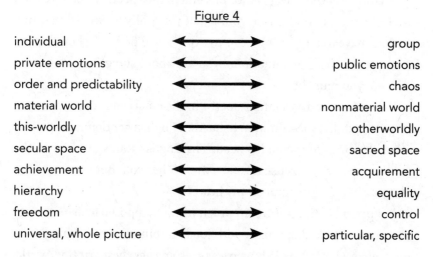

Figure 4

individual	group
private emotions	public emotions
order and predictability	chaos
material world	nonmaterial world
this-worldly	otherworldly
secular space	sacred space
achievement	acquirement
hierarchy	equality
freedom	control
universal, whole picture	particular, specific

Excerpt from *Transforming Worldviews* by Paul G. Hiebert, copyright © 2008. Used by permission of Baker Academic, a division of Baker Publishing Group.

Let's go through each of these spectra with a little more specificity.

Individual versus Group

A culture at the individual end of this spectrum values the individual—you have the right to do whatever makes you happy. But in a culture at the group end of the spectrum, your identity comes more from your belonging in a group. In the West when a couple gets married, it's the bride's day! But in Asia when a couple gets married, the day belongs to the parents. Most of the guests will be invited by the parents and won't know the couple. The marriage ceremony is just as much a celebration of the parents' achievements as the couple's. This makes it more of a group effort, like a graduation ceremony for the parents.

Or let's say you are a high school student and you ask your guidance counselor what you should do for a career. If you are a student in California, your counselor will say, "What do you want to do?" But if you're a student in Singapore, your counselor will say, "What do your parents want you to do?"

Private Emotions versus Public Emotions

A culture at the private emotions end of the spectrum believes you should keep your emotions to yourself. If you really believe something, you don't have to rely on emotions to express it. The truth should speak for itself, and the more emotional you are about something, the more insincere you must be.

When I worked as a junior doctor in the emergency department of a large hospital, it was common to have an English gentleman approach with a bleeding wound on his head. The Englishman would say to the triage nurse dryly, "Excuse me. Sorry to bother you. But there appears to be a rather large wound on my head."

But patients from cultures in which you are supposed to demonstrate your emotion would approach with loud, gasping shrieks of pain. One time a nurse wheeled in a lady who was grasping her chest, panting, writhing, and moaning in pain. I asked the nurse about the lady's condition.

The Mosh Pit Wars

The difference between a public emotion culture and a private emotion culture is of significance in Christian conferences run for teenagers. When the older generation sees the youth jumping, hooting, and hollering to loud Christian music in the mosh pit at the front, what do they usually think? In my tradition the older generation shakes their heads with disapproval because to them it's too emotional. But to the youth, if the Christian faith is true, then you should be emotional about it.

If these were African teenagers jumping and dancing to loud music, we would approve because it is consistent with their culture. But if it's Anglo teenagers doing it, we disapprove because we think it's inconsistent with their culture. But maybe the real problem is that it's inconsistent with our culture.

If we don't take time to understand culture, we will come up with sophisticated arguments for why people shouldn't do something, when in essence we're saying, "I'm not used to it" or, "It's not how I do it." We often have theological debates that are actually cultural debates.

The nurse, rolling her eyes, said to me, "She says she's having a heart attack. Let's do a quick EKG on her and send her back out into the waiting room." But when we did the EKG, it showed that the lady really was having a heart attack! None of us had believed her because she was showing more emotion than we expected. She came from a public emotion culture, but we came from a private emotion culture.

Order and Predictability versus Chaos

In many Western countries—Australia, New Zealand, Canada, UK, USA—the traffic lane markings tell you to stay in your lane. If you even dare drift from your lane into the next one, the car in the next lane will honk to tell you to get back into your lane.

But if you live in other countries—and I dare not name any!—the traffic markings are merely a suggestion. Why have only three lanes of traffic when you can have nine or thirteen squeezed in? Traffic here is much more organic. We are like fish in the ocean. If I drift into your lane, that's okay. You can drift into someone else's lane. There's plenty of room for everyone. If I honk my horn, it's out of courtesy, to politely warn you that I'm about to come into your lane.

Material World versus Nonmaterial World; This-Worldly versus Otherworldly

In our Western, scientific, post-Enlightenment culture, we usually believe that everything is only atoms and molecules. If we can't see it or touch it, then it doesn't exist. We pay lip service to angels, prayer, and heaven, but many people do not live as if they are real. This life in the here and now is all we have to live. We'd better make the most of it. You only live once!

But in most other cultures people believe in spirits and the unseen. This is a conscious part of everyday life. If you get sick, it's not enough only to see the doctor for some medicine. You should also try out alternative medicine, acupuncture, and the local priest. In other cultures people also hold the belief that there is more than just this life to live. Our actions have consequences on both the spirit world and our afterlife.

Secular Space versus Sacred Space

In our Western culture almost all space is secular—trains, planes, schools, libraries, town halls, taxis, bars, restaurants, cinemas. Only a handful of spaces are designated as sacred—churches and maybe the privacy of your own home. That's where you pray and worship your God. But you certainly don't do that in a secular space. There is a strong sacred-secular divide.

But in most other cultures there is no sacred-secular divide. Your Asian restaurant owner will have a little shrine set up in public to her gods. Your Hindu taxi driver will have a religious symbol on his dashboard. Your Muslim neighbor will wear clothing that publicly displays her faith. In these cultures all space is sacred.

Achievement versus Acquirement

In achievement-based cultures, we are all blank slates. We have to earn our success, status, and honor. But in an acquirement-based culture, although achievements are still important, who your parents are and which tribe you belong to also matter.

Our Californian dude, Kai, comes from an achievement-based culture. When Kai goes surfing, every surfer is on equal footing. It doesn't matter who your parents are, whether you're a CEO or a cleaner, or what car you drive. You all have to fight for the same parking spots. You all have to fight for the same waves. You have to earn your place in the water with your surfing skills and let your surfing do the talking.

Kate, the Asian American, comes from more of an acquirement-based culture. Although she studies hard, gains acceptance into an Ivy League college, and becomes a lawyer, she will still not be accepted into the ruling elites of her social order. She has the wrong parents. She comes from the wrong village.

Hierarchy versus Equality

Western countries such as Australia and New Zealand are off-the-charts down the equality end of this spectrum. People call each other by their first names. Titles are shunned. If you insist on being called "Professor" or "Doctor," then you will come across as snooty, snobby, and self-aggrandizing.

But in most other countries, there is a hierarchy. It would be rude to call someone by their first name. It is respectful to call people by their titles.

You Gave Up Medicine?

Sometimes when I give talks to high school students, the MC will introduce me in the following way: "Sam Chan used to be a medical doctor, but he gave up medicine to go into full-time Christian ministry."

At this moment I can see many Asian students gasp. *Wait. He got into medicine and he gave it up? Either he's stupid or this Christianity must have something to it!* In their culture of hierarchy, group, and control, I gave up something that promised honor to my parents. I gave up security. But maybe more important, it shouldn't have been my decision to make. My parents had given up everything to move to Australia to give me a better future. But then I disrespectfully threw it all away.

But I can see that the Anglo students are unmoved. *Good for you. You have to do what makes you happy.* In their culture of individualism and freedom, what I've done is underwhelmingly mundane. Whether Christianity is true is irrelevant. In the end only I can decide what makes me happy. *So you gave up medicine? Big deal.* Yawn.

Freedom versus Control

The word free exists in the national anthems of the USA, Canada, Australia, and New Zealand. When I was a schoolboy, I sang these words at my school assemblies: "Australians all let us rejoice, for we are young and free." In Australia we don't worship God or king. We worship freedom.

I find it amazing that Singapore, with its Asian collectivism and Asian worldview, can ban chewing gum. And people happily comply. Singaporeans are happy to give up their individual rights (the right to chew gum) if it results in a greater good for the collective society (cleaner sidewalks).

The Prodigal Son: Comedy or Horror Story?

I've seen and heard the retelling of the prodigal son parable (Luke 15) in many talks, puppet shows, and skits. Usually, it's a bit of a comedy. When the younger son takes his father's money, leaves home, and experiments with wild living—rock and roll, alcohol, and parties—we all have a bit of a laugh. This is because the younger son's actions make perfect sense to our Western ears. The younger son has done exactly what Western parents want their children to do: leave home, travel, make some mistakes, and return older and wiser. Western parents encourage their children to do this. In the UK it even has a name: the gap year. If the prodigal son had lived in the UK, he wouldn't have had to ask his father for money. His father would have happily paid for his son's gap year.

In Western culture there is something wrong if your children are older than eighteen but still live at home. You have failed as a parent! In the West your children shame you by continuing to live at home with you.

But in traditional Asian cultures the prodigal son story has the opposite effect. Children are not supposed to leave home until they get married. If your child leaves you before this, then you have failed as a parent. In Asia your children shame you by leaving your home too soon. As much as they might try, a Western audience will never feel the full gravity of the shame, horror, and abomination of what the prodigal son did to his father.

But in the USA they tried to ban alcohol during prohibition, which was spectacularly unsuccessful. In many states in the USA, they cannot make you wear a helmet when you ride a motorcycle. You have a God-given right to do with your head whatever you want!

I love how New Hampshire has its famous state motto "Live Free or Die" emblazoned on its license plates. I would rather die without a motorcycle helmet than be forced to wear one. I can't imagine them banning chewing gum in New Hampshire.

Whole Picture versus Particular

In the West we concentrate on the particular: "Just the facts." If there is a car accident, we focus only on who is in the wrong. Which car failed to stop at the stop sign? End of story.

But many other cultures will take in the whole picture. It matters if it's the village chief who was driving the car. It matters if someone was visiting their sick grandmother. It matters if someone let their car get hit! "Why did you let the other car hit you? Couldn't you see it shooting through the stop sign?"

Combining the Spectra

Paul Hiebert shows how we can gain further nuance and insight by combining some of these spectra. For example, we can form a grid by combining the freedom-control and hierarchy-equality spectra. (See fig. 5.)

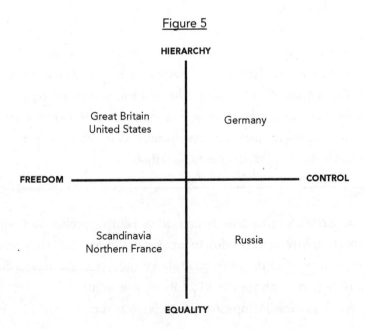

Figure 5

Here we see how not all Western cultures are exactly the same. Cultures in Scandinavia, northern France, and Russia place a high value on equality. But Scandinavia and northern France value freedom, while Russia lives under more collective control. Cultures in Great Britain, the USA, and Germany have a bigger emphasis on hierarchy. But Germany values control, while Great Britain and the USA prefer freedom.

When I taught this to my class in Sydney, I asked them where Australia belonged on this grid. Someone quickly joked, "We're in the center!" Of course, the joke is that every culture thinks it is in the center. We are the neutral, normal culture, while every other culture is the weird, wacky, zany one.

This is why many US maps of the world have the USA in the middle, even if it means Asia has to be split into two sections on the edges of the map. This is why China calls itself the Middle Kingdom. This is why Britain calls its time zone Greenwich Mean Time. They are the reference point for the rest of the world. All our clocks are set to their time.

Kate and Kai Live on Opposite Ends of Each Spectrum

Here's something I find interesting. On these spectra of themes and counterthemes, our Asian American friend, Kate, exists on the group, private emotions, order, nonmaterial world, otherworldly, sacred space, acquirement, hierarchy, control, and whole picture ends of the spectra.

But our Californian dude, Kai, exists on the opposite ends of the spectra. Kai's culture is at the individual, public emotions, chaos, material, this-worldly, sacred-secular divide, achievement, equality, freedom, and particular ends of the spectra.

Of course, there is some overlap between Kate's culture and Kai's. They watch the same movies, eat the same fast food, study the same plays by Shakespeare. But these are superficial similarities. When push comes to shove, we must acknowledge that Kate and Kai exist in different universes. What Kate sees as true, good, right, and beautiful is the opposite of what Kai sees as such.

There are at least three significances we can draw from this for our preaching. First, it explains why ethnic churches thrive. When I lived in Chicago for five years, I attended a Chinese church rather than an Anglo church. When my Asian Australian brother, Simon, lived in Montreal for one year, he attended a Chinese church. When my flatmate (an Asian Australian), David, lived in Toronto for one year, he also attended a Chinese church. None of us could speak Chinese! English was our one and only language. But we found a better cultural fit with Asian Americans and Asian Canadians than we did with Anglo North Americans.

Often my Anglo friends complain that Chinese churches are an example of the homogenous unit principle (HUP). But that's because my Anglo friends can't see that their churches are also examples of HUP. They are Anglocentric HUP churches. They just can't see their own culture, so they view their church as the neutral, normal, non-HUP church.

When my Anglo friends complain that ethnic churches are a poor witness to the gospel—which ought to transcend culture, language, and tribe—they assume their church transcends culture, language, and tribe, in the same way Hollywood movies transcend culture. I once heard Timothy Keller quote Don Carson (so it must be true!) as saying that although the gospel transcends culture, it still has to come enculturated, in a particular culture.

Second, right now the traditional Christian message has much appeal to Kate. She comes from a culture that is high on duty, obligation, superstitious rituals, fear of the spiritual realm, hierarchy, and delayed gratification. To her the Christian gospel makes sense: *Of course God must punish us if we have wronged him!* To Kate, Jesus offers freedom from fear, shame, and darkness. The gospel is great news! This explains why the gospel holds disproportionate attraction for people from the majority world cultures—Africa, Asia, Latin America, and the Middle East—that have much cultural overlap with Kate.

But the traditional Christian message has lost its appeal to Kai.

He comes from a culture that is high on autonomy, individualism, and immediate gratification. To him the Christian gospel makes little sense: *If God can't accept me for who I am, then God's got the problem, not me.* He may fear the Christian life will be one of duty, obligation, superstitious rituals, fear of the spiritual realm, hierarchy, and delayed gratification. To Kai, Jesus offers the loss of freedom and a return to fear, shame, and darkness. This is the complete opposite of how Kate hears the gospel. It explains why churched Westerners like Kai are choosing deconversion stories. In many ways Kate comes from a pre-Christendom culture, while Kai comes from a post-Christendom culture.

Third, now more than ever we need to preach with high cultural intelligence (CQ) to both Kate and Kai. Just as we might try hard to enter Kate's culture before challenging it, we need to do the same with Kai. His culture is just as foreign to Christianity as Kate's. But his entry points will be different from Kate's. It's time we explore the wider variety of entry points the Bible offers us.[6]

3. What Is Its Storyline?

I once learned from Timothy Keller that each culture has its own storyline.[7] Keller explains that a story needs three elements:

1. A mission
2. Bad guys that stop you from achieving this mission
3. Good guys that help you achieve this mission

Let's take the story of Cinderella. "Cinderella goes to the ball" is not a story. It's only an event. "Cinderella wants to go to the ball (the mission), but her wicked stepsisters (the bad guys) won't let her go, but the fairy godmother (the good guy) helps Cinderella go" is a story.

To interpret a culture, we ask, what is its storyline? What is its mission? What do we want this world to look like? What is the happily-ever-after ending we're looking for? What would the opposite—a sad ending—look like? What must we have to be fulfilled? Where are we going? Where do we want to be? Who are the bad guys? What is wrong with this world? What will stop us from achieving our mission? Who are the good guys? Who are the heroes? What will help us achieve this mission?

What is Kate's mission? She says it's to get into law school. But is that really her mission? Because, let's face it, she'd be equally happy studying medicine. So it's not really law school she's after; it's status, honor, and security. In Kate's world, if she gets into law, she will elevate her standing among her peers. Her parents will be honored among their peers. Their decision to emigrate to the USA will be validated. Kate will also achieve security. She will never be poor. Her children will go to good schools. Her parents won't end up in a run-down old persons' home.

Who are the bad guys in Kate's world? They are anything that stops her from studying: parties, sports, leisure, friends, peers, jocks—people like Kai!

Who are the good guys in Kate's world? They are anyone who will help her get into law school: authority figures, like teachers, parents, and tutors.

So where does the Christian church fit into her storyline? On the one hand, the church is one of the good guys. It's an authority figure. It teaches discipline, duty, and obligation. On the other hand, the church can be a bad guy if it takes Kate away from her studies. Kate will be at Friday night youth group when she should be doing homework. At my Chinese church's Friday night youth group, the youth do their homework at church in the thirty to sixty minutes before youth group starts. At a friend's Chinese church, the leaders schedule time for study at their youth retreat. If they didn't do this, the parents wouldn't let their kids go to the youth group.

Let's now look at Kai, the Californian surfer dude. What is his mission? He says it's to go surfing every day. But let's face it, it could be fishing or hiking instead. So it's not really surfing he's after; it's freedom. In Kai's world, if he gets to go surfing whenever he wants, that represents freedom. He will be his own boss. He won't have to listen to what anyone else tells him to do. He will be doing whatever he wants in order to be happy.

Contextualization Is a Double-Edged Sword

The more my message is contextualized, the sharper and more focused it will be for my target group. But this automatically makes it poorly contextualized for another group.

If I preach in English, this is well contextualized for English speakers but poorly contextualized for Spanish speakers. If my message is focused on Chinese restaurant workers who can meet only outside of work on Tuesdays, then my message will exclude German train drivers who can meet only on Wednesdays. If my message is sharply contextualized for the hip-hop culture of the South Side of Chicago, it will be meaningless for the professional Chinese accountant in North Vancouver.

But if I try to abstract my message in order to be as inclusive to as many groups as possible, then it will lose its edge. My audience will hear me speak about something, but they won't hear me speaking to them.

This should result in three things. First, we need to be humble about our preaching. If we think we have a well-contextualized message, it also means our preaching is poorly contextualized for a different audience. Whatever is working for our audience right now won't work so well with other listeners.

Second, we should be less critical of others' preaching. We might not like their style, delivery, tone, humor, or illustrations. But that's probably because it's well contextualized for their audience and not ours. It's not what we would do, but it might be exactly what they need to do for their audience.

Third, if our preaching works on Kate in her cultural storyline, then it's probably not going to work on Kai in his cultural storyline. We need to explore new biblical metaphors to enter and challenge his storyline.

Who are the bad guys in Kai's world? They are anything that stops him from doing what he wants to do. They are authority figures, like teachers, parents, and tutors. And Asian nerds like Kate!

Who are the good guys in Kai's world? They are anything that helps him to do what he wants to do: parties, sports, leisure, friends, peers, jocks.

Where does the Christian church fit into Kai's storyline? The church is easily the bad guy. It is an authority figure. The church is full of rules and regulations. It tells him what to do and what not to do.

Can you see what's happened? Kate's good guys are Kai's bad guys. And Kai's good guys are Kate's bad guys. They're flipped.

There's a reason why the gospel seems to be doing disproportionately better among the majority world than in the West. There's a reason why, when you go to a Christian group at a university campus, the Asians will be disproportionately represented. There's a reason why, when your church runs an evangelistic event, many Asians will choose to follow Jesus, but not their Anglo counterparts. And it's this: Kate and Kai live two storylines. Right now the gospel is the hero in Kate's storyline, but it is the villain in Kai's storyline.

Consciously or unconsciously, we have stumbled into a contextualized message for Kate's storyline. But the very thing that makes it well contextualized for Kate's storyline is what makes it poorly contextualized for Kai's storyline. It's time that we relearned how to enter and challenge Kai's storyline as well as Kate's.

Enter the Culture's Storyline

We can enter any cultural storyline—no matter how hostile or foreign it is to the gospel—because of our theological doctrines of common grace, general revelation, image of God, and hearts that cry for eternity. All goodness is God's goodness, all truth is God's truth, and all beauty is God's beauty.

As a result, if we search our audience's cultural texts, we will find something good, true, beautiful, divine, and transcendent that we can agree on. We then describe their storyline back to them, show that we understand, and demonstrate empathy for it. Who of us doesn't want the same thing? Who of us doesn't feel the same way?

Our example is Paul in Athens (Acts 17). Paul saw the multiple idols of the Athenians and was grieved (v. 16). He had every right to go through that city with a whip, the way Jesus did in the temple, and clean out the idols. He had every theological justification to condemn the people for breaking at least the first two of God's ten commandments. He would have been correct to denounce the people as idolators, lawbreakers, and transgressors.

Instead Paul decided to enter their culture. He searched their cultural texts—in this case, their idols and their altar to the Unknown God (v. 23)—for something good, true, beautiful, divine, or transcendent that a Christian could agree with. Paul found this: they were religious (v. 22). They had hearts that cried for eternity. They were searching for the transcendent.

Paul then spoke their storyline back to them. "I see that in every way you are very religious" (v. 22). At this point Paul resonated with his audience. They were nodding their heads in agreement. "Yep. That's us. You've got us. You understand us."

In the same way, we can enter Kate's culture. Her cultural text is her need to study, prove herself, and get into law school. We can describe this back to her and show that we understand where she's coming from. It's good that she wants to be disciplined in her studies. It's true that law can open doors. It's beautiful that she wants to honor her parents. It's divine that she will one day protect the rights of the weak, poor, and marginalized. She has a heart that cries for eternity—she has a transcendent longing for security. Who of us doesn't want the same thing?

At this point we can say something like this to Kate: "We all long for security. One way to find it is by getting into a secure profession. That's why many of us study so hard and deny ourselves so many immediate pleasures." If we get this right, Kate will say, "Yep. That's me. You understand my world. You get me."

We can also enter Kai's culture. His cultural text is his need to go surfing. We can describe this back to him and show that we understand where he's coming from. It's good that he can surf. It's true that the outdoors is necessary for a balanced lifestyle. It's beautiful to enjoy God's creation. It's divine to have control over the wind and the waves. Kai has a heart that cries for eternity—the transcendent longing for freedom. Who of us doesn't feel the same way?

We can say something like this to Kai: "We all long for freedom. One way to find this is to get away, escape to the outdoors, and surf all day long. Because in that moment we are free. Free from boredom. Free from having to do what someone else tells us to do. Free to do whatever we want to do." If we get this right, Kai will say, "Yep. That's me. You understand my world. You get me."

Challenge the Culture's Storyline

After entering a culture's storyline—and only after—we can now challenge that storyline. We can do this because every culture has a way of running away from God, falling short of God's glory, suppressing God's truth, distorting God's goodness, and breaking God's law.

We do this by deconstructing their storyline. Usually, it will have one or two flaws. There may be a deficiency—something is lacking. Their storyline is incomplete. It cannot achieve its happily ever after until this deficiency is filled.

Or there is a dissonance—two clashing truths that can't coexist. I call this the "you can't have it both ways" problem. You have to hang on to one of the truths and let the other one go. But you can't keep hanging on to both of them at the same time.

Let's go back to Paul in Athens. After entering the Athenians' storyline, Paul then challenged it. He demonstrated a deficiency. Their altar was to an unknown god. They were ignorant of the God they worshiped (Acts 17:23). Their storyline was incomplete. They could not worship and appease this God if they didn't know his name! There would be no happily ever after until they knew who this God was.

Paul also demonstrated a dissonance in their storyline. On one hand, this God had made the world. Even their own poets recognized this: "In him we live and move and have our being" (v. 28). But on the other hand, if this God made everything, then he didn't live in temples built by human hands; you couldn't worship him with handmade idols (v. 24). This is the "you can't have it both ways" problem. Either this God made everything, or he's merely a human-made idol. But you can't have it both ways. You have to let one of these clashing truths go.

In the same way, we can challenge Kate's storyline. There is a deficiency: she's after security, but she won't find it in law. In the end law is only a college degree. It's only a qualification. It's only an achievement. It's only an income. But security is a state of being. It's based on something else. There's still a hole in Kate's storyline. She's not going to get her happily ever after from a law degree.

There is also a dissonance: she can't have it both ways. On the one hand, she believes she can find security in law—through the degree, achievements, and income. But on the other hand, all these things are relative, because there's always another postgraduate degree. There's always another qualification. There's always another achievement—perhaps becoming a partner. But will the law firm be big enough? Will there be a bigger one in San Francisco? What about New York? What about Shanghai? And her income will never feel like enough, because she'll need a bigger car, a bigger house, a bigger city. The dissonance is this: security is supposed to be absolute, but she has based it on relative markers of success. Becoming a lawyer won't guarantee her security; if anything, it will make her feel less secure.

Similarly, we can challenge Kai's storyline. There is a deficiency. Surfing represents freedom *from*. When Kai surfs, he is free from stress, worry, and anxiety. He is free from authority figures—parents and teachers. He is free from study and work. But what is he free *for*? He needs to be part of something bigger than himself, but what could that be?

There is also a dissonance in Kai's storyline. On one hand, he's free to do whatever his heart desires. But on the other hand, if he has to do whatever his heart desires, then he's a slave to those desires. According to the ancient Greeks, true freedom isn't being able to do whatever you desire; true freedom is not having to do whatever you desire.

Complete the Culture's Storyline with the Gospel

After entering and challenging the culture's storyline, we can now complete it with the gospel. The culture has a God-given, legitimate existential cry—for meaning, purpose, hope, security, freedom, redemption, forgiveness, and salvation. This cry is a result of common grace, general revelation, the image of God, and hearts that yearn for eternity. Until now, because of human fallenness, the people of this culture have been looking in the wrong places. But we can now show them that Jesus is the happily ever after they have been looking for. He is the only way to achieve a happily ever after, and he is a far better happily ever after than they dared to dream of.[8]

We can do this by showing that Jesus fills the deficiency in their storyline. Until they find Jesus, there is no chance of a happily ever after. But with Jesus their storyline will be completed. Or we can show them how Jesus resolves the dissonance in their storyline. If they're prepared to leave behind one of their clashing beliefs and replace it with the gospel, then the dissonance in their storyline will be resolved. They will find their happily ever after.

The deficiency in the Athenians' storyline was that they didn't know the name of the God they needed to worship. So Paul filled this deficiency by telling them about Jesus (Acts 17:31). The Athenians also had a dissonance in their storyline: they were trying to worship a God who made everything, but with idols and temples built by human hands. They had to let one of those things go. If they wanted to worship the God who made everything, they needed to abandon their idols and temples and replace them with Jesus, the true image and temple of God.

In the same way, we can complete Kate's storyline. The deficiency and dissonance in her storyline is that she is after security but is trying to find it with a qualification and profession, which will always ask more of her. We can show Kate that she can find security in Jesus. In Jesus, Kate will find a God who doesn't require her to be perfect. This God will adopt Kate as his child. She will forever be part of God's kingdom, not because of her achievements or qualifications but because of the achievements and qualifications of Jesus.

We can also complete Kai's storyline. The deficiency and dissonance in his storyline is that he is after freedom, but if all he has is surfing, then he will end up empty and self-absorbed. He will be trapped by his desires. But if he loves, worships, and follows Jesus, then his heart will be changed to desire right things. He will be set free to live for a story bigger than his own. He will live a full and fulfilled life—something Jesus calls eternal life.

Quote Their Author before Quoting Our Author[9]

From Paul's speech in Athens, we learn a helpful sequence. He describes one of the Athenians' texts—in this case, their idols (Acts 17:23)—before describing his own texts. He references one of their authors—in this case, one of their poets (v. 28)—before quoting his own authors.

We can do the same thing. We should first quote from one of our audience's texts and authors—a song, a movie, a poem, a novel, a play, a *New York Times* op-ed piece, a TED Talk, a *New Yorker* article, an NPR podcast. After we've done this, because of God's common grace and general revelation, we can find one of our own texts—a verse from the Bible, a quote from a Christian writer, or a lyric from a Christian singer—that says the same thing.

This is a good persuasive and pedagogical sequence. Begin from a known before you take them to an unknown. Begin in their world before you take them into your world.

KATE AND KAI, REVISITED

We began this chapter with the story of Kate and Kai. We thought we were preaching a neutral, culture-free sermon to them. They were the ones with the wacky cultures, not us. But until we realize that we also have a culture, we will speak to them in ways that are culturally naive. We will misinterpret their culture as hostile to the gospel, when it could simply be that their culture is different from ours. We will also impose our culture on them as if it were a gospel norm. In doing so, we will be guilty of both syncretism and legalism.

The early church also struggled with this. The original Jewish converts wanted to force the Greek converts to submit to Jewish cultural norms as if they were gospel norms. But the council of Jerusalem (Acts 15) clearly resolved that Greek converts did not have to submit to Jewish cultural norms. They were free to be Christians in their own culture.

The theological significance of the incarnation is that Jesus became one of us. The gospel can be translated into any culture. In the visions of Revelation, Christians worship the Lamb, but still in their own tribes, languages, and cultures. When we become Christians, we don't give up our culture to follow Jesus. We follow Jesus *in* our culture. Just as Jesus incarnated himself into a culture, we too incarnate our Christian faith into our culture. If we are from a Vietnamese culture, we can be Christians and still Vietnamese. If we are from a Tanzanian culture, we can be Christians and still Tanzanian. If we are a high-achieving Asian American like Kate, we can follow Jesus as a high-achieving Asian American. If we are a Californian surfer dude like Kai, we can follow Jesus as a Californian surfer dude.

The homiletical significance of this is that our sermons can also be incarnated into any culture. We preach the Bible in its culture, from our culture, to our audience in their culture. It will be a challenge. But if we work on our sermon's CQ as hard as we work on our sermon's EQ and IQ, then our preaching will connect with our audience—intellectually, emotionally, and culturally.

What If I'm Speaking to Both Kate and Kai?

The double-edged sword of contextualization is that if I sharply contextualize my message so that it speaks pointedly to one cultural group, then I cannot speak as relevantly to another cultural group. Jesus' metaphor of living water spoke to the needs of the Samaritan woman (John 4:10), but it probably would not have spoken as sharply to those of the man born blind (John 9). Conversely, Jesus' metaphor "I am the light of the world" (John 9:5) spoke keenly to the man born blind, but it probably wouldn't have to the Samaritan woman at the well.

So what can we do if we're preaching to both Kate and Kai? We could do what Jesus did. In John's gospel, Jesus spoke separately to the Samaritan woman and the man born blind. Why not preach to Kate this week and to Kai next week!

But if we have only one talk to give, then we can acknowledge how both audiences are hearing the talk. We can say, "Now, if you're Asian like me, then you're not going to understand the big deal about freedom. But if you're from the West, then you're totally going to get it." Or, "If you're not an Asian, then you're not going to understand how studying hard is a way of honoring your parents. But if you're Asian like me, then you're going to get it." The advantages of this method are that it allows both audiences to step outside of their culture and see what they look like to outsiders, and it invites them to appreciate the strengths of other cultures.

It also relativizes their cultural objections. We can say, "If you're from the West, then you cannot fathom how giving up your rights allows you to be more free. But if you're Asian, you understand that this is exactly what people in Singapore gladly do—they give up their God-given right to chew gum so their footpaths are clean and free to walk on without getting gum on their shoes."

Or, "If you're from Asia, then you cannot believe that students question their teachers. But in many American colleges, they actually give students 10 percent of the grade for speaking up in class. Their students don't just memorize data but also learn to be critical thinkers, to be communicators, to be collaborative, creative, and independent."

If Kate hears what you say to Kai, she might learn that there's more to life than social advancement through studies and degrees. And if Kai hears what you say to Kate, he might learn that there's more to life than just chasing your dreams. At that moment you will have "emptied their worldview cups," and they will be ready for you to fill those cups with the gospel.

CHAPTER 7

HOW TO ADDRESS A TOPIC PASTORALLY

What Ministry Wisdom Do I Need?

MALCOLM GILL

I grew up in an independent church that was part of the Open Brethren movement that started in Dublin, Ireland, in the early 1800s. As a young movement, the Brethren had several doctrines that they held dear to their heart, but perhaps the most important was the priesthood of all believers. Responding to the clergy-laity divide of traditional denominations, the early Brethren broke away and formed a group that sought to reestablish the priority of ordinary individuals within the church.

In my childhood church, everyone bought into this ethos. Each of us participated in some form of ministry; we understood this to be the biblical model. The church employed no paid staff. Our plural eldership was made up entirely of older men who had faithfully served at the church over the years. All of the sermons preached were delivered by members of the church, none of whom had formal theological training, and I was regularly told by older members of the congregation that Bible college ruined folks. Everything needed for the Christian life, you already had: the Bible and the Holy Spirit. My church was an earnest place of worshipers who took the Scriptures and personal holiness very seriously.

As a teenager, I was shocked to discover there were Christians from other traditions, and I wasn't impressed. The Baptists? They were irreverent. The Anglicans? They were superstitious. The Pentecostals? Where does one even begin? In my mind our church was the only one that really understood the Scriptures. We were the faithful remnant in this world. Whenever someone asked me what sort of church I belonged to, I rolled out a cliché answer I'd picked up from others in church: "We are simply a New Testament kind of church." There's no comeback to that—or so I thought.

One day one of those cunning Baptist types approached me and asked the question about the distinctives of our church. I responded with my usual line: "We are simply a New Testament kind of church." He retorted, "Which one? Are you like Corinth? Or Galatia? Or Ephesus? What's your church's dysfunction?"

I had no comeback. My mind was blown. He was right; it wasn't quite as simple as saying we were like the New Testament church, because even then there was no uniform gathering of God's people. If there was any uniformity in the New Testament churches, it was that they were uniformly broken.

There is no such thing as the perfect church. Someone once told me that if you find the perfect church, don't join it, because then *you* will ruin it! All churches are flawed because they are made up of frail people who live in a world fractured by sin, and because of this brokenness, we need sermons that are not only theologically accurate but also delivered with pastoral care and warmth. We need messages that are not only scripturally nuanced but also compassionate in tone and delivery.

Pastoral preaching is exemplified by a commitment to communicating God's truth in a manner that reflects the shepherding heart of God. The one who preaches pastorally is concerned not only with biblical fidelity but also with the spiritual condition of those listening.

This type of preaching recognizes that the sermon is not only a discourse of biblical truth but also an exhortation delivered to God's flock (1 Peter 5:2).

BE PASTORALLY SENSITIVE TO THE NATURE OF YOUR TOPIC

Many topics are sensitive by nature. If you speak on a topic such as bullying, divorce, depression, death, or global warming, you will discover that the topic itself will often evoke an emotional response. Though there may be a spectrum of emotions that your audience might feel toward these topics, you should be mindful of the weight such issues carry for the listener. While it is not possible to know or address all the sensitivities people have toward every issue, we need to at least try to be conscious of them.

There are numerous topics in life that people feel strongly about. Some of these are directly dealt with in the Scriptures, while many are not.

Sensitive Moral Topics

There are topics in life that bring to the fore issues of right and wrong. Those such as murder or theft will be black and white, while others may illicit stronger responses from some people than from others. Certain moral issues will be met with conviction by some but indifference by others.

In a mixed audience of believers and unbelievers, in particular, you will often see stark differences surrounding morality. Christians, because of their belief in the authority of Scripture, might hold one ethical position because they feel God has addressed it. Unbelievers might feel just as strongly about a different position, one not based on an understanding of Scripture but based on their experience and how they perceive the social-moral mores of the world.

Think of the subjects in figure 6.

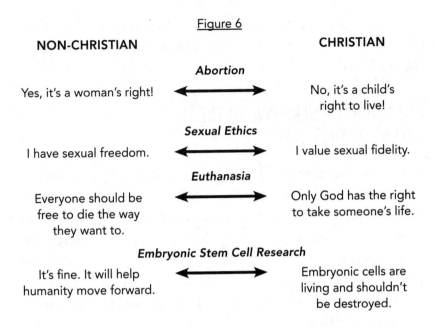

Figure 6

NON-CHRISTIAN   **CHRISTIAN**

Abortion

Yes, it's a woman's right!   ⟵⟶   No, it's a child's right to live!

Sexual Ethics

I have sexual freedom.   ⟵⟶   I value sexual fidelity.

Euthanasia

Everyone should be free to die the way they want to.   ⟵⟶   Only God has the right to take someone's life.

Embryonic Stem Cell Research

It's fine. It will help humanity move forward.   ⟵⟶   Embryonic cells are living and shouldn't be destroyed.

In these examples, there is a significant contrast born of the competing ideologies. The Christian worldview and ethics are derived from reflection on the Scriptures. The unbeliever's worldview stems from a different set of presuppositions. While not every Christian and non-Christian agrees with the positions in their respective columns (fig. 6), their sources of authority and worldviews clearly influence their perceptions of important moral issues—often in opposing ways.

Pastorally sensitive preaching recognizes that in any given audience these competing worldviews may be present. Preachers are not called to deny their biblical convictions, but they should preach with a cognizance of the diverse ideologies that may exist in their audiences.

Even among Christians some moral issues seem straightforward, while others are less clear-cut. Issues on which faithful Christians disagree include the following:

- gambling on sports events
- issues of social justice
- alcohol consumption

- socialized medicine
- global warming
- political activism
- veganism
- prayer in school
- purchasing ethical products

In these moral areas we find considerable degrees of conviction. Some people feel strongly about these topics, while others have no emotional skin in the game. Because we find people all along the spectrum in these areas, we need to be strategic in how we canvass the issues in our preaching.

Let's say I have been asked to give a topical sermon called "Caring for God's World" in my church. In particular, the church would like me to help them understand what a Christian worldview on climate change should be. As I prepare to speak on this topic, I assume there will be a range of views among my audience. (See fig. 7.)

Figure 7

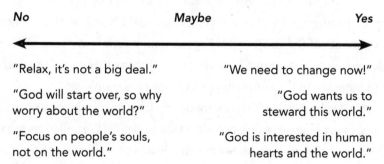

SHOULD WE CARE ABOUT CLIMATE CHANGE?

No	*Maybe*	*Yes*

"Relax, it's not a big deal."   "We need to change now!"

"God will start over, so why   "God wants us to
worry about the world?"   steward this world."

"Focus on people's souls,   "God is interested in human
not on the world."   hearts and the world."

Likely, some will feel a strong moral obligation regarding this issue. These folks are committed to renewable energy, they ride their bicycles to church rather than drive, they compost rather than throw things in the trash, and they might even protest over climate change. For these folks the issue of caring for God's world is not something to merely tip the hat to; it's a topic we must act on.

Others in the audience will feel indifferent toward the issue. Such people feel that the topic is not a right-or-wrong type of issue as much as it is a personal preference. While they are not averse to hearing a sermon on stewardship of God's world, they don't feel any strong conviction about the subject. They are not emotionally invested in the issue at hand.

Still others in the audience will view this topic with suspicion or even antagonism. Climate change, they will argue, is a manmade conspiracy that has too large of a profile in mainstream media and is subsequently having a negative impact on the world's economy. For these folks, climate change is a distraction to life, and the subject is irrelevant to the Christian life. The issue of climate change, for these listeners, is negative, and they will likely be morally opposed to such a sermon.

In this case the issue of morality—what is right and wrong—is keenly felt by some in the congregation but not by others. Some will view this as a critical issue, others will shrug their shoulders, while still others may be angry the issue is even being canvassed.

Regardless of where I go in my sermon, however, I need to preach in a way that acknowledges the moral tensions and even the anger the audience might feel toward the topic. If I simply talk with a matter-of-fact disposition, whatever my position, I will likely lose the attention of segments of the audience. If I speak with a dismissive tone or fail to acknowledge other significant views, I will convey the idea that either I am ignorant of the different opinions or I just don't care.

While the Bible addresses many moral issues in black-and-white terms, many other areas are not addressed as clearly. We will likely preach about moral issues that some consider clear-cut, while others disagree. When such topics arise, we need to be sensitive to the different positions people might hold. This is not to say we shouldn't have conviction, argue for clear moral positions, or preach what we believe the Bible teaches. Rather it is to say we must demonstrate a considerate tone that appropriately highlights our recognition of the topic's importance to the listener.

Right Message, Wrong Tone

Jason is twenty-four years old and in his second year of study at a theological college. Learning all sorts of ideas on biblical and systematic theology, Jason is keen to put some of them into practice. He desires to go into vocational Christian ministry and figures the best way to learn is to get involved. Fortunately for Jason, his college is running a series of events in a local church, and as a result Jason gets his chance. He is asked to speak at a special event, on the topic "What Would Jesus Say about Cancer?"

In preparation Jason hits the books. A tough topic demands careful consideration. Pouring over multiple works, he formulates an outline, develops a series of arguments, and provides a few illustrations for his talk. On the night of the event, a group of about fifteen people join him in the church hall, where he delivers his presentation. A question or two follow his talk, and then the evening draws to a close. *That went well,* Jason thinks.

When he evaluates his talk, he feels he has accomplished what he wanted to do.

- Share statistical data on cancer. Check.
- Explain the brokenness of our world. Check.
- Demonstrate God's awareness of the world's brokenness. Check.
- Speak of God's desire to make things new. Check.
- Tell of Jesus' defeating cancer and death through resurrection. Check.

Looking at his list, one can easily see why Jason thinks his message went well. He covered all the bases. He acknowledged

> the reality of cancer, outlined God's solution to the problem, and concluded with the hope of Jesus.
>
> The next day, however, someone asks one of the Christian ladies in the congregation how the evening went. She says, "That was one of the clearest presentations I've heard on cancer. It is a pity there was zero compassion in the message." Ouch! Evidently, Jason's message, while right in content, still had something missing. His talk was true but lacked sensitivity regarding the nature of the topic being addressed.

Sensitive Personal Topics

Elise and Pedro Rodriguez, in their early thirties, are committed members of their church, where they serve as volunteer leaders of the junior high ministry. The couple, who have been married for eight years, have boundless energy and a genuine passion to see young people come to Christ. They are the sort of volunteers that church staffs love.

Yet behind the smiles and enthusiastic demeanor is a deep pain that few see and fewer know about. For the past five years, Elise and Pedro have tried to begin their family, but with no success. Concerned, the couple went to their physician, and after several medical tests the devastating news came back: Elise is infertile, and because of further complications, she will not be able to have children naturally. The Rodriguezes are heartbroken.

Kristen is a single mother of two typical teenage kids. Her fifteen-year-old son, Jack, speaks to her with grunts. Her thirteen-year-old daughter, Caitlin, is becoming something of a handful and is often moody. Kristen is doing her best to raise her kids, but it has not been easy. Six years earlier her husband decided to abandon Kristen for a younger colleague at work.

Though the divorce was years ago, Kristen still feels a great sense of shame and loss as she reflects on her marriage. She feels embarrassed to explain to others that she no longer has a husband, and she still feels vulnerable and untrusting when it comes to relationships. Though she has found consolation in her church, Kristen still has a ways to go in regard to healing her personal hurts.

Arthur is a retired army officer. A man of few words, Arthur has spent most of his seventy-nine years serving others. On a Sunday morning Arthur is almost always the first to church and is eager to extend his warm hand of welcome to all of those visiting for the first time. Regimented, honorable, and displaying old-school manners, Arthur is loved by everyone.

Although he doesn't express much, Arthur seems to have lost a bit of his mojo recently. While this could be because of his age, the change is more likely because of the recent passing of his wife of fifty-eight years, Cheryl, after her long bout with dementia. Arthur loves to talk about most topics, but any mention of Cheryl causes Arthur to tear up. Arthur misses his wife.

Though their experiences and life circumstances are different, Elise and Pedro, Kristen, and Arthur are all feeling the painful effects of personal heartbreak. For the Rodriguez couple it is infertility. For Kristen it is divorce. And for Arthur it is death and grief. These are real issues of real life in a real world that is broken.

While you and I as preachers may never know the full details of the hurt in the lives of our listeners, some topics by nature impact people personally. These topics should be addressed with deep pastoral sensitivity.

Let's say you are preaching through a topical series titled "God's Plan for Marriage and Family." Among other parts of the series, you might choose to cover the following topics.

- Who should I marry?
- What about divorce?
- How do we raise kids?

As you prepare your sermons, your pastoral intuition should flag the topics that might be delicate with your audience. You may not be in the position to address all of these concerns in your sermon, but you should be aware of as many of them as possible. It may even be helpful to anticipate some of the areas in which people might have particular sorrow regarding the topic. Here are a few examples.

Sermon Topic: Who Should I Marry?
Pastoral preparation question: Who might find the topic of marriage difficult?

- those who desire to get married but have never found anyone
- those who are widowed or divorced and wonder whether they should remarry
- those in difficult marriages who wonder if they have made a mistake

Sermon Topic: What about Divorce?
Pastoral preparation question: Who might find the topic of divorce difficult?

- those who have been divorced
- the children of those who have been divorced
- parents who have divorced children or grandchildren

Sermon Topic: How Do We Raise Kids?
Pastoral preparation question: Who might find the topic of raising children difficult?

- infertile couples
- single people who would love to have children but have found no one to marry
- couples who marry later in life and aren't able to have children
- couples who have lost a child through a miscarriage or some other tragedy
- those who have regrets about the way they raised their children

- those who have children with special needs, who require additional help
- people who have had a child taken out of their care because of divorce, abuse, or some other reason

Many topics could create angst in some of your listeners. Although you may not always be able to alleviate their tension or address their concerns, pastoral preaching requires that you prayerfully consider the difficulties your topic will present to your audience.

Right Message, Wrong Delivery

Several years ago, while watching the evening news, I was disturbed to hear a report on a tragedy that had occurred overseas. Though I was saddened to learn of the event, I was not disturbed by the nature of the story as much as by the body language and delivery of the presenter. The young reporter was too casual in his reporting, almost smiling as he explained the story.

Now, while I want to give the reporter the benefit of the doubt—he might not have realized how he came across—I was disturbed because the delivery of the message didn't correlate with the nature of the topic. The reporter seemed remarkably unaffected by the sadness of the words coming out of his mouth. The words cried tragedy, but they were delivered from a messenger who resonated happiness. When I watched that report, I was simultaneously sad, angry, and confused.

When we preach, our delivery style should reflect our topic. If we are speaking of sensitive issues related to bullying or abusive behavior, then there is no room for flippancy or jesting. To speak of death or illness with glibness or to make an offhand comment about mental health is unbefitting of a preacher.

While there is often a place for a humorous anecdote or a lighthearted comment in preaching, these things are detrimental with certain topics and sermons. A snippet from a movie, an interesting illustration, or a prop may work in many messages, but they may hinder others. While some of us are naturally bubbly and vibrant in our personalities and delivery, we may need to rein this in, depending on the issue at hand.

As preachers, we should be wary of sending mixed messages through delivery that doesn't match the nature of our topic. If you have a sensitive topic, be sensitive in your delivery. Don't deliver the right message the wrong way!

Sensitive Theological Issues

We Christians are an unusual bunch. A few years ago I was listening to a roundtable discussion on eschatology, the study of last things. The panel was made up of scholars representing different viewpoints on the timing of Jesus' final reign. The thing I remember most from this is a presenter's observation about the millennium discussion. He said, "Does anyone else feel that it is ironic that Christians love to fight over the thousand years of peace?" Yes, it is ironic! But sadly, that is what we do with many areas of the Christian life.

Unfortunately, the Christian community doesn't have a great track record at managing issues of disagreement. Sometimes, even in the context of sincere ministry, Christians can betray their commitment to unity through harsh words and belittlement of those with whom they disagree. We squabble over the best way to do evangelism. We bicker over how to sing praise to God. We wrangle over techniques of discipleship. Sadly, if we are not careful, our preaching can be a poor model of how to engage with theological diversity.

One of the subtle dangers a preacher faces in the pulpit is the temptation to speak rigidly about disputed and sensitive theological topics. This often shows itself in sermons that are condescending of positions other than that of the speaker. You and I can be correct in our theological positions, but if we speak without charity and temperance, then our messages may win neither the argument nor the audience. Our sermons may be thoroughly orthodox and yet miss the mark. As the apostle Paul reminded the Corinthians, "If I speak in the tongues of men or of angels, but do not have love, I am only a resounding gong or a clanging cymbal. If I have the gift of prophecy and can fathom all mysteries and all knowledge, and if I have a faith that can move mountains, but do not have love, I am nothing" (1 Cor. 13:1–2). Preachers must handle sensitive theological issues with precision and love. We must speak theological truth in the spirit of charity.

Issues of Primary and Secondary Importance

There are, within our Christian faith, hills we should die on—truths we should hold to be nonnegotiable in areas of faith and practice. The inspiration of the Scriptures, the sufficiency of Jesus' death and resurrection, the nature of the triune God—these areas are of primary importance to the Christian life.

Other hills, however, are not worth dying on. These secondary issues may still be important, but they are not essential. For faithful Christians, there is some latitude in these areas regarding faith and practice, and they do not determine whether one is an orthodox Christian. While Christians must believe that Jesus Christ is Lord (an area of primary importance), they do not need to prescribe to a particular translation of the Bible or worship with a certain style (areas of secondary importance).

The challenge for many Christians, of course, lies in recognizing the difference between the primary and secondary matters of Christian belief. Depending on our Christian tradition, certain things can sometimes be treated as defining markers of orthodoxy, when they are not core Christian beliefs.

In my parents' generation, markers of faithful Christians included the following.

They dressed conservatively. "Would you turn up wearing those clothes if you were meeting a king? Well, at church you are meeting the King of Kings, so show it in how you dress for church!"

They worshiped with a particular style. "We sing only hymns because they are theologically robust. Those trite choruses are for those who lack biblical wisdom and understanding."

They preached a certain way. "Back in my day, people preached the Word! We heard hour-long sermons straight from the KJV, none of these contextualized sermons with wandering microphones and visuals. Nowadays people preach sermonettes that produce Christianettes."

They were defined by what they didn't do. "People who love Jesus do not do anything on the Sabbath. You do not read the paper or go out. Can you imagine if Jesus returned and you were in a theater watching a movie? Oh, the shame!"

While these examples may seem mildly ridiculous in our day and age, a generation or two ago many Christians used such markers to define who was in and who was out of the Christian community.

Outsiders and Insiders

Our Christian traditions can sometimes, even if well-intentioned, make the same error. We have our own defining markers of who is in and who is out, who is weak and who is strong, who is committed and who is uncommitted. Consider the following differences regarding Christian belief.

Premillennial	Amillennial
Theistic evolution	Seven-day creation
Spiritual gifts have ceased	Spiritual gifts continue
Homeschooling is biblical	Public schooling is fine
Infant baptism	Believer's baptism

Sole pastor	Plural eldership
Formal membership	No membership
Mixed-church leadership	Male-only leadership

For each of these categories, you will find people with biblical convictions. They each feel that their position stems not merely from preference but from what the Bible teaches. The challenge, of course, is that you might have three people sitting in the same pew who represent three positions with three levels of conviction. How do you preach in that context? What do you do when you know that one, two, or possibly all three of them will disagree with your theological position?

The key when preaching on contested theological topics is that you need to be mindful of your audience in your sermon preparation as well as in your delivery. Just as you develop a pastorally responsive approach to your audience's feelings about sensitive moral and personal topics, you also need to be mindful of hot-button theological issues that might evoke strong feelings in your listeners.

Let me be clear: I'm not suggesting for a minute that you minimize, downplay, or dilute the gospel or your convictions. No, you need to preach God's truth! I'm suggesting that in your sermon development and delivery, you pay particular attention to the *manner* in which you address theological differences.

Over the years, I have often taken note of preachers who handle delicate theological topics with wisdom and sensitivity. Three things always seem to stand out about their delivery.

1. Such preachers generally seek to remove the heat from the situation by acknowledging that Bible-believing Christians may disagree on the issue. Acknowledging that there are multiple views held by other genuine, Bible-believing Christians removes the outsider-insider divide.
2. Pastorally sensitive preachers not only recognize theological differences but also present them in a way that honors others.

People can see a straw man argument coming from a mile away. While some audiences thrive on perpetuating misconceptions about other views, the preacher must not stoke such falsehood. Integrity demands that we seek to represent other theological views kindly and fairly, even if we disagree with them. This may require us to read and listen to those outside of our camp, but if we are to be charitable in preaching, we should aim to be nuanced and careful in how we speak of others.

3. Preachers who address sensitive theological areas effectively not only distinguish between what is of first and second importance but also know how to help the audience navigate those distinctions.

When we preach, we will naturally canvass passages and doctrines about which members of our audience will disagree. Some topics, often because of people's theological background or denomination, might create angst in members of your audience, especially if they have a strong commitment to a particular view. As a preacher, you should be aware of your own theological biases as well as those of your listeners. While you should preach with conviction, you should also remember that Christian unity doesn't always equal theological uniformity.

BE PASTORALLY SENSITIVE TO THE NEEDS OF YOUR AUDIENCE

Every time you get up to preach, you can assume there are people in your audience who are burdened by life. While some people in your audience will appear to have it all together, privately many will not. People will have battle wounds from life. Some will have addictions, others fractured relationships, and some will be wrestling with health issues. Most will be tired. It is within this framework that you and I are often placed to speak God's words of hope to those who are yearning for encouragement, direction, and healing.

The church can and should be a safe place for all those who are broken. The gathered people of God should provide a haven for the weary, the erring, the shattered, and the downcast. Jesus invited such people to himself when he said, "Come to me, all you who are weary and burdened, and I will give you rest. Take my yoke upon you and learn from me, for I am gentle and humble in heart, and you will find rest for your souls" (Matt. 11:28–29). Elsewhere the people of God are exhorted to "cast all your anxiety on him because he cares for you" (1 Peter 5:7).

While the comfort of the gospel is most keenly felt by those who have come to the end of themselves, through sin or circumstance, the reality is that we all need grace. We all have needs and challenges, spoken or unspoken, that only God can meet. As those who preach the grace of God (1 Peter 5:12), we must keep this in mind. We are not in the pulpit to present happy vibes or mantras to live by; we are there to address the specific pastoral needs of our particular audience by communicating the gospel message. But how do we pastorally apply the gospel to our different audiences?

At the back end of his ministry life, Paul concludes his final letter to Timothy with the following charge: "Preach the word; be prepared in season and out of season; correct, rebuke and encourage—with great patience and careful instruction" (2 Tim. 4:2). While much ink has been spilled on the celebrated directive "preach the word," less attention has been paid to the commands that follow—"correct, rebuke and encourage." Consideration of these three commands, however, is crucial, for they provide insight into the nature of the preaching that Timothy, and by extension we, are being called to. Pastoral preaching is not simply presenting the text of the Bible; it also involves using wisdom to know how the Scriptures should be applied to the listener.

Preaching Involves Correction

In caring for those to whom we preach, we must be committed to helping them facilitate a worldview that is consistent with Scripture. Sometimes this will require helping our listeners rewire the way they think about certain topics.

If I were addressing the topic of heaven, people in my audience may hold a variety of views that I would need to correct in my talk, as they would not be in alignment with God's truth. Such common errors include the following:

- People get into heaven if they're basically good.
- Heaven is where we lose our bodies to live as celestial spirits.
- Heaven is a boring place where people just sing and strum harps.
- Heaven is a place of nothingness.
- In heaven we will no longer work.

If I care for my audience, I will seek to correct such views. If I allow the listeners to perpetuate error, then I am passively endorsing their ignorance of God's will. While it is sometimes uncomfortable to address inaccurate thinking, if I care for my audience's spiritual well-being, then it is incumbent on me to redirect them to truth so they might be spiritually rewired through the renewing of their minds (Rom. 12:2).

Concerning Paul's exhortation to correct, Robert W. Yarbrough comments, "Pastoral preaching must often help people stay on their desired path by addressing errant tendencies. The preacher or spiritual counselor must not only disseminate information or offer engrossing talks but actually deter digression and herd sheep back toward where they belong."[1] We sheep tend to look for grass wherever we can find it, and sometimes that can be in the wrong field. The pastoral preacher helps the flock by directing them to safe pasture. Pastoral preaching helps the listener align their worldview with God's through correction.

Preaching Involves Rebuke

I saw a meme floating around the internet a little while ago that said, "When someone yells 'Stop,' I never know if it's in the name of love, Hammer-time, or I should collaborate and listen." I, too, know that confusion!

The Value of a Timely Rebuke

Several years ago I was preaching through a series on the book of Romans. In my message about our relationship to civil authorities, which was based on Romans 13, I gave an illustration relating to our political leaders. I made a comment about a chance meeting I'd had earlier in the year with the Australian prime minister, John Howard. In my sermon I referred to our country's leader with the moniker "Little Johnny," which was quite commonplace in our society—just an offhand Aussie comment that meant no harm.

After the sermon, however, a godly older lady in the congregation made a beeline toward me. "Pastor," she said, "Prime Minister Howard is our God-given leader at the time. The Bible says we are to honor our leaders. By referring to him as 'Little Johnny' in your sermon, I don't think you honored ours. You shouldn't do that again." Ouch.

I was stunned. It was hard to hear, especially from someone I looked up to. After my initial shock, I was convicted. She was correct in her assessment, and her rebuke was warranted. In this case it was the preacher who was rebuked, not the congregation! I learned my lesson that day as I took her rebuke on board. I sincerely apologized and have refrained from making such comments since.

As preachers, we will periodically need to rebuke God's people in regard to their behavior. It might feel hard, and some of us may wish to avoid it, but from my experience as one who has been reproved on more than one occasion, I can honestly say I'm thankful for those in the past who have loved me enough to rebuke me.

Apart from admonishing my teenage kids to stop looking at their phones, I rarely exhort people to halt an activity. While every now and then I meet someone who appears to have the spiritual gift of criticism, most of us don't like confrontation. Yet calling others to account through rebuke is one of the ways we can pastorally care for people. Exhorting people to refrain from a wrong belief or unbiblical activity is, though uncomfortable at times, the best thing we can do for them.

Sometimes pastoral preaching requires that we rebuke our listeners by confronting them with truth. Jesus used this same term in Luke 17:3, where he urged his disciples to rebuke each other in regard to sin, with the hope of bringing about repentance. Rebuking is not about belittling people or bullying someone into submission. Rather it is confronting a behavior or attitude that is out of step with God's character, with the hope that the listener will respond by changing their ways.

To love people, we must periodically confront and rebuke them. The pastoral goal of such preaching is, of course, repentance and realignment with God and his vision for the world.

Preaching Involves Encouragement

In contemporary speech the term *preaching* is not always, or often, positive.

"I'm not preaching at you!"
"I don't mean to preach, but . . ."
"Quit preaching at me!"

In these contexts, the term is used pejoratively and paints the picture of someone looking down their nose and offering a word of condescension. Preaching is understood as negative.

In the New Testament, however, *preaching* is generally a positive word. At its heart is the idea of proclamation. There are several aspects to proclamation, but the content and nature of the proclamation normally centers on the good news message of Jesus' appearance and the redemption that his life, death, and resurrection now offer.

Pastoral preaching builds up people by reminding them of these wonderful truths. Preaching edifies listeners by fortifying their faith through the proclamation of truth claims about a believer's status. To care for your people, you don't preach to build an identity for your listener; rather you preach to expose your listener to the reality of their existing identity in Christ. When you explain the truth of the gospel of grace, you strengthen your people so they can continue in their faith. Pastoral preaching heartens the listener. It encourages.

Consider the Appropriate Need for Your Context

That pastoral preaching involves correcting, rebuking, and encouraging is little disputed. The challenge for the practitioner, however, is to wisely discern which of these is most appropriate for any given audience. When approaching a topic, you must ask yourself, "How do I determine whether my audience needs to be corrected, rebuked, or encouraged?"

Ultimately, there is probably no right or wrong approach to preaching to your audience. Even within one audience, some will need to have their worldview corrected, others will need to be rebuked, and all will need to be encouraged. Knowledge of your audience and prayerful consideration of their needs should factor into which aspect you emphasize.

Let's say you have decided to speak on the issue "Money" at your church. In your preparation you consider the possible avenues you might take to exhort your people on the topic. You have a few possibilities.

You Might Correct Erroneous Thinking about Money

Correct:

- Money can be used for good or ill.
- Money can be an idol.
- Money can ruin people.

Biblical wisdom:

- Life is more than money (James 4:13–15).
- Wealth is fleeting (Prov. 23:5).
- Fear of the Lord is better than wealth (Prov. 15:16).

Gospel focus:

- God's generosity has been shown to us in Christ (2 Cor. 8:9).
- Set your mind on things above, not on fading treasure (Col. 3:2).

You Might Rebuke Wrong Behavior or Attitudes toward Money

Rebuke:

- Stop being greedy with your money.
- Cease making riches an idol.
- Quit trusting in your wealth for your security.

Biblical wisdom:

- "The love of money is a root of all kinds of evil" (1 Tim. 6:10).
- Wealth doesn't provide security (Prov. 18:11).

Gospel focus:

- God's way of eternal security in Christ, in contrast to fleeting wealth, is assured.

You Might Encourage Continued Obedience regarding Money

Encourage:

- Continue to seek eternal things.
- Persist in giving generously to others.
- Keep trusting the Lord to provide.

Biblical wisdom:

- God supplies all that you need (Phil. 4:19).
- Don't worry; God will care for you (Luke 12:22–31).
- True security is found in God, not in fleeting wealth (Prov. 18:10–11).

Gospel focus:

- God has met your needs in Christ, so you can trust him with your future.

- God's generosity to you frees you to be generous to others (2 Cor. 8:9).

In speaking on money, I could take any of the foregoing approaches. There is biblical precedent to correct, rebuke, and encourage people regarding the topic of money. I could have a smattering of each aspect in the body of my sermon. If I were to preach this, I would need to prayerfully consider which aspect is most needed among the people to whom I am ministering.

If I were addressing this issue with college students who were beginning their journey toward professional careers, I might try to correct the way they think about money. They might have ideas on wealth, stemming from their upbringing or from external influences, that are not in alignment with God's vision, and as a result I would offer a biblical corrective to their worldview.

Alternately, if this sermon were being preached to a comfortable and affluent church in the suburbs, I might focus on challenging the members to be more generous in their giving. A gentle rebuke and challenge might be in order. I might point to the folly of greed or the fleeting nature of money before putting before them a positive vision of how the gospel is more appealing than transient wealth.

If I were speaking in a small, multicultural church in the inner city that was committed to generously sharing Christ through financial giving and partnership, I would encourage them to continue. I would affirm their actions and cheer them on to further acts of obedience. I would remind them of the motivation of the gospel in our giving and encourage them to continue their pursuit of eternal things.

A PASTORAL DISPOSITION

Pastoral preaching is not so much about a method as it is about a disposition. Preaching with pastoral sensitivity requires a commitment to an attitude of awareness that seeks to serve listeners by carefully considering how they may feel regarding topics close to their heart. This type of preaching values the audience by reflecting on their moral, personal, and theological dilemmas and mindfully acknowledging those in both the tone and content of the sermon.

Preaching difficult topics requires an element of wisdom, as the preacher needs to discern what a particular audience needs to hear. At times pastoral preaching will involve confrontation. At other times the focus will be to encourage existing behavior or challenge a listener's worldview through a biblical correction.

When we address topics, we must be aware that the audience to whom we preach is not there simply to absorb abstract theological propositions. We need to remember that we are bringing God's vision for the world before his flock—people who are broken, tired, hurt, and in need of the balm of his grace in Christ.

CHAPTER 8

HOW TO TRACE THE TOPIC TO CHRIST

Can Topical Preaching Point to Jesus?

SAM CHAN

If you want to start an endless debate with pizza lovers, ask them, "Does pineapple belong on a pizza?" Half the room will tell you that a pizza must never have pineapple as a topping. The other half will firmly believe that pineapple is a legitimate—even necessary—topping.

If you want to start an endless debate with expository preachers, ask them, "Does every sermon have to preach Christ?" Half the room will shout, "No!" We need to let the text speak to us on its own terms. Preach the pericope. Focus on the tree in all its intricate and unique detail and not just the forest it belongs to. Sometimes it's about the journey rather than the destination. Take the scenic route and smell the roses.

The other half of the room will shout, "Yes!" We need to preach Christ each and every time. The text belongs in a canonical context. Preach the overarching metastory and not just the individual chapter. See the forest and not just the tree. The whole point of the journey is to end up at the destination. Don't get lost along the way.

This robust dialectical argument shows that there is some truth to both sides of the debate. There is a time and place for pineapple on your pizza, but not always! Similarly, sometimes we do need to preach Christ, and maybe at other times we can enjoy the text on its own terms.

The Difference between Implicit and Explicit

Let's say my wife and I are getting dressed to attend a friend's wedding. When it's time to leave, my wife comes out of the bedroom wearing a classy evening dress. But she sees me in shorts and a T-shirt. Her face falls in disappointment. She wants me to be more dressed up than I am. How can she tell me this?

My wife has a spectrum of ways to do this, ranging from indirect to direct communication.

- She can say nothing. Her mere presence in a classy dress should be enough to make me change into something more appropriate.
- She can ask me a question. "Is that what you're wearing?"
- She can hint. "I love it when you dress up."
- She can pray out aloud. "Dear God, why can't you give me a husband who dresses up for weddings?"
- She can sing a song by ZZ Top. "'Cause every girl crazy 'bout a sharp-dressed man."
- She can tell me a story. "Mama bear wore shorts and a T-shirt to a wedding and was very sad. Papa bear wore shorts and a T-shirt to a wedding and was very sad. But baby bear got dressed up for the wedding and was very happy."
- She can give me an example. "Your friend Tom is getting dressed up for this."
- Or she can give me a direct command. "Get changed out of that into something dressy."

> In each of these examples, my wife has communicated to me the same message: "Change out of the shorts and T-shirt into something dressy." But she has a variety of ways to do that, ranging from super indirect to super direct.
>
> It's the same with preaching Christ. We have the same variety of options. We don't have to be blunt and explicit every time. Sometimes we can be indirect, but we're still preaching the same message.

But this is a book on topical preaching. In some ways we are spared this debate. The aim of topical preaching is to preach the topic. We can be excused for preaching only the topic and not Christ. We don't have to look for imaginative, affective, and cognitive links between our topic and Christ.

But this is also a book on Christian topical preaching. We want to do more than just preach about a topic. We want to give the Christian perspective on it. We want to do more than just summarize a Wikipedia article or a TED Talk about our topic. But what does this "more than" look like? How can we give a Christian talk on this topic? In this chapter we will explore a variety of ways to preach Christ from any topic.

Here are eight ways to preach Christ in a topical sermon, ranging from the indirect to the direct.

1. CHRISTO-EMBODIED

The sermon preaches Christ because the preacher is in Christ.

Much of ethical theory focuses on the action itself: what should you do? *Can I steal? Can I gamble? Can I support the Yankees?* But in virtue ethics, we focus on the actor: who should you be? *What is my character? What is my motive? Is this the person I want to become?*

Similarly, in preaching we often focus on the art and craft of delivering a message: what should you say? But we can argue that preaching is as much about the messenger: who should you be? The messenger is the message embodied. In this sense my talk preaches Christ simply because, as a Christian, I embody Christ. I am in Christ. I am indwelt by his Spirit. I am being shaped into his image (2 Cor. 3:18). I am his ambassador (2 Cor. 5:20).

Even if my talk doesn't explicitly mention Christ, or even if I'm not allowed to identify myself as a Christian, I am still preaching the words of Christ on behalf of Christ. I am his Spirit-anointed and appointed messenger.

Preaching and Speech Act Theory

How can my words be the words of Christ?

In my previous book on preaching, *Preaching as the Word of God*, I answered this question with the use of speech act theory. Let's say you're my CEO, and I am your manager. You want me to go to a conference and deliver a message from you. How can you choose to do this?

You could dictate a letter to me, which I would type up and take on your behalf. Here my words are the exact same words as your words, one for one. Or I could write the letter in my own words, and you would approve of it with your signature on the bottom. Here my words have been appropriated by you as your words. Or you could send me as your ambassador to speak on your behalf. Here my words are your words because I am performing the same speech act that you would have performed if you had been there in person. My words count as your words.

It's the same when we preach. In God's covenant, he has appointed us to be his Spirit-anointed ambassadors who speak on his behalf. That's why the job of topical preaching is a theological task, as we covered in chapter 4, because we are asking ourselves, "What would God say about this topic?" Whenever we do this, we are performing Christ's speech act. That's how our words count as Christ's words.

2. CHRISTO-CONTEXT

The sermon preaches Christ because it is preached in a Christian context.

I've often heard this critique of a sermon that doesn't explicitly preach Christ: "That same message could've been preached in a Jewish synagogue or a Muslim mosque." But the obvious counter to this is that the sermon wasn't preached in a synagogue or mosque. It was preached in a Christian context, by a Christian speaker in a Christian setting.

Context is everything! Almost every talk you can find on YouTube tells you the original context of the talk—when and where the talk was given, by whom, and to whom. This influences its meaning.

That's why memes and TikTok videos are so funny. They lift talks out of their original setting and replant them in a different context, changing their meaning. In the same way, if someone lifted your talk from its Christian setting and replanted it in a synagogue or mosque, then of course it would have a different meaning.

In my job with City Bible Forum, I often give talks in neutral, secular settings such as cinemas, bars, or restaurants. But the advertising makes it clear that I am a Christian speaker from a Christian organization giving a Christian talk on the topic. Even if my talk doesn't explicitly mention Christ, the talk is still a *Christian* talk.

Example: A Talk on Money

Let's say I'm giving a talk on the topic of money to young urban professionals in their first five years of work. The topic can sound neutral: "Everything to Know about Money before It's Too Late." The venue can be neutral: a pub where people go for drinks after work.

But my details on the advertising let people know that this comes from a Christian speaker: "Sam Chan is a global citizen. He was born in Hong Kong, studied medicine in Sydney, and got his PhD from Chicago. Just like you, he senses that our world has changed—we work more but are less happy. Sam loves helping people rediscover the joy that comes from faith, spirituality, and the Christian tradition. But he also knows that Australians don't want to be too serious. That's why Sam has discovered humorous ways to talk about the important issues in life."

3. CHRISTO-WISDOM

The sermon preaches Christ because it preaches the wisdom of Christ.

In the Bible, Christ is revealed as King, Judge, and Savior. When we preach Christ, we preach the need to submit to his rule, repent of our sins, and trust in his atoning sacrifice. But in the Bible, Christ is also revealed as Sage. When we preach wisdom, we also preach Christ. He is the wisdom from God. Christ is the Logos—the logic of creation. We need to live in harmony with this logic that God has programmed into his creation (Proverbs 8).

Example: A Talk on Parenting

Let's say I'm giving a talk on the topic of parenting. I might speak directly about specific aspects of parenting: spending time with children, teaching them emotional literacy, and adjusting your role to their different stages of life (zero to four years, four to fourteen years, fourteen to eighteen years).

Although the Bible might implicitly teach these aspects of parenting, much of this wisdom is too specific to be found directly in the Bible. It is specialized knowledge found elsewhere, as in books and seminars from child psychologists and pediatricians.

But it is still God's wisdom because it is consistent with the wisdom that is interwoven in the fabric of his universe. All wisdom is God's wisdom. By preaching wisdom—even if it is extrabiblical—I am still preaching Christ, who is wisdom from God.

4. CHRISTO-EXEMPLAR

The sermon preaches Christ because it gives you the example of Christ to follow.

Many of the debates in preaching focus on whether we can use Old and New Testament characters as examples to follow. When David fights Goliath, can we use David as a positive example to follow, as someone who bravely trusts God? The argument against this is that it leads to moralism and legalism. A better way to preach this would be to focus on the story's salvation-historical significance. David is God's Spirit-anointed deliverer who saves his people, much in the same way Christ will one day be God's Spirit-anointed deliverer for us. This shifts the focus to God (what does God do?) rather than humans (what do I have to do?).

But much of this debate is unnecessary because the Bible itself uses David as both an example to follow (Heb. 11:32) and a type of Christ (Ps. 2:6). We need to see both the trees and the forest.

In the same way, much of our preaching rightly focuses on the salvation-historical significance of Christ. He is God's Spirit-anointed deliverer whose atoning death and resurrection saves us from our sins (1 Peter 3:18). But the Bible also uses Christ as an example to follow. When the apostle Peter talks about Christ's suffering in 1 Peter 2:21, it is both "for you" (our substitutionary atonement) and "an example" to follow.

Example: A Talk on Leadership

If we have to give a talk on the topic of leadership, we can preach Christ by showing people the countercultural example of Christ's servant leadership. Jesus did not lord over those he led. He even washed their feet. From Christ we can draw out important principles of leadership such as humility, service, and sacrifice.

179

5. CHRISTO-EMPATHY

The sermon preaches Christ because Christ knows how you feel (Heb. 4:15).

When we focus on Christ as King, Judge, and Savior, we usually focus on the fallenness of our human condition. We are the rebels against the King. We are the guilty ones before the Judge. We are the lost who need a Savior.

But we can also focus on Christ as our brother (Heb. 2:5–18). Then we can concentrate on the humanness of our human condition. Jesus became one of us and knows what it's like to be one of us.

Here we might point out how Jesus was tempted in the same ways that we get tempted to sin (Matt. 4:1–11; Heb. 4:15). If we're ever tempted to become lawbreakers, then we can draw strength from knowing that Christ has gone before us. Again, here we are concentrating on the fallenness of our human condition.

But we can also point out that Jesus has experienced the humanness of our human condition. Jesus knows what it's like to yearn for basic human needs. He got tired (John 4:6). He got thirsty (John 4:7). He got hungry (Matt. 4:2). He even got peopled-out and sent his disciples to do the shopping and face the crowds (John 4:8)!

But it's more than that. Jesus also knows what it's like to suffer the brokenness of our human condition. He wasn't just tempted to become a lawbreaker; he also became the Broken One. He grieved over the death of his friend Lazarus (John 11:35). He was angered and distressed by people's stubbornness (Mark 3:5). He was betrayed by an insider (Matt. 26:21). He was abandoned by his disciples and friends (Mark 14:50). He suffered unjustly (1 Peter 2:20–23).

Example: A Talk on Work

If we have to give a talk on work to those who work in large corporations—banks, law firms, technology companies—we can preach Christ by telling them that he knows how they feel. If they are anxious about their job security, Jesus experienced that kind of anxiety. He was once in a desert not knowing when he would eat next. If they are tempted to take ethical shortcuts to get to the top, we can point out that Jesus was tempted to achieve power and position in all the wrong ways. And if they are hurt by office politics and workplace bullying, then we can mention that people often plotted against Jesus. He suffered unjustly, and he is grieved, distressed, and angry about what has happened to them.

6. CHRISTO-EMPOWERMENT

The sermon preaches Christ because it empowers you with Christ.

Often, topical talks can be quite overwhelming for audiences because they are left disempowered. The audience feels powerless to implement the action points: How do I become a wise parent? How do I invest my money wisely? How do I become an inspiring leader? But we can empower our audience by showing them the difference Jesus can make.

Example: A Talk on Parenting

Let's go back to our talk on the topic of parenting. The logical flow of our talk could go like this:

"A lot of us live through our children—their successes and failures. We project on them our fears and insecurities and impose on them our idols of perfectionism. Our status, security, and self-worth depend on their victories at school, sports, and society. They become our trophy children. They end up not living their own lives but living our lives.

"So how can we stop this? We need to find our status, security, and self-worth in Jesus. We need to trust in his finished work on the cross for us. We need to celebrate our honored status as children of God and coheirs with Christ. We need to let the Spirit dwell in us and cry out, 'Abba, Father' on our behalf.

"In this way, Christ empowers us to be the parents God wants us to be. We are set free from the hold our idols of perfectionism have on us. We are set free from projecting our projects of perfectionism on our children. We are set free from our insecurities. We already have all the perfection we need in Christ."

Example: A Talk on Leadership

Here's a second example. The logical flow of our talk on leadership could go like this:

"Most leaders make the mistake of becoming too task orientated rather than relationship orientated. They also become obsessed with personal glory rather than the good of the people. Often this stems from insecurity and narcissistic personality traits.

"But how can we stop this? On one level, we have the positive example of Jesus, who did not seek personal glory. His sacrificial love is an example for leaders. But the Bible goes farther than this. On a deeper level, Jesus empowers us to become the leaders we want to be. His Spirit dwells in us to form us more and more into the image of Christ. Furthermore, in Jesus we have all the glory and status we need, so we don't have to seek them in all the wrong places."

7. CHRISTO-FULFILLMENT

The sermon preaches Christ because the topic is ultimately fulfilled in Christ.

C. S. Lewis believed God has placed "seeds of the gospel" in every culture's stories, fables, and myths. Emil Brunner believed there is an *Anknupfungspunkt* ("contact point") between every culture and the gospel. With this in mind, we can trace seeds of the gospel and contact points from our topic to Christ. For example, our sermon can demonstrate how Christ ultimately fulfills people's deepest desires in regard to this topic.

Example: A Talk on Happiness

Let's say we have to give a talk on the topic of happiness. The logical flow of our talk could go like this:

"Our Western world is obsessed with happiness. The USA's Declaration of Independence famously lists the pursuit of happiness as its chief goal. The mantra of the West is, 'Be true to yourself and do whatever it takes to be happy.' But somehow our unprecedented material wealth and comfort has led to less happiness rather than more.[1] What is going on?

"Part of the reason for this is that we're chasing all the wrong things in order to be happy—we work more hours to make more money to buy more things. But in the end it's not what we do or what we own that correlates with happiness; it's who we have in our lives. Studies show that the quality of our relationships determines our level of happiness.[2] Simply put, do we love someone, and does someone love us?

"In the end Jesus is that ultimate Someone who loves us. Our pursuit of happiness should be a pursuit of Jesus."

8. CHRISTO-CENTRIC

The sermon preaches Christ because the topic properly belongs under the headship of Christ.

At creation everything was created good. But at the fall creation ended up sinful, broken, and cursed. With Christ's redeeming work we can once again enjoy God's creation under Christ's headship. Work was cursed after the fall (Gen. 3:17–19) but is now repurposed "as working for the Lord, not for human masters" (Col. 3:23). Human relationships were doomed to dysfunction at the fall (Gen. 3:16) but can now function "as is fitting in the Lord" (Col. 3:18).

This is because the goal of the universe is for all things to end up under the headship of Christ (Eph. 1:22). Everything finds its proper place if it is in Christ, for Christ, and under Christ (Col. 1:15–20; Acts 17:28). If this is true, then our talk should aim to demonstrate how our topic properly belongs under the headship of Christ.

Example: A Talk on Freedom

If we have to give a talk on the topic of freedom, the logical flow of our talk could go like this:

"Our Western world celebrates the freedom of the individual. The word freedom is found in many national anthems in these countries. We are free from the authority of our parents, teachers, and religious figures. We alone can choose to do whatever it takes to make ourselves happy.

"But if we are so free, then why are we so miserable, tired, and stressed? We know what we are free *from*, but we don't know what we're free *for*. To figure that out, we need to know why we're here and what we're designed for. True freedom comes, then, not from doing whatever we want to do but from doing what we're designed to do. To do that, we need to know the Designer.

"The Bible tells us that Jesus is the Logos. He is the organizing principle behind the universe. He is both the Design and the Designer. If we know Jesus, then we will know who we are, why we're here, and what our purpose is. In discovering these things, we will find what we're free for. That's why Jesus is the truth who will set us truly free."

Example: A Talk on Work

As another example, the logical flow of our talk on work could go like this:

"We spend most of our waking hours at work. This creates two problems: First, if we work only to earn enough money to pay the bills, then our work becomes empty and unsatisfying. But second, if work becomes too important, it ends up consuming and destroying us. So what can we do?

"The Bible tells us to work as if for the Lord. Ultimately, Jesus is our boss, and we are working for him. Our work becomes meaningful, not because it pays the bills but because it is for Jesus. Somehow our work fits into Jesus' bigger purpose for this universe. Our work now has infinite value because it is our service, our offering, and our worship to Jesus. He is glorified by our work."

IF YOU ONLY HAVE A HAMMER . . .

Many people criticize expository preaching that preaches Christ from every text, because it makes each sermon sound the same. No matter how unique and different each text is, somehow the sermon ends up with the same main theme: kingdom, promise, or covenant. Another criticism is that it feels like a deus ex machina moment. Jesus suddenly appears—ta-da!—in a gear-crunching moment.

I'm sure that the same criticism can be leveled at topical preaching that preaches Christ from every topic. Just as a magician pulls a rabbit out of a hat, the topical preacher somehow pulls Jesus out from a topic, no matter how secular or extrabiblical.

Maybe the solution to this is not to do less of it but to do more. With a more generous understanding of what preaching Christ means and a broader variety of tools to do so, topical (and expository!) sermons can still feel diverse and can avoid the deus ex machina moment. People say that if you only have a hammer, then everything looks like a nail. It's the same with preaching Christ. If we only have one method, then every ta-da moment will look the same.

This chapter has given us eight ways to preach Christ, but I'm sure you can think of more. There is one Christ. But there is a rich variety of connections between Christ and each topic. Part of the joy and wonder of preaching Christ from topics is to discover, explore, and demonstrate this variety of imaginative, affective, and cognitive connections.

Topical Preaching Teaches Our Listeners How to Exegete Topics

I've heard it said many times that the goal of expository preaching is to teach our listeners how to exegete the Bible for themselves. I don't believe this is true, but I can understand why people say it. I'm sure there are many times when listeners have walked away from an expository sermon buzzed with fresh insights into the biblical text.

Maybe this is also true of topical preaching! Although it's not our primary goal to teach our listeners how to exegete a topic, I'm sure that will end up happening. If so, our topical preaching will equip our listeners with new and exciting ways to discover seeds of the gospel in all topics, in a far richer and more complex way than they had previously dared imagine.

In recent years I've been blogging at *EspressoTheology.com* for this very reason. The goal of the blog is to start from a seemingly random topic and end up at Jesus—in sixty seconds! I hope readers can see the rich variety of connections from any topic to the gospel. So far I've managed to cover topics as varied as the mason jar, K-pop, chess, Baby Shark, slime, and the poo emoji. Check out the blog and see what connections you would have made to get from those topics to Jesus.

CHAPTER 9

HOW TO CONNECT WITH YOUR AUDIENCE

Know Yourself and Your People

MALCOLM GILL

Jasmine is a keen student of the Bible. She loves God's Word. She has attended several Bible conferences, every week for the past decade she has listened intently to radio Bible teaching, and more recently she has taken to podcasts. She just can't get enough of listening to the Scriptures. There is one place, however, where Jasmine has struggled: the Sunday sermon. Though she loves her church and is actively involved in ministry in the Sunday school program, Jasmine, as hard as she tries, struggles to engage with the preaching.

Though she wants to engage with God's Word at church, she finds the Sunday sermons lackluster and at times downright boring. She feels bad about this and has often questioned herself. *Is it my fault I'm not engaged? Are my expectations too high? Is my heart becoming hard to the gospel?* While she may be right to ask such questions, for many the struggle to listen to dry and lifeless preaching is not the fault of the listener. Rather the burden must fall on the preacher.

I don't think there are too many travesties greater than boring preaching. Taking God's living and active Word and putting people to sleep with it or boring them to distraction, often under the guise of faithfulness, is a real problem, and we should own it. If you want to bore people, speak to them privately about the migrating patterns of whales. Talk to them about the different types of soil in outback Australia. Chatter away about internet-based conspiracies regarding the death of Elvis. But please, preacher, don't bore people with the life-giving Word of God! The English preacher Charles Spurgeon is right on the money when he states,

> Over the head of military announcements our English officers always place the word "ATTENTION!" in large capitals, and we need some such word over all our sermons. We need the earnest, candid, wakeful, continued attention of all those who are in the congregation. If men's minds are wandering far away they cannot receive the truth, and it is much the same if they are inactive. Sin cannot be taken out of men, as Eve was taken out of the side of Adam, while they are fast asleep. They must be awake, understanding what we are saying, and feeling its force, or else we may as well go to sleep too. There are preachers who care very little whether they are attended to or not; so long as they can hold on through the allotted time it is of very small importance to them whether their people hear for eternity, or hear in vain: the sooner such ministers sleep in the churchyard and preach by the verse on their gravestones the better.[1]

While not every preacher may be dynamic in delivery, nor will every passage jump off the page, there is no justification for lulling people into mental oblivion through lifeless and disconnected sermons. In particular, if you are preaching a topical sermon, it is assumed you are doing so because you desire your audience to engage with a particular issue of the world in which they live. If you think your topic is worthy of a sermon, surely you need to make sure you present it in such a way that people will want to remain mentally engaged.

The good news, however, is that regardless of our different skills, abilities, and personalities, there are things each of us can do to improve our delivery to make sure God's Word is heard. As communicators, we can stop doing some things and start doing others to facilitate better engagement.

KNOW YOURSELF

One of the most freeing aspects of the preaching ministry is discovering the truth that you and I have not been created to look or sound the same. There is not one right style, sermon length, structure, or delivery manner. God did not create Peter to be Paul, nor Phoebe to be Priscilla. Even a cursory glance at church history reveals that preachers through the centuries have ranged from learned hermits in monasteries to uneducated farmers, from trained pastors to lay-preaching tradesmen. God has used everyone from those preaching from vaulted pulpits in cathedrals to those preaching from outdoor platforms in arenas. He has provided for each of us different backgrounds, experiences, giftings, and abilities. He has used circumstances in our lives and backgrounds to shape who we are. Not one person in God's making is alike, and this uniqueness is something to be embraced rather than shunned.

In addressing the Corinthian church, the apostle Paul highlighted the beauty of diversity when he wrote, "If the whole body were an eye, where would the sense of hearing be? If the whole body were an ear, where would the sense of smell be? But in fact God has placed the parts in the body, every one of them, just as he wanted them to be. If they were all one part, where would the body be? As it is, there are many parts, but one body" (1 Cor. 12:17–20). God, in his wisdom, created us to contribute, each in our own unique way, to the building up of his people for their good and his glory.

While many of us would acknowledge and even value the aforementioned diversity, many preachers feel uncomfortable in their own skin. Although there may be a variety of reasons for this, one of the chief factors seems to be the rise of online sermons. Whereas once upon a time, the members of a congregation might have listened only to their pastor or on occasion a visiting preacher, nowadays people can listen to a sermon on any part of Scripture they want, when they want, from whomever they want.

When I get up to preach on Sunday, I can safely assume that for some people sitting in the pews, this is the fourth or fifth sermon they've heard during the week. They've listened to the daily Bible teaching of their favorite radio ministry. On their daily commute they've tuned in to the weekly sermon of the pastor of a huge church. They may have watched the livestream of a seamless worship production followed by a stellar sermon at a church in a different city or even country. When it is your turn to preach on Sunday morning, this can lead to feelings of insecurity. We can begin to doubt ourselves. "I can't preach with the dynamism of that megachurch pastor." "I don't know the Greek or Hebrew like that minister." "Where does that preacher find his illustrations? I can't find any good ones."

Rather than being excited that some of our congregants are learning from other voices during the week, many of us feel intimidated as we wrestle with comparison. We begin to think we should adapt our style to imitate those to whom our congregants are listening.

Now, I'm not for a moment suggesting there isn't a place for your people to listen to other preachers, be it online, at a Bible conference, or in some other format. What I'm saying, however, is that if you put the burden of comparison on yourself, you will more than likely end up discouraged. There will always be a speaker more engaging than you. There will always be someone out there who is more dynamic, more educated, more humorous, more incisive. Comparing yourself with such people will push you to feelings of inadequacy, and copying them is not the solution.

Rather than trying to be like other preachers—even very fine preachers—work on developing yourself and becoming comfortable with who you are. In my experience, a less fluent and even homiletically rough sermon delivered with authenticity and relationship always triumphs over the polished homily that is remote and detached from the audience. The sooner you and I can shake the burden of comparison off our back, the better. Learn to be yourself.

We Don't Need Karaoke Preaching

Over the past few years, many of us have grown to love and appreciate the ease and availability of online sermons. With just the click of a button, we can download messages from our favorite speaker. It is amazing.

One of the most influential Christian speakers in recent years has been pastor Tim Keller, and for good reason.[2] An insightful, engaged, and nuanced preacher, Keller has had an effective ministry reaching out to postmodern thinkers in New York City. I certainly have been refreshed listening to Pastor Keller's sermons.

But here's the thing: Tim Keller is preaching to real people in a real context—his people. And here is the problem: his people are not your people or my people.

Many have sought, despite the consistent pleas of Tim Keller, to emulate his style, thinking that by mimicking his sermons, they will somehow have the same impact.[3] More and more, as I listen to local speakers, I have observed that their illustration choices, their applications, and their sermon structures sound vaguely familiar. Then it clicks. They're imitating Tim Keller. It feels like karaoke preaching—the same sermon but with a different voice, and never as good as the original!

The problem with this, of course, lies not with Tim Keller but with those trying to copy his style. Keller's sermons connect because he has taken time to understand his audience in New York City, and he is communicating in language that is appropriate to them. If you live somewhere else, you will realize that the questions,

> the needs, and the style of reasoning of your audience may be very different from those of his. Tim Keller's messages, though excellent, may not be the most suitable for your context.
>
> Learn from the best, yes, but develop your own voice for your own people.

Know How God Has Wired You

Matthias is in the third year of his master of divinity program. An easygoing guy with a great sense of humor, Matty is good with people and is naturally engaging. He hopes to go into pastoral ministry, so he takes all the preaching classes he can. Something dramatic occurs, however, when he gets up in front of his preaching class. Matthias's personality suddenly shifts from relaxed and personable to solemn and reflective.

In his sermons, Matthias abandons his normal conversational language in favor of a more elevated and technical vernacular. Out of nowhere come references to chiastic structures, hapax legomena, and textual variants. The unfamiliar nomenclature of these terms is matched only by the equally alien references to scholars like Barth, Brueggemann, and Bock. The normal tone of Matthias's voice also gives way to a new and slightly higher-pitched voice that, while urgent, seems unnatural. The transformation is pronounced and complete. Matthias, it appears, has morphed from normal person to nuanced preacher.

Matthias's behavior is something I've seen dozens of times in both the classroom and the pulpit. Well-intentioned and serious students of the Bible want to communicate God's truth, but in doing so, they feel they need to change who they are to be more effective. The reason for such a mentality is not always the same. While some may be motivated by a desire to impress others, most change because they sense a level of expectation, whether real or imagined. Perhaps they have heard a solemn preacher and have benefited from them. Perhaps they have engaged with a highly intellectual preacher and want others to experience that same delight. Perhaps they have witnessed the passion of another preacher and seek to emulate that. Whatever the motivation, preachers often adopt the belief that they should be like others.

The reality is, of course, that God made Matthias and you and me to be who *we* are. I constantly have to exhort students that God doesn't need a second Matt Chandler, Nancy Guthrie, or Voddie Baucham. God has wired each of us to be different. In your experience, your cultural background, and your personal engagement with the Scriptures, you bring something to the pulpit that is distinctly yours. Your voice is unique. While we can learn from other preachers, God has not called them to be you, nor you to be them. The sooner you and I realize this and are comfortable with being ourselves, the more our preaching will engage those who hear us.

Being ourselves does not mean, however, that we are a finished product. One of the greatest challenges I have in training preachers lies in the process of helping them to discover their own unique voice. I say "process" because that is exactly what it is. Like all skills, the ability to preach is not something you simply acquire from a seminary course; it is a competency that requires constant refining and development. And in the process of growing as a preacher, you need to develop an awareness of how you're wired.

Some of us are wired as storytellers, others are humorous, some are passionate, and still others are introspective, pensive, and thoughtful. Rather than seeking to change your personality and makeup, work hard to be the best version of you that you can be. You might be humorous, but to be effective, you might need to keep that in check. You might be a storyteller, but you have a propensity to waffle. You might be passionate, but that can wear people out. You might be dull and need to work on vocal variety. Ask those closest to you to provide their honest reflections on your sermons. Inviting feedback from those who know you well can help you retain your unique voice while also knocking the rough edges off your style and delivery.

Know how God has wired you. And as much as you're able, be the same person in the pulpit as out of the pulpit.

Be Transparent

One of the central features of early Christian leadership was the integral relationship between word and deed, what one preached and how one lived. Writing to the Thessalonians, Paul explained, "Because we loved you so much, we were delighted to share with you not only the gospel of God but our lives as well" (1 Thess. 2:8). Effective preaching happens when there is concord between the message and the messenger. Listeners are not necessarily looking for the most polished product; they are looking to you as a preacher and asking, "Do they really believe it?"

The little church I grew up in had the same few applications for every sermon. It didn't matter the text; I knew that the application for every message was going to be "Pray more," "Spend time with God's people," and most important, "Read the Bible." So with earnest desire I would go home each week after church and try my best. I would do okay on the prayer front and didn't find it hard to enjoy some fellowship, but I stumbled badly at reading the Scriptures. I began with enthusiasm as I made my way through Genesis and Exodus, but once I arrived at Leviticus, I halted to a screeching stop. I had no idea what I was reading, and I quit. As a result, during every subsequent sermon I felt terrible. Every week I was told to read the Bible, but clearly, unlike the preacher, I was an incompetent Christian because I had tried and failed.

Then one Sunday a visiting preacher came and preached about the importance of Scripture in the Christian life. As guilt started to make its way over me again, the preacher paused and explained how *he* struggled with reading the Bible. He shared his struggles with both consistency and content. He confided with us that reading the Bible was not easy; it was actually quite hard. I couldn't believe what I was hearing. *The preacher struggles with things much like I do? The pastor doesn't have it all together? He too wrestles with personal weakness and experiences discouragement?* The transparency of the preacher built instant rapport not only with me but also, I discovered, with many in the audience who resonated with the same struggle. The preacher then offered some hope and practical suggestions on some strategies he was seeking to employ in his own life to work on this discipline. I was astonished.

Now, it should be said that preaching with transparency does not mean sharing every one of your shortcomings with your audience. I remember while at seminary a student confessing in a chapel service that he felt convicted about his problem with lust. Given that nearly half of the audience were of the opposite sex, his transparency, though well intended, felt inappropriate and a little creepy. While he was hoping to build rapport with his audience, he probably lost it. The preacher should be real with an audience but at the same time use discretion to avoid losing credibility through oversharing.

In preaching we should also be open about our positive experiences in following the Lord. While it can be encouraging to hear others share about their struggles in evangelism or Bible reading, if a preacher speaks only of his or her failures, then the audience might lose heart or lose confidence in the preacher. Positively share what God is teaching you. With humility reveal a growth area, an answered prayer, or a good-news story from your life. Transparency in your discipleship journey can provide great encouragement to fellow disciples.

Our sermons carry genuine freight when we preach with personal transparency. People often feel inadequate about their Christian struggles, and they don't need a picture of perfection. Rather they need an authentic word from a fellow sojourner. If you have struggles in your Christian life, share them with people. If you've recently experienced a moment of joy in your Christian walk, communicate it. If you've wrestled with obeying an application of Scripture, tell that to your people. Be transparent with your audience.

Give People Water from a Flowing Stream

One way we can demonstrate our authenticity is to share from what God is currently teaching us. Sometimes the preacher can seem to have it all together. As authorities declaring what the Lord says in his Word, speakers can give the impression that they have a mastery of the issues at hand and that the sermon is only for the listener in the pew. In reality the preacher needs to sit under the Word as much as does every member of the audience.

What's Your Story?

One of the features of postmodernism is the movement away from proposition-based truth claims and toward experience as a means of testing truth. People are less inclined to accept propositions that we merely state. They are, however, more likely to hear us out if we share with them something from our life experiences. Effective preachers should capitalize on this by embedding in their sermons personal stories of their journey with God. How do we do this?

First, share common experiences. One of the reasons we share our experiences in the sermon is because we seek to invite our listeners to consider what God may be saying to them in their context. Struggling with doubt, wrestling with God in prayer, or contending with fear in evangelism are common experiences many in your audience will resonate with. Sharing common experiences invites listeners to consider the truth in their lives.

Second, in sharing your personal stories, be careful not to present yourself too often as the hero—or as the villain. Some people are inclined to share only the positive stories of their Christian experience. They talk about leading people to Christ, God's specific answers to their prayers, their always-obedient children, or their highly successful ministry. While such stories can

---

inspire, they can also draw too much attention to the preacher and leave the listener feeling inadequate.

Conversely, some preachers share too much of their own struggles. They may share too often of their doubt in prayer, their struggle with suffering, or their failures in sharing their faith. They want to share their weakness, but they fall into danger of losing all credibility with their audience. When we share our personal experiences, we should humbly share our small victories as well as our struggles and defeats. Don't talk about yourself as only the hero or the villain.

Third, use your personal story to speak of a greater story. When Jesus healed the demoniac in Mark 5, he exhorted the man, "Go home to your own people and tell them how much the *Lord* has done for you" (Mark 5:19, emphasis mine). Jesus wanted the man to tell his story, but the purpose of his testimony was to convey to those closest to him what the Lord had done. When we integrate our experiences into the sermon, it should always be to exalt Christ, not ourselves. It is good to share our experiences, but we must remember that the larger goal is to draw attention not to ourselves but to our Savior.

When we preach, we must make it clear that we have been and are considering Scripture's relevance to our own lives just as much as how it pertains to the lives of all listeners. Much contemporary preaching lacks passion because preachers have failed to consider how the text first and foremost challenges them. If you are going to speak about generosity and giving, share what that looks like for you now. If you are preaching on forgiveness, reveal what that looks like in your present-day experience. Don't simply recount stories of when you shared your faith five years ago; show how you are seeking to do that in your current context.

When you preach, show what difference the text is making in your own experience. Share how it has challenged you this week. Reveal what you have found encouraging, sobering, and convicting in your study of God's Word. Preachers are tempted to give people water from the stagnant well of past experience, but the most effective preacher shares from the fresh overflow of what they are currently learning.

KNOW YOUR AUDIENCE

If you are to be an effective communicator, you must develop an awareness of and appreciation for the dynamic between you, the sender of a message, and those who receive it. Traditionally, preaching has often been practiced as a one-way monologue that is highly sender oriented. In this approach preachers work hard in their studies. They exegete the text and reflect on the theology, and this culminates in the sermon, in which they proclaim their observations and reflections to the audience. Such sermons are often characterized by the use of high-context language and assumed theological knowledge and competency. The problem with this approach, however, is that most of the receptors of the message, the audience, do not move in the same world as the preacher. Those hearing the message might find it difficult to engage, because they have to make the jump from their world to the world of the preacher.

This problem is nothing new. Addressing his students in the 1800s, Charles Spurgeon stated, "The people in the marketplace cannot learn the language of the academy, so the people of the academy must learn the language of the marketplace. It is the pastor's job to translate."[4] Spurgeon understood that the preacher's job is to engage with the world of the person on the street, not to expect that person to enter the theological sphere of the preacher.

Receptor-Oriented Preaching

Those who communicate effectively take seriously the world of their audience. Engaged preaching is often the result of a receptor orientation rather than a sender orientation. Recently Tim Keller has focused on this dynamic. Addressing church planters, he writes,

> Listeners ("receptors") automatically interpret communication from the perspective of their own context. It is an extremely tiring and difficult process for a receptor to comprehend communication which is not provided within his or her frame of reference. Can you imagine reading a technical computer journal if you have no background at all in the field? The technical journal makes no effort to begin with a beginner's frame of reference. Soon you, the receptor, "tune out" and become numb. By a "frame of reference" we mean a person's culture, beliefs, language, vocabulary, life situation, perceived needs, and so on.
>
> There are two basic approaches to communication: sender-oriented and receptor-oriented. When the communicator designates his frame of reference as the one in which communication takes place, the receptor must make most or all the adjustments. As we have seen, this is quite tiring, difficult, and often unsuccessful. The receptor in this case is in a dependent position. He must ask many questions, listen, deal with many strange and uncomfortable concepts and conditions, look up many words, ask for a great deal of help, and constantly check and re-check meanings. In short, the receptor is forced into a vulnerable position. However, when the communicator designates the receptor's frame of reference as that in which the communication will take place, the roles are reversed! Now, the communicator is in a dependent position. He must ask the questions, he must listen, he must deal with many strange and uncomfortable concepts and conditions, look up many words, ask for a great deal of help, and constantly check and re-check meanings. He has become vulnerable. "Sender-oriented" communication is "1-way" communication for the sender, but "2-way" for the receptor. But "receptor-oriented" communication is "2-way" communication throughout. The latter is much harder and more complex for the sender, but far more comfortable for the receptor and far more successful.[5]

Why Everybody Needs to Learn
Receptor-Orientated Communication

My (Sam's) three young boys have swimming lessons after school at the public swimming pool. This gets complicated because each boy has a different skill level. Each boy is in a different class, with a different instructor, at a different time of day, in a different swimming pool lane. But it gets more complicated than that, because with the start of each new term, the school places my boys in new classes, with new instructors, at new times of day, in new swimming pool lanes.

Every time we begin a new term, every parent has to go to the pool notice board to see what the new arrangements will be for their children. And there is only one notice board. As a result, a scrum of fifty sets of parents fight each other to find the names of their children on the notice board. But to our dismay, the information is grouped according to the names of the instructors. Under the names of the instructors is the skill level of their class. Under the skill level is the time of the class and then the swimming pool lane. Finally, under all of this appear the names of the students in the class.

This means I have to check out the names of all the instructors and their classes to look for my child's name. From this I can work out what class my child is in and when and where this new lesson will be. I have to do this three times—once for each of my boys—in a crowd of other parents trying to do the same thing.

What's wrong with this picture? The information is true, factual, and correct. But the information is sender orientated. The school organizes the information according to how it makes sense to them. It's the roster they hand out to their instructors, telling them who is in their class and when and where they should turn up. But from the parents' perspective, they couldn't pick a less helpful way to reveal our children's lesson times.

How should the information have been organized? It should have been receptor orientated, organized according to how it makes sense to us parents. They should have listed the lesson times under the names of our children in alphabetical order. Then we could quickly look up our children's names to discover their lesson times and lanes. That's how it would make the most sense to us.

The difference between receptor- and sender-orientated communication is crucial, but I see this mistake often, especially when I look at websites for churches. Usually, the church's home webpage displays information according to what is most important to the church organization: the origin story of the church, the church governance, and something about their leadership team.

But what information is most important for visitors to see on the webpage? *Where are you located? What is your address? What times do you meet?* Yet this information is often missing. And if it exists, I have to scroll down to the bottom to find it. Even then, nothing on the page tells me which state or country the church is in. You say you're located in the suburb of Springfield—is that in Illinois, California, or Scotland?

We preachers need to learn from this. When we research and prepare a sermon, we usually organize the information according to how it makes sense to us. But we need to organize and deliver the information according to how it makes sense to our listeners.

If we are to communicate the gospel clearly, it is critical that we adopt a receptor-oriented disposition in our preaching. As Keller and others have noted, this model of receptor-oriented communication is seen in the gospel through Jesus' incarnation. God takes on flesh and descends to make himself known by becoming one of us. The gospel is inherently receptor oriented, and we should follow its lead.

There are three significant ways in which we can work on becoming better receptor-oriented preachers. We can work on understanding who our people are, how they learn, and how they speak.

Who Am I Speaking To?

One of the very first questions we should consider when preaching is, who am I speaking to? When we preach, we are involved in the proclamation of ideas, but we do so in the context of relationship. Ideally, preaching should be done with some connectedness between the sender and the receptor, between the preacher and the audience. Those who understand the world of their audience and have some form of relationship with their listeners tend to make the most significant impact when they speak.

Relationship is the soil from which fruitful preaching grows. I remember once preaching at a church with which I had been heavily involved. I was six weeks into a twenty-three-part series in Romans—the sermon was on the faith of Abraham in Romans 4—when a lady approached me. She began, "Thanks for the sermon, Pastor. I found what you said about Abraham interesting . . ." Then she fell apart. "Pastor, I think my daughter might be on drugs!"

Drugs? How was this a response to my Romans 4 sermon? She wasn't inquiring about the use of Psalm 32 in Paul's reflection of faith. She wasn't wanting to engage with issues about Abraham's faith. This dear lady wanted direction regarding her struggles.

As I later reflected on that conversation—and many others since—I have come to discover that the regular preaching of God's Word to people you know, love, and pray for is often the basis for meaningful ministry. Preaching builds rapport, which lays a platform for pastoral care. This is certainly not to undermine the importance of declarative preaching. It is a reminder that effective preaching is intrinsically tied to *people*. We shouldn't present generic homilies from the file; rather we should aim to proclaim audience-specific truth to souls we care about.

Something Is Missing from This Sermon

Several years ago, while teaching at a seminary in the US, one of my graduate students, Scott, researched the dynamic of multicampus church ministry. In particular, Scott was interested in how large churches incorporated recorded video sermons of the lead pastor into smaller community gatherings.

After interviewing a variety of churches, he discovered that while people generally listened to video sermons, these pastors appeared distant, since they had almost zero personal connection with the audience. While the preachers' messages were compelling and polished, something was missing from their delivery: relationship.

Know Your People

There are numerous ways to get to know people. First, an old-fashioned yet always productive way to develop connection is to spend quality time with them. Getting to know people through hospitality—whether in your home, a coffee shop, or somewhere else—is a helpful way to cultivate relationship. Contexts in which you listen to others and hear their struggles, their joys, and their doubts will enrich your love for your people as well as shape your commitment to preaching God's truth to them.

Second, get to know your people by praying for them. As small as it may seem, sending an email, a note, or a text message to let people know you are praying for them will help you cultivate your pastoral commitments to them. And it will assure them of your genuine concern. By praying for those to whom you preach, you will strengthen your ministry and overall gospel effectiveness. Take and create opportunities to pray with and for your people. It will impact your preaching dynamic.

Can You Preach at My Son's Birthday Party?

Many years ago I served at a ministry in which I did a lot of evangelistic preaching. People would call our ministry and ask for speakers to come and preach at special events. Most of the events were typical outreach-style meetings: a men's breakfast, a youth service, a mothers' group. One day, however, I received an unusual request. A sincere and soft-spoken man called our office to request an evangelist for a special event he was hosting. In broken English he said, "I would like you to come and speak at my son's birthday party."

Wow. I'd never had a request like that before, but I was more than happy to do it. I put it on the calendar and told the gentleman I would be in touch.

A week or so before the event, I gave the gentleman a call to get a few more specifics about the birthday party sermon I was set to deliver. I am so glad I called him. He said, "Two months ago my son was released from prison. He has had a rough few years. This week he is turning twenty-one years old, and we are throwing him a party to assure him of our unconditional love for him. There will be about ninety of his non-Christian friends at the event, and we would like you to share with him and his friends the good news message of Jesus."

After hearing this, I needed to pick my jaw up off the floor. It was a prodigal son story. What a powerful act of love, grace, and commitment from this family.

Needless to say, my vision of the birthday sermon was radically altered after that phone call. Instead of an animated Bible talk to sugar-filled eight-year-old kids, I found myself sharing the message of Christ with a large gathering of non-Christians under a large, open tent in someone's back yard. It pays to ask, who am I speaking to?

Third, make genuine efforts to keep your feet in the world of your audience. Sometimes I hear sermons from those in ministry who clearly haven't been out in the real world for quite some time. One of the great dangers that ministry people face is that we can become so focused on rosters, services, and committees that we lose touch with the challenges of the people we are trying to serve.

Many preachers would benefit from getting to know people by entering their world. Sign up to be a soccer coach. Join the school PTA. Take a college course on photography. Getting into the world of your audience will help you better see the challenges of life they must navigate. Seeing the world through their eyes will sharpen your awareness of how you might connect God's Word to them in the sermon.

Know How to Engage Your People

To communicate effectively with an audience, we must develop an awareness of everchanging patterns of communication.

While some of us may have grown up in contexts where it was not unusual to hear a forty-minute sermon, for many nowadays listening to an extended monologue is not only unusual, it's almost impossible. For better or for worse, our world has thousands of voices all vying for our attention. The result is that it is hard for many to hear with clarity any message of length.

Those sitting in our pews are often sympathetic to our sermons, but they are highly distracted. Emails, tweets, Instagram images, Facebook posts, and podcasts are only ever a click away on a smartphone. Even in church, the simple vibration of a phone can pull an audience member's attention from what is going on in a service.

The battle for a listener's attention feels like climbing Mount Everest. It appears too difficult and the odds seemed stacked against us. In spite of this, if we are willing to observe mainstream cultural communication trends and learn why many of them are effective, we can in small ways leverage our preaching to better connect.

I See What You're Talking About

Studies show that when we add a visual to an auditory message, comprehension levels rise significantly. There is great value in offering things that people can see to help consolidate what they hear. Throughout the Bible physical objects are often used as visual tools to teach God's people lessons. We find altars established, memorial stones arranged, and a Passover lamb provided. Jesus himself used bread and wine to remind us of his death until he comes again.

In church history we also have physical sites and objects that were used to teach and disciple God's people. Go to almost any old church in Europe, and you will find paintings and stained glass windows that make visible the gospel story of Scripture. In the days long before multimedia, churches used their windows as their storybooks.

In preaching, visuals used effectively, be they onscreen or a physical prop, can greatly consolidate a message. A metaphor of fruit growing on a vine, the yoke of an animal, olive oil being poured out, or a sandal being untied can have much more impact if you display it physically before an audience.

Likewise, if you're using an illustration, a physical item in front of your people can bring it to life. Once I preached on abiding in Christ and illustrated it with a tea bag and a cup. I demonstrated, through making a cup of tea, that a tea bag needs to remain in the water for a period of time in order for the tea to permeate. The longer the tea bag abides in the cup, the richer the flavor. I then transitioned to letting Christ's word abide in us. Though it was a simple illustration, having the item in front of the audience reinforced the idea in a way that words alone would not have done.

Take visuals for example. Studies have shown that "in the world of social media, visual content is forty times more likely to get shared, and articles that feature an image every seventy-five to one hundred words receive double the social media shares than those with text alone."[6] Words matter, but it seems that for those words to best be received, visual content should be strongly considered as well. This dynamic, called pictorial superiority, has been studied and has revealed that the use of visuals in any verbal communication embeds ideas far more effectively than words alone.[7] Along with hearing a message, seeing the message engages the listener in a way that words alone, whether written or spoken, can't.[8]

Using images in a sermon, whether through the use of visuals on a screen or physical props, can enhance the clarity of your sermon as well as the memorability of your message. Just as previous generations of preachers used large charts, overhead projectors, and PowerPoint images, the preacher ought always to consider effective visuals.

While communication fads will rise and fall, the effective preacher should be open to new and innovative ways to enhance communication, not simply to keep in step with mainstream culture but to leverage the familiar learning patterns of those to whom they preach.

Know Your People's Language

Several years ago I was grading online essays for a seminary evangelism class. The assessment required the student to write an evangelistic letter to a friend or family member, outlining to them the gospel message of Christ. Students would be marked on both clarity of language and gospel content. While most of the essays were balanced and comprehensible, several of them highlighted the challenge of translating Christian terms into everyday language.

One student urged his grandfather, "Pop, we have all transgressed and fallen short of God's glory. The good news, however, is that the Lamb of God has borne our iniquity. Redemption and propitiation have been secured for all who will repent and believe. Therefore call

207

upon the name of the Lord!" The letter assumed that his unchurched grandfather understood concepts such as transgression, propitiation, and repentance and could identify the Lamb of God. At that point the student might as well have been speaking Gaelic or Latvian to his relative. The terms, though rich to him, were virtually a foreign language to his grandfather.

Mind Your Language!

Many years ago I completed an undergraduate degree in the United States. As an international student from Australia, I thoroughly enjoyed living abroad and particularly loved living in the great city of Chicago. Though Australia is not far removed from America culturally, some language differences threw me off more than once.

I discovered early on that a bum is someone perceived as lazy or a vagrant. In my country *bum* refers to your buttocks. In America a thong is a skimpy piece of swimwear, whereas in my country thongs are what you wear on your feet to the beach. In Australia a torch is a light you use when camping. In the States a torch is a stick covered on one end with burning tar. What I referred to as a torch, my American friends call a flashlight.

One time a young lady from college called to ask how I was doing. I responded, "I'm knackered," which is a typical Australian way of saying, "I'm exhausted." On hearing this, the girl promptly hung up the phone. I later asked why she ended the call. She said, "It was inappropriate for you to tell me you were *naked* on the telephone." Yikes! The words we use and what we mean by them are shaped by our context, background, and culture and will not always be heard the way we intend.

One of the common mistakes that preachers make is to

assume their words will always be understood and interpreted correctly. The problem, however, is that often preachers use words that are unknown, unfamiliar, or mean different things to different people.

When we refer to a pericope, the divided kingdom, or the gentiles, we must not assume the audience understands our language. *Wrath, righteousness,* and *exile* probably mean something to you, but these words might be foreign to your audience. As my beloved seminary professor Howard Hendricks would say to us, "There are people in your audience who think that an epistle is the wife of an apostle!" His point? Don't assume people know what you mean, especially in regard to Christian jargon. Work hard on your language skills. It is better to be clear and comprehended than murky and misunderstood.

I wish I could say that the error of jargon-heavy language was an issue just for those outside the church who lack familiarity with the Bible. The reality, however, is that in pulpits all over the world, sermons are going out every week that are unintelligible to the people of God.

About a year ago we sang a beautiful song in church which has as one of its refrains, "Calvary covers it all." After the service I quizzed a few members of the audience, as well as those who had led the singing. "What is Calvary?" The answers surprised me. "Calvary means Jesus' death." "Calvary is about forgiveness." "Calvary signifies Jesus on the cross." While all of those things are sort of in the ballpark, most of these people didn't know what Calvary actually was.

"The name Calvary," I explained to them, "was from the Latin *calvaria*, which means 'skull.' The reference is to the place where Jesus died. In the Bible this place is usually referred to by the Aramaic term *Golgotha*" (see Matt. 27:33). After I offered this simple explanation, I could see the lights come on for them. I wondered how many more people in church were singing this song with no comprehension of the word Calvary. I suspected quite a few.

Whether in a sermon or in a song, our language should convey meaning that is appropriate to our audience. As I pointed out earlier, many of us preach sender-oriented messages. We share our ideas using language that was useful in our preparation. But we need to translate those valuable ideas into a receptor-oriented form. We need, as it were, to assume their ears when we pen our manuscripts. To do this, I often ask myself a series of questions.

- Would someone who doesn't speak English as their native language grasp what I am saying?
- Would a new Christian understand the concepts I am articulating?
- Would a young teen comprehend what I am saying?
- What in this message do I need to make clearer?

While it is not always possible to make yourself understood by every group or individual, simplicity of language and ideas should be constantly on your mind as you prepare to speak to others.

CHAPTER 10

HOW TO DELIVER A MESSAGE WORTH HEARING

Know Your Craft, Not Just Your Content

MALCOLM GILL

Several years ago I heard a sermon from a young student minister who was busy preparing for vocational ministry at a theological college. He began his sermon by telling a dad joke based on a pun. After a few courtesy laughs from some of the faithful, the student promptly announced, "Okay, now that I've told a token joke, let's look at Philippians chapter 2, verse 1."

I was dumbfounded. Not only was I disappointed with the quality of his dad joke (it could have been way better—meaning, way worse), but I was even more disappointed with the perfunctory nature of his introduction. The poor young student either didn't know what was involved in a sermon introduction or simply didn't value such a thing. Either way he displayed a low view of the form of the sermon.

While I don't want to be too harsh on the poor student minister (what preacher hasn't told a bad joke from the pulpit?), the mindset that he expressed is all too familiar. For many, the craft and science of homiletics is superfluous to the real task of preaching. Such preachers feel that the shaping of structures, use of illustrations, and reflections on application are nice if you have time, but they are not crucial. This mentality sometimes goes even farther by pitting the content of the sermon against the form, rather than viewing both as essential. Such a dichotomy, however, is not only unnecessary but unhelpful.

I'm not sure where this phrase originated, but I've heard people say, "When we preach, someone suffers. Either you suffer in your study, or your congregation suffers on a Sunday morning!" There are no shortcuts to effective preaching; it is simply hard work. Wrestling with the biblical text and identifying the theological ideas behind it is the necessary and significant process by which we develop sermons. But we must not neglect the hard work of shaping the sermon itself.

In thinking through the relationship between the content of the message and the final crafting of the sermon, Tim Keller accurately observes, "It is not enough to just harvest the wheat; it must be prepared in some edible form or it can't nourish and delight."[1] To preach effectively, we must take seriously not only the content of material but also the best form in which we might communicate it.

In contrast to expository sermons that typically follow the contours of a passage, the topical sermon requires a slightly different skill set to provide a sermon's shape and form. As seen in the previous chapters, the topical sermon may, for example, build itself around a theological or christological idea. Rather than being shaped by the boundaries of a particular passage of Scripture, the topical sermon is flexible because it can be shaped to the purpose of the context in which it is delivered.

Although many of the basic principles of oral delivery are the same as those of expository preaching, there are at least three ways we can seek to enhance our topical sermons. We can develop clear outlines, cultivate conciseness, and learn from others.

DEVELOP CLEAR OUTLINES

The late Haddon Robinson famously quipped, "A mist in the pulpit can easily become a fog in the pew."[2] True words. As someone who for many years was paid to listen to hundreds of sermons every year, I have witnessed more fog in pulpits than in a San Francisco winter.

David recently preached a sermon in class. At the conclusion of his sermon, I asked the audience what they thought was the main thrust of the sermon. Rachel responded, "Be generous with your resources." Kit followed this up with, "Love your neighbor through acts of service." Geoff, anticipating the answer, chimed in with, "Jesus is Lord." While all of these statements are factually true, none of them reflected David's actual point. From the diversity of responses, David quickly saw that his sermon was not as clear as he thought it was, and that was likely because of its structure.

Often in preaching we have terrific ideas that are biblical and true, but we need to make those ideas clear. Outlines are our friend in this regard. Outlines give our sermons structure and direction. A good outline acts as a mental road map that takes us on a journey to a destination. Now, I know some people like to go on trips without a clear route to their destination. Such people are happy to look outside the window and take it all in. They don't care if they're on a highway, a byway, or a skyway. They know they'll eventually get to their destination, and they are happy to just be on the journey.

Others, however, find this approach highly frustrating. Such folks, while still interested in the destination, would like to know where they are along the way. They don't want to simply drive; they also want to know what signposts to look for during the trip. These folks look to their GPS devices on their smartphones to indicate the way to their destinations. While they might still enjoy the view, they find directions helpful.

What is true of a journey is generally true of a sermon. While some listeners don't mind if a sermon meanders all over the place to get to an end point, most listeners want to know where they are headed.

By providing a clear structure, the preacher doesn't simply speak of a destination but points out signposts along the way that will help the listener understand where they are and where they are going.

Structures are flexible, and we must view them as such. A topical message on wealth might use a problem-solution-application format. A traditional expository message might follow the two or three main movements of the text. A parable or narrative text might be suited to a storytelling structure that moves from disequilibrium to an aha moment that brings about a new equilibrium.[3] Whatever model one uses, the goal should be to make things clearer. The structure serves the clarity of the sermon rather than simply existing for itself.

The 2:00 a.m. Oral Clarity Test

One way to test your oral clarity is what I call the "2:00 a.m. test." Let's say the night before you preach, I (in a noncreepy way) come to your bedroom and shake you from your slumber and ask, "What are you preaching on tomorrow? What is the shape of your message and your main thrust?" If you can tell me your main thrust and structure clearly—before you call the police—then you'll likely be clear during the sermon. If, however, you start waffling, then I suspect your message will likely be unclear when you preach it. Work hard to bring clarity through crisp and careful outlines.

CULTIVATE CONCISENESS

A lot of preaching I hear is what I call "dump truck preaching." The preacher, having studied all week, dumps truckloads of information on the unsuspecting audience. The listeners turn up to church and may even be excited about the Scripture reading of the day, but when the preacher starts, the information piles up. The audience hears about the historical background of ancient Corinth. They learn about rhetorical features within the text. They are asked to consider five interpretive understandings of an issue, and if they are lucky, they might even learn a new Greek word which they can later roll out at a party to impress their friends.

While I'm not against information-laden sermons, the overload of information is often less effective than a message that is pointed and concise. The maxim "Less is more" is usually true in regard to preaching. This requires effort by the preacher, however, as it is much harder to preach a tight, twenty-five-minute sermon than to deliver one that is forty-five minutes.

Clear preaching is often marked by concise and intentional speaking rather than verbose and exhaustive explanation. But how do you develop the preaching skill of clarity and conciseness? Here are a couple of suggestions.

Manuscript Your Content

When I prepare to preach, I always manuscript what I intend to say. By writing (or typing) out my sermon, I think through what I would like to say and how I plan to say it. I do this for a few reasons.

First, it forces me to think through the logic of the message. As I link each movement of the sermon, I'm reflecting on the connectedness of each part of the message.

Second, it helps me make sure I'm covering my topic or passage. I can look at my manuscript and see that I have adequately covered either the subject or verses at hand.

Third, it guides me in my time management. After writing manuscripts for more than twenty years, I can tell—knowing how fast I speak —how long the sermon will go, based on how many words I've written.

Fourth, completing a manuscript allows me to check my sermon for imbalances. I can identify when I have too much information or when an illustration is too long. As I compose my sermon, I can edit, remove, or add until I feel I have the right message to deliver.

Should I Preach with a Manuscript?

Some of the common questions that people raise in their development as a preacher are, what role does the manuscript play in the delivery of the sermon? And, doesn't the use of a manuscript minimize the Holy Spirit's prompting in a sermon?

In regard to the manuscript's role in the delivery of a sermon, it should be observed that there are no hard-and-fast rules. There is, however, common wisdom we should learn from the field of effective verbal communication.

First and foremost, the most effective tools that speakers have in their toolbox are their eyes. I'm not talking about whether one has large or small eyes or whether they are brown, blue, or green. Rather we best communicate when our eyes make contact with our listeners. The best public speakers almost always maintain strong eye contact. This is not debated. Most studies show that people who make little eye contact are often viewed with suspicion! Eye contact between the speaker and the audience is crucial because it builds trust.

If you and I want our people to engage with the content we are preaching, then we must work especially hard to maintain eye contact with our audience when we preach. If we choose to use a manuscript in our delivery, we should make sure it does not hamper our eye contact.

Second, a wooden reading of a manuscript makes people zone out. I've heard many sermons like this. These messages have sounded more like dull news reports than impassioned words from the Lord. The content is often okay, but the monotone and stifled delivery keep the content from being heard. I often wonder why the preacher doesn't simply email the congregation the sermon to read at their leisure. An ineffective verbal delivery of a manuscript will prevent the message from getting through to the receiver.

Third, a manuscript can and often does act as a safety net for the speaker. Many an anxious speaker has found comfort in the twelve-point Times New Roman font on a printed page rather than in the earnest faces of an audience. Such communicators would prefer to bury their heads in the manuscript than get it wrong.

While such a speaker may succeed in a word-perfect delivery of their content, perfect words don't mean much if no one is listening.

In regard to the role of the Holy Spirit in the preaching of the sermon, some have, erroneously, misunderstood Jesus' promise "do not worry about what to say or how to say it. At that time you will be given what to say" (Matt 10:19) to mean that preaching should be impromptu as one is moved by the Spirit. Apart from the fact that this is a misunderstanding of the passage, because Jesus is addressing how the disciples were to respond to being arrested, this approach incorrectly suggests that the Holy Spirit uses only the act of preaching and does not work during sermon development.

Whenever I sit down to write a sermon, I constantly ask the Spirit of God to direct my words. From constructing an outline to the use of illustration to shaping a big idea, I constantly ask God to aid me. It is incorrect to think that the sermon alone is the place where God leads us. As preachers, we must be open to God's leading from exegesis to explanation, from structure development to sermon delivery.

Do I ever depart from the sermon manuscript? Yes. Do I ever omit details or add an application or illustration on the fly? I do. However, if I've covered my sermon in prayer during the process of preparing it, I should trust that the Holy Spirit will do his work as the sermon is delivered.

> The preacher, in prayerful dependence, ought to trust not in the precision of every word of the manuscript but in the God whose Word they are proclaiming. In light of the real dangers a manuscript can present, a preacher should use it sparingly during the sermon.

Fifth, after reading my manuscript six, seven, eight times prior to the sermon, I should be familiar enough with the content that I can deliver my message with good eye contact. Writing out a manuscript is time consuming, but it will help you add a crispness to your message.

Follow a Plan

Contrary to popular belief, I'm not a high-performance athlete. I'll never score forty-five points for the Chicago Bulls or a Test century for the Australia cricket team, and there is very little chance I will ever surf a big break at Jaws. Though I may lack the athletic prowess of an elite sports star, I have discovered that I can learn much from them.

Athletes who compete at the top level almost never get there through luck. Sports stars often talk about things like muscle memory and getting the one-percenters right. Practice, regularity, and consistency are all required if athletes are to excel in their sporting disciplines.

In preaching, the same disciplines of practice, regularity, and consistency often set apart the great communicators from the average ones. While there is an element of natural giftedness in public speaking, many great speakers I hear are not endowed with inherent ability. They've simply worked hard to get better, by cultivating a routine.

In writing your sermon, establish some consistent patterns. You could work on your message on the same day every week. You might set aside a specific time to read, pray, and write. Limit how much time you spend on each task. Set up a template document for a topical, textual, or expository message. For each movement in your sermon, you might set up a section to state, explain, illustrate, and apply each point. Aim to have your message complete by a certain time to digest your manuscript.

Each message will be different, of course, but having regularity and structure in your preparation will help you to develop muscle memory in your delivery. While you may want to mix up your preaching style, built-in preparation consistency will aid you in being concise and disciplined.

Read and Review

Jason has recently started his first full-time ministry position as a youth pastor. Keen to make an impact, he works hard on his talks. Jason has been invited to speak at a gathering of multiple youth groups. At the event there will be games, testimonies, and a band, and then Jason will have fifteen minutes to share an evangelistic message on the topic "Why Jesus Makes a Difference." Jason is excited. As the event draws closer, a run sheet of the evening is sent around. People must stick to their allotted times because parents will be at the venue to pick up kids at 9:30 p.m. *No worries,* Jason thinks.

As the evening unfolds, everything runs smoothly. There is plenty of pizza and some helpful interviews, and then it is time for Jason to preach. Jason is confident and the message starts well. His introduction contains a personal story of how he came to faith. Everything seems to be going fine, until Jason sees the clock.

He is shocked to see that he has gone for twelve minutes but has just started on the first point of his message! He notices the furrowed brows of youth pastors who can see this blowing out. He observes a few parents milling around the back of the hall. Jason speeds up and tries to boil down the body of the message.

Jason does his best for a few more minutes. But seeing that he is now over his time, rather than landing this plane, he turns off the engine and takes a nosedive. What started with great promise ends in a crash.

I wish I could say Jason's dilemma is unique to him, but it is not. Time gets away from most preachers without discipline. That's why in our preparation it is important to read and review our sermons.

During my seminary days I was required to take several preaching classes, for which I am very grateful. I not only received excellent homiletic teaching, but I also learned a great deal from my fellow students. As a non-American, I found it particularly enjoyable to hear the different styles of preaching from those in my class.

Bob was from one of the southern states of America. He wore cowboy boots, a shiny belt buckle, and a bolo necktie to class. Bob made me feel like I was in a spaghetti western; it was fantastic! When Bob's turn to preach arrived, I was excited. He took off his cowboy hat, straightened his bolo tie, and preached with a toothpick in his mouth. Bob spoke slowly with a Texas drawl, and I was thoroughly engaged.

Jay was a city boy from the east coast of America. He was sharp, witty, and spoke with confidence. While Jay was a no-nonsense kind of guy, he was immensely likeable. When he rose to preach, I was enthralled, but in a different way. Jay was animated and moved around the stage freely. He spoke quickly, gestured frantically, and offered his points with crispness and precision.

The differences between Bob's and Jay's styles were stark. One was laid back and reserved, while the other was intense and frenetic. One was slow and steady, while the other raced along. There were similarities as well. Both sermons were biblical, both preachers had written full manuscripts beforehand, and both deliveries went approximately fifteen minutes.

Though the pace of the sermons was dissimilar, the time of each sermon was almost identical. This could have been because of the clock at the back of the classroom, but more likely it was because all of us needed to submit our manuscripts forty-eight hours before class. We had to preach without notes, which required us to practice what we intended to say. We were told that the message should be fifteen minutes, so we prepared accordingly.

I suspect that if you and I had examined the manuscripts of Bob and Jay, we would have noted quite a difference in length. Bob seemed to drag out sentences because of his southern drawl, whereas Jay seemed to get more words into one minute than was humanly possible. Both speakers, however, knew their own pace and style, and that was reflected in how much they included in their manuscripts.

After years of writing full manuscripts for my sermons, I know what works for me. I know with an element of precision how many minutes a sermon will be, judging by the size of my manuscript. This is helpful because I can discover whether a sermon is too long (seldom is it too short!) by noting the number of pages written.

In my early years of ministry, I refrained from writing manuscripts and usually went with bare-bones outlines. The danger of this, which was revealed in many of my sermons, was that the sermon could easily blow out timewise. Using a manuscript and reading it out loud multiple times will help you manage your time well.

When I reread the manuscript in preparation, I'm not only looking at the length of time but also checking the balance of my sermon. I ask myself a series of questions.

- Have I stated my ideas and structure clearly enough?
- Is there enough time dedicated to explaining the biblical text and theological idea?
- Have I illustrated my major ideas appropriately?
- Are there enough snapshots of relevance from everyday life to engage people?

When rereading the manuscript, I may notice that I've given considerable time to the explanation section of my sermon but I've failed to give people a mental break. I will then consider either reducing the size of my explanation or inserting a brief illustration or aspect of relevance to provide relief or clarity.

At other times I might look at the introduction or illustration and feel that it is too long. I then go over that section and ask myself, "What can I remove from this section that is not needed?" I want to make sure that my sermon is appropriately balanced to achieve the goals of the sermon. An expository sermon may contain more explanation than an evangelistic sermon. A topical sermon might use more illustrations than a text-based message. Rereading the manuscript allows me to edit, add, and remove material to ensure a more concise message.

LEARN FROM OTHERS

One way we can improve our communication, particularly in the field of speaking on topics, is to learn from those who do it well. Fortunately, in our day and age we can watch and listen to world-class communicators with the click of a mouse or a swipe on our phone. There are hundreds of thousands of sermons, podcasts, and YouTube videos that feature people speaking in public contexts. Not all of these, of course, are stellar models of good communication, but we can learn much from watching and listening to others.

In recent years one of the most frequently watched sources of public speaking has been TED Talks. This international forum facilitates a variety of speakers who address their areas of interest and specialty. TED stands for Technology, Entertainment, Design, and the subjects covered in these talks are broad and usually unfamiliar.

- "Six Tips for Better Sleep"
- "The Japanese Folktale of the Selfish Scholar"
- "What Foods Did Your Ancestors Love?"
- "How Bumble Bees Inspired a Network of Tiny Museums"

While I'm not always interested in the content of "The Evolution of the Coffee Cup Lid" or "How Corn Conquered the World," I am fascinated with how people deliver their messages. (And yes, all of these are actual TED Talks you can watch online.) Because almost all of the

TED talks online revolve around single issues, there is much we can glean from them about how best to communicate on a topic. Let me highlight a few lessons we can learn from TED talks.

Effective Communicators Are Passionate

Surf through any of the TED Talks, and you will see people who love what they are talking about. Whether it is learning a language, solving a science problem, or exploring caves, the presenters always seem to bubble with enthusiasm. Now, it should be said that we all express passion differently. Some of us wear our hearts on our sleeve and are physically animated in our delivery. Others are more reserved but just as passionate.

Passion shows itself differently, but it should show itself in one form or another. When you watch a TED Talk, you see people express, through their own personalities, delight in and passion for their subjects. Even more so, preachers should feel passion about what we've been learning in our preparation.

Now, admittedly, not all topics float our boats or get the blood pumping. Some topics are difficult and unfamiliar. Some, and probably many, topics require effort to learn about. In the midst of our sermon development, we might not feel overly joyous or passionate about the material. But when we move to how the gospel intersects with the issue, we should develop an earnestness about it because the topic provides us an opportunity to point people to the beauty, wisdom, and grace of Jesus. This is what should drive our passion.

Effective Communicators Know Their Subject Well

One of the features of an effective TED Talk is the confidence of the speaker. Notice I said confidence, not arrogance. When you listen to an engaging speaker, you get the sense that they really know what they are talking about. In many of these talks, I get the feeling that were I to get the presenter alone, they would talk for hours about their topic. Their demeanor is confident because they have spent significant time thinking about and investigating the subject matter.

As preachers, we need to emulate such confidence, not trusting in our ability or skill set but rather trusting that God's Word is one of truth and power. Our confidence flows from the fact that we've studied, reflected on, and prayed through our message, and we believe God will speak through it.

A good TED presenter knows their material and speaks with authority because they have enmeshed themselves in the topic. We preachers commissioned to speak God's Word to the world must, more than all others, seek to know our subject matter well and let our confidence in God's Word spill out in our delivery.

Effective Communicators Are Concise

I know I've emphasized this several times in this chapter, but it's important: be concise. As a general rule, TED Talks go for ten to fifteen minutes. They are short, punchy, and on point. There is not a lot of waffle in TED Talks. While the context is slightly different in a sermon—and I'm certainly not suggesting that all sermons should be ten to fifteen minutes—there is something compelling about a direct message.

As stated earlier, short sermons are harder to craft and deliver than long ones. But would you rather linger too long and have people zone out, or finish with people wanting more? Do TED speakers have more to say on their topic than fifteen minutes allows? Undoubtedly. However, they know what they want to say, they say it, and they finish. A TED Talk will never be exhaustive on the subject of interest, but it will drill down on an important idea. Effective preaching should be equally pointed in its focus.

Effective Communicators Maintain Eye Contact

Standing on a red dot in the middle of a stage, TED presenters simply speak. There are no physical barriers such as a lectern or music stand. There is no place to hide. The best communicators don't have their heads in a set of notes or their eyes on the floor. Rather they maintain excellent eye contact with their audiences.

A Preacher Walked into a Bar . . .

There are only three main forms of communication in which a speaker monologues for ten to twenty minutes to an audience: sermons, TED Talks, and stand-up comedy.

I (Sam) firmly believe we can learn a lot from watching TED Talks, both from the content and from the styles of delivery. The only problem with TED Talks is that most of us have no chance of becoming a TED speaker, so we can only watch but never try out the skills required to deliver TED Talks.

So Malcolm and I decided to give stand-up comedy a shot. We both signed up for a five-week course in which we learned from comedians how to talk to an audience. We learned the art of rhythm, timing, tone, using a microphone, speaking without notes, and many other things.

The number one thing I learned about preaching from stand-up comedy is this: we don't speak the same way that we write. In written communication the unit of thought is a paragraph, which contains a primary sentence and some supporting secondary sentences. These paragraphs can be very long. You might write a lot of secondary sentences before you move on to the next paragraph.

But in oral communication the unit of thought is a spoken module, which contains a set-up, premise, and punch line. The modules have to be as brief as possible. There can be no wasted words. You must move on to the next module as quickly as you can.

If you're wondering, Malcolm and I have already performed some comedy gigs in front of real audiences. If our preaching ministries ever end, both of us can fall back on stand-up comedy!

To preach effectively, preachers should learn to communicate in a similar manner. While there is nothing wrong with a lectern or music stand to hold your Bible and/or manuscript, be careful not to be drawn into looking down. As I mentioned earlier, the most effective preachers maintain good eye contact with their listeners.

Look at the people you are speaking to. Do they care if you get your sermon word-perfect? No! They don't even know what you intended to say. It is better to maintain visual contact with your audience than to bury your head in a script, even if it is quality work. TED Talks remind us of the importance of engaging people through eye contact.

Effective Communicators Use Visuals to Enhance Their Talk

People generally learn and retain far more from seeing and listening than from listening alone. TED speakers know and understand this. Appropriately used visuals—an image on a large screen or an object—can help consolidate an idea. Frequently in TED Talks, the speaker uses images to make visible the concept that they are verbally expressing. Preachers would do well to capitalize on this well-accepted notion that people learn best by listening and seeing.

Effective Communicators Share Why the Topic Means Something to Them

Driving most TED Talks is an obvious desire to communicate an idea the speaker believes is important. The goal of a TED Talk is not simply to transfer information about a topic, as important as that is; rather it is to persuade the audience to think, feel, or do something differently.

A TED Talk may confront the listener with an uncomfortable reality. It might challenge the listener to think more broadly or to respond to an issue with an action. A talk may simply drive the audience to a place of curiosity or wonder.

TED Talks, however, are not merely a well of factual information. They are messages from people who are seeking to persuade listeners of something important to them. Speakers almost always have a personal connection or background that links them to their topic.

In a similar vein, effective preaching occurs when the messenger and their message are tightly connected. Some people feel that preaching is primarily about transferring biblical information. Application and relevance, such folks argue, are God's work, not ours. This type of preaching often produces smarter sinners but doesn't necessarily penetrate the heart.

Effective preaching is certainly built on a biblical and theological foundation, but it also should exhort the preacher and audience to change. Any preacher calling others to respond to God's Word should first demonstrate in some form how it has impacted them. TED Talks remind us of the importance and power of connecting the message with the person delivering it.

Effective Communicators End Intentionally

Coming to the end of his TED Talk called "Why I Became an Actor," David Wenham concludes, "I'm an actor. Why? Because stories make us human."[4] In his final statement he brings full circle the purpose of his twelve-minute message. With just four words—"stories make us human"—the speaker summarizes the whole purpose of his talk. His conclusion is succinct, memorable, and intentional. The audience hearing this conclusion responds with applause.

Watch most TED Talks, and you will observe a pattern similar to that of Wenham's. Generally, in the last thirty seconds of the speech, the heart of the speaker comes through with a crisp statement, an assertion, a summary, or a challenge. TED Talks provide good examples of how to land a message effectively.

A good conclusion is like landing a plane. It should be smooth and intentional. As preachers, we must not only prepare the body of a sermon but also end our sermon well. More often than not, however, I hear sermons in which the preacher enters a long, drawn-out flight pattern that has them slowly circling and descending but taking way too long to reach the ground. Effective sermons should end intentionally.

A sermon should end by answering the big questions it raised in the introduction. The conclusion should provide a summary of the main idea(s) being communicated. It should provide both clarity and challenge. TED presenters want listeners to leave with some key ideas ringing in their ears. Preachers would do well to follow their lead.

CONCLUSION
What's the Recipe for Your Favorite Go-To Sermon?

SAM CHAN

M y wife, Stephanie, loves to make a cobbler for dessert. She learned the recipe when we were living in Chicago. It's easy to make. The basic ingredients are typical of what you find in most desserts: flour, butter, sugar, baking powder, and milk. It's also versatile. If she adds peaches, then it's a peach cobbler. If she adds pears, then it's a pear cobbler. If she adds blueberries—you get the idea.

The cobbler is my wife's go-to dish for whenever she cooks a dessert. If we invite people over for a meal, she makes cobbler. If we have to bring a dish to someone else's dinner, my wife makes cobbler. If we go to a school fair—again, you get the idea.

The only problem is that my wife often gets the proportion of ingredients mixed up. If she doubles the amount of flour because we're cooking for a larger crowd than usual, she will forget to double the baking powder. If she triples the amount of butter, she will forget to triple the milk. As a result, we end up with some sort of dessert, but it's no longer a cobbler. It's still a great-tasting dessert. We simply have to rename it. If it's flat, we call it a pancake. If it's shaped like a brick, we call it a loaf. If it's round, we call it a muffin. If it's puffy, we call it a soufflé. If it's crumbly, we call it a ... crumble. Many desserts have essentially the same ingredients. But we call them different names according to their shapes, sizes, and ingredient proportions.

Maybe it's the same with sermons. We have names for all kinds of sermons—expository, propositional, didactic, inductive, deductive, narrative, first-person, storytelling, and topical. But they're more similar than we realize. They should all contain the same ingredients: biblical truth, illustrations, examples, personal insights, stories, worldly wisdom, cultural exegesis, practical advice, and contemporary relevancy.

The differences between these sermon types come down to shape, sequence of information, and ingredient proportions. If a sermon begins with biblical truth and then traces that to cultural relevancy, we might call it an expository sermon. But if we flip the sequence, and the sermon begins with cultural relevancy and then traces that to a biblical truth, then we might call it a topical sermon.

What we do in topical preaching is not too different from what we're already doing in expository preaching. We already have the ingredients that we need. We just need to double or triple some ingredients and throw in less of others.

This book has taken you farther. It has equipped you with additional tools and skills for topical preaching. It has fired up your imagination with some practical examples. And it has empowered you to take your ingredients and skills and try out new recipes. Hopefully, by now you no longer dread giving a topical sermon you've been asked to preach, and instead feel excited to do so.

We hope and pray that your topical sermon will rise like a soufflé. And if all fails, you can always call it a pancake.

APPENDIX 1

Topical Preaching and the COVID-19 Pandemic

SAM CHAN

B y the time this book comes out, we hope, the COVID-19 pandemic will be well and truly over. But as we write this book, in 2020 and 2021, there's still no guarantee the pandemic will be over quickly. Whenever we think we've flattened the curve, the virus surges back with yet another wave. Even though we now have vaccines, it's still a race between the vaccine and viral variants. But even when the pandemic is a distant memory and we've all moved on to a new normal, the influence of this global event will be felt in all aspects of life. Preaching, I suspect, will be no different.

In this section I will outline some ways that my preaching changed during the COVID-19 pandemic. Like it or not, some of these changes will continue for years to come. There will be no going back to "normal"—the way we preached before 2020. Instead we will have a post-normal way of preaching.[1]

MY AUDIENCE'S CULTURAL STORYLINE CHANGED

At the level of cultural exegesis, I needed at least to read and interpret what COVID-19 was doing to the Western cultural storyline. The key features of the West's storyline I took for granted included rugged individualism, freedom, choice, and certainty. But the pandemic dismantled that storyline. It replaced individualism with collective responsibility, freedom with lockdowns, choice with restrictions, and certainty with uncertainty. Suddenly we couldn't plan what we were going to do next week—let alone next year. Travel, work, and vacation plans were left in tatters. We had no control over our destiny. Personal autonomy was exposed to be an illusion.

As a result, the Western storyline was deconstructed. Like a house of Jenga blocks, it crumbled and fell. While Asian cultures were largely willing to forego individual rights for government control and embrace collective responsibility for the sake of communal well-being, Western cultures chafed at the idea of lockdowns and masks. While Asian cultures are largely comfortable with a high level of contingency, Western cultures required a high level of autonomy and control. (Think of how you can control a clock in American sports such as football and basketball—down to a tenth of a second!) As a result, Western countries fared disproportionately worse during the global pandemic.[2]

Prior to the pandemic the storyline of the West was one of infinite progress. We put people on the moon. We had seedless watermelons. We had driverless cars. We were invincible. But overnight we discovered that we were powerless against an invisible virus. It felt like we had gone backward—all the way back to the 1918 flu pandemic. Our story of progress was replaced by one of regression.

My sermons needed to acknowledge this new cultural storyline of uncertainty. There was no guarantee of a better future. We weren't necessarily going to live longer, own more things, or be smarter. Our happily ever after was taken away by a tiny virus, and I don't expect that storyline to quickly revert to the old one once vaccinations are widespread and restaurants reopen.

MY AUDIENCE'S EMOTIONAL NEEDS CHANGED

But it wasn't only our macro Western storyline that changed. Most of us did not fare well at a micro, individual level. I work a few days a week as a medical doctor. Prior to the pandemic this was a safe, secure, high-status job. But during the pandemic, being a healthcare worker was a danger- ous occupation because we were at high risk of encountering the virus. Our job security also became shaky. The government shut down elective surgery without any warning. We were left without an income for several weeks. At the time we didn't know if it would be weeks, months, or years. It felt like we were falling down a hole without knowing when we would hit the bottom. Many other professions experienced similar levels of uncertainty, and some, like the food service industry, fared worse.

Therefore it's understandable that mental health declined during the pandemic; there were increased levels of stress, anxiety, and depression.[3] These days when I preach, my audience is likely not coping well on the inside, in private. They are putting on a brave face, but deep down they probably are not doing well. As a result, my preaching can explore these different emotional needs of my audience.

Here I learned a lot from a sermon Timothy Keller once preached on Acts 16, in which three types of people are evangelized by Paul and Silas. First, we have Lydia the businessperson who is reasoned into the gospel with a discussion. Second, we have the servant girl who is under the control of an evil spirit and earthly masters. But she has a powerful encounter with Jesus and is set free. Third, we have the jailer who fails at his job. He is shamed and dishonored. But he sees a way of life that works in Paul and Silas and wants to experience the shalom they enjoy.

Prior to the pandemic much of our preaching was similar to that of Paul and Silas to Lydia. We used reason, discussion, and logic. But during the pandemic our audience became more like the servant girl, gripped by the fear and control of the dark, the unknown, the unseen. Now my preaching can offer them the same freedom that Paul and Silas offered the servant girl. Jesus has power over a virus. Also, our audience experienced much shame during the pandemic—even hoarding alcohol and toilet paper! Many of us don't like who we became during the pandemic.[4] But our preaching can now offer them the same shalom Paul and Silas offered the jailer.

THE TOPICS OF MY SERMONS CHANGED

During 2020 and 2021, COVID-19 dominated blogs, podcasts, news feeds, and social media. My preaching needed to address the virus as a topic. It was the hot topic of the year. To not mention COVID-19 would have been tone-deaf to what was going on in the hearts and minds of my audience.

I was given the topic "Fear and Uncertainty" to speak on at a pub for a TED-style message to a mixed audience of nonbelievers and believers. I was sharing the platform with a state politician—a member of the House of Representatives. He would give the government's point of view, and I would give the Christian point of view.

The date was March 2020, just days before a total lockdown. But the event had been organized half a year earlier, before there was a COVID-19 outbreak and before most people had even heard of a coronavirus. Both the politician and I had prepared to speak on topics such as the economic recession, unemployment, and the cost of living. Those were the big things causing fear and uncertainty until February 2020.

But by the time the event arrived, we were in a pandemic. There was a feeling of impending doom. Panic was setting in. People were beginning to hoard supplies. Suddenly my topic was no longer the economic recession. It was COVID-19, whether I liked it or not.

Sample Sermon: Fear and Uncertainty

(Available at https://youtu.be/iLl4gKBmSQc.)

Here is the talk I gave at a pub on the topic "Fear and Uncertainty" in March 2020. In the introduction I set up the talk's question as, "Should I be afraid of the future?" After all, we have so much to be afraid about: economic recessions, loss of lifestyle, and now a global pandemic. So how afraid should we be of the future?

In my first point I affirmed my audience's fears. It is good to be afraid. Fear is what keeps us alive from snakes, spiders, and saber-toothed tigers. Fear stops us from taking stupid risks. Fear makes us study for exams and prepare wisely for the future. We need a reasonable amount of fear to function well. This is why the Bible tells us that the fear of the Lord is a wise thing—it puts us in a healthy relationship with God and his universe.

But in my second point I noted that it's hard to know what exactly is a reasonable fear. Peter Sandman, a risk advisor, says the fears of our hearts (emotion) and heads (reason) are usually out of synch.[5] When our hearts are afraid of things our heads aren't afraid of—our hearts fear shark attacks even though our heads tell us those attacks are highly unlikely—then that is an example of an irrational fear. But when our hearts aren't afraid of something our heads tell us we should be afraid of—we are more likely to die from cigarette smoking than from a terrorist hijacking—that is an example of an irrational calm. In both examples our hearts are usually wrong, but our heads are right.

But what if, for a change, our hearts are right but our heads are wrong? Sandman says this is what happens in a pandemic. Our heads don't want to panic in case we look silly or are guilty of overreacting. Yet our hearts feel that maybe we do need to fear this virus, sooner rather than later! But here's the thing: we can't ever know for sure. And that is the essence of fear—the loss of certainty and control.

But what if someone else is in control? In my final point I explained that we have three choices. First, I have to control everything, which is pretty much the Western storyline. Second, there is no one in control; control is merely an illusion. Third, the Christian worldview gives us a different choice: there is a loving and powerful God who is in control, and that frees us up to control what is our responsibility to control. We need to take precautions—wearing a mask, washing hands, social distancing. But we also have to trust God with everything we can't control, such as how long this pandemic will last.

You may have heard this saying: "Peace isn't being in control. Peace is knowing that someone else is in control." That is what God offers us. Someone else is in control. Or maybe you've heard another saying: "The opposite of fear is love. Fear came knocking at the door.

Love answered. And fear ran away." That is what God offers us. At the end of the day, no matter what happens, we know we are loved by God. My biggest priority is to worry about my relationship with God. That is something I can control. This is why Jesus can say something like, "Do not worry. . . . But seek first his kingdom. . . . Do not worry about tomorrow, for tomorrow will worry about itself" (Matt. 6:25–34).

Sample Sermon: What COVID-19 Teaches Us about Christmas
(Available at: https://youtu.be/GJa1oxJxCiM.)

In December 2020 my Christmas sermon was titled "How Can I Find Joy in a Joyless Year? What COVID Teaches Us about Christmas." I preached this sermon to mixed audiences—believers and nonbelievers—in workplaces. I also preached it at my church on Christmas day.

In the introduction I recalled how I once gave my wife a vacuum cleaner for Christmas. It was the latest cordless model. I thought my wife would be impressed, but she was thoroughly unimpressed. That was a joyless Christmas. But the Christmas of 2020 promises to be even more joyless, especially with the pandemic. So our question is this: "How can I find joy in a joyless year?"

In my first point I affirmed the audience's lack of joy. Twenty twenty was indeed a year of unmet expectations. Our plans for work, school, sports, travel, and vacations were canceled. But isn't that what Christmas is all about? The original Christmas was also one of unmet expectations. Joseph and Mary couldn't find a room. And I'm sure baby Jesus cried and cried all night, despite what the Christmas carols tell us.

In my second point I said that 2020 was the year that forced us to slow down and recalibrate. I once put big wheels on my Jeep. As a result, when I thought I was going 55 mph, I was probably doing 65 mph. I couldn't work out why every other car was going much slower than me. That's when I realized I needed to recalibrate my speedometer to my bigger wheels and slow down.

That's exactly what COVID-19 did to us. It forced us to slow down and recalibrate. We were stuck at home and couldn't travel, so we got back into things that take time: making sourdough, cleaning out the house, and exercise. It forced us to declutter our lives, get back to basics, and concentrate on what's most important.

Isn't this what the original Christmas was all about? Jesus Christ, the Son of God, born in a manger. Talk about keeping it real. No baby showers. No Instagram photos. No relatives or friends. Just a few shepherds and barn animals. It was a moment of decluttering.

In my final point I explained that COVID-19 exposed the quality of our relationships. During the lockdown we all became experts at Zoom meetings. We knew how to fake our background. We knew how to fake what we were wearing—just worry about your shirt and not your pants. We even knew how to fake our attention—let's face it, many of us were on YouTube or Minecraft during our meetings. But there's one thing we couldn't fake during the COVID-19 pandemic: the quality of our relationships. The lockdown was a great time with our roommates, buddies, families, and spouses—if our relationships were healthy and functional. But lockdown was a horrible time if our relationships were stressful. It exposed our loneliness, our dysfunctional relationships. It showed we lacked someone to love us.

In the end, once you strip everything away, happiness comes from the quality of our relationships. Life's ultimate question is this: "Am I loved, and do I have someone to love?" But that was the whole point of the original Christmas. Jesus comes to us so that he can be that ultimate Somebody—someone to love us, and someone for us to love.

And that is why the Bible calls Jesus "Immanuel"! He is "God with us." Christmas is about God being with us so we have Someone to love and Someone to love us.

In the conclusion I pointed out that COVID-19 closed a lot of doors. But it also opened a lot of other doors. So this Christmas, more than any other, was a time to close the door on sin, guilt, shame, and brokenness. And it was a time to open the door to peace with God—Someone to love us, and Someone for us to love.

Sample Sermon: Easter 2021 and COVID-19

(Available at: https://youtu.be/bH7h6oIRoIY.)

In 2021 my Easter sermon was titled "How Easter Gives Me the Reboot I'm Looking For." I preached this sermon to mixed audiences—believers and nonbelievers—in workplaces.

In the introduction I pointed out that COVID-19 got us doing the strangest things: exercising, making sourdough, and missing working in the office. But there's one thing we don't miss about the office: the photocopier, especially with its paper jams.

Isn't that how 2020 felt? It was the paper jam year. Wildfires. Floods. Pandemic. So 2021 feels like the year of the reset. This is when we can reboot and start all over again. But that's not how 2021 started. We still have wildfires and floods, and there's no guarantee the COVID-19 pandemic is over. Twenty twenty-one has begun not as a reboot but as a repeat. I then set up this question: "How can we find the reboot we're looking for?" Then I suggested, "What if Easter is the only guarantee of finding the reboot we're looking for?" But how?

In my first point I affirmed the need to grieve. I said, "Easter tells us that, yep, last year was messed up." I explained how, in sports, we need bad guys. In baseball the bad guys are the Yankees. In basketball it's the Lakers. In football it's the Patriots. And in 2020 the bad guy was COVID-19.

But in Mother Nature there are no bad guys. In dinosaurs versus asteroids, there are no bad guys. It's just something that happened. Get over it. It's Mother Nature doing what Mother Nature does. In grizzly bears versus salmons, there are no bad guys. It's just something that happens. Get over it. It's Mother Nature doing what Mother Nature does. Using the same logic, in COVID-19 versus humans, there are no bad guys.

But something in us says no! The pandemic was bad. People lost jobs. Children missed out on school. Loved ones died. But where do we get this from? We can't get it from Mother Nature. We need Easter to tell us that this was messed up.

At the original Easter, Jesus became one of us. He was disturbed by sickness. He sobbed at his friend's funeral. He called out religious hypocrites. And he groaned in agony when it was his turn to die. He sweated drops of blood. He cried out, "Why?" to God as he hung on a cross to die. Jesus affirms our need to grieve, groan, get angry, and cry out, "Why?" This world is messed up and isn't how it should be.

In my second point I said that Easter gives us the hope we're looking for. I'm hopeless at marathons. My times get slower and slower. When I ran my last marathon, I ended up unconscious in a medical tent, with an IV drip. After that marathon my wife asked me, "Why do you do these things if you're so bad at them?" Ouch! What a knife to the heart. But my wife had a point. Why do I do these things when I'm so hopeless at them?

If all we have is Mother Nature, then we have no hope. This is a world where bodies age and get slower. Societies break down and collapse. The universe is destined to implode. So why do we think life will get any better?

Yet Barack Obama famously said, "The arc of history is long . . . and it bends towards justice." And so we march for justice at Black Lives Matter rallies. We call out oppressors in the #MeToo movement. We call on people to care for the environment and make a difference.

We live as if there is a direction to this universe. There is hope. There is the chance for a reboot. But we can get that only from the Easter story, in which Jesus rose from the dead and promised to come back again to right all wrongs. Easter tells us that the arc of history bends toward justice, love, mercy, hope, and freedom.

But where does that leave us? In my final point I said that Easter gives us the personal reboot we're looking for. Think about it: without Easter we are stressed at unprecedented levels. We have to maintain a facade of perfectionism. We have to virtue signal and demonstrate our worthiness and loyalty to our tribe. We fear being shamed, cut off, or canceled. There is no forgiveness if we've ever done wrong. That's why no one says sorry anymore—there's no point.

A Seismic Shift in Communication

In the history of the Christian church, there have been seismic shifts in communications, with profound ramifications. The first seismic shift was Pax Romana and the Roman roads. The effect was this: when the apostle Paul wrote one letter from a prison cell, possibly in Rome, to a church in Ephesus, that letter was widely circulated and read by many other churches, both then and now. Paul's letter was read by the original audience in Ephesus in AD 60. But it is also being read more than two thousand years later by other audiences in, say, Dayton, Ohio. I'm sure Paul had never heard of Dayton, Ohio, but that is now his audience, whether he intended it or not.

The second seismic shift was the invention of the printing press. The effect was this: Luther wrote and preached a sermon in 1522 to a church in Wittenberg, Germany. But that same sermon is now read five hundred years later by a shopkeeper in Arequipa, Peru, or a university professor in Nairobi, Kenya.

The third seismic shift is the COVID-19 pandemic. It has forced us to preach to camera. In the same way that Luther's sermons became tracts, our sermons have become videos. In the same way that Luther's sermons reached a wider audience than intended, our sermons are now uploaded onto the internet. The sermons we preach today will go to a wider audience tomorrow, next week, next year, and next century—in Sydney, Shanghai, and San Diego.

Our intended audience has shifted. The definitions of space and time have shifted. We thought we were preaching only to the 9:00 a.m. congregation at our local church. We are now doing way more than that.

But Jesus is perfect, so we don't have to pretend to be perfect. More than that, Jesus became our scapegoat. He became the called-out, shunned, shamed, canceled one. He took our place so we can be included. We can find belonging. We can find forgiveness. And now we can belong to Team Jesus.

In the conclusion I talk about the Slinky effect in rush-hour traffic. There are moments when we speed up to ridiculous speeds, only to slam on our brakes. It's like a Slinky expanding and contracting. Why do we do this? Why do we rush, knowing we're going to have to stop again? Will it be different this time? Somehow we always think so.

Isn't that what life is like? We rush from place to place. We promise ourselves that this year will be different—this year I will fix myself up, fix my relationships, and fix my well-being. Then we hit gridlock again.

What if Easter gives us a genuine reboot? And not just a reboot but a resurrection—a rebirth, in which our old self dies with Jesus and a new self rises with him. In this new self we are the person we want to be, the person God needs us to be.

PREACHING TO CAMERA: THE NEW NORMAL

When we entered lockdown during the pandemic, we faced the new challenge of preaching to a camera. This happened almost overnight. We had only days to adjust to this new normal. Until COVID-19 many of us had clocked up our ten thousand hours of preaching experience. We were experts at this!

But now we were starting all over again. We had zero prior experience. There were no experts to consult. We all became newbies again. There were no textbooks or manuals to consult. In the entire history of the church, we have never had to preach to a camera from our studies, bedrooms, or closets. This was n = 0.

So we had to pivot. Yes, *pivot* became the new buzzword. But it wasn't only the preacher who needed to pivot. Everything in our world of preaching also pivoted. Here are some features of our new normal, whether we like it or not. We can choose to see these as threats to our status quo, or we can see them as opportunities to leverage, in the same way that Paul used Pax Romana and Luther used the printing press.

First, we pivoted from analog to digital. Prior to COVID-19, people first encountered our preaching in person. They came to our church, conference, or event. They heard us preach live. If they were interested, they later went online to check out our other resources—the church website, the archived sermons. The sequence was analog to digital.

But now, because of COVID-19, it's the other way around. People first encounter our preaching online. They hear us preaching to them on the internet. We are a digital face and voice on their electronic device—phone, tablet, laptop. If they are interested, they click on a link for more information, perhaps to contact the church. When things are safe, they might meet us in person at church. They might sign up to attend a small group, conference, or seminar. But only because they first heard us online. The sequence is now digital to analog.[6]

Second, our studies pivoted to become our studios. Before the pandemic the study was our place for sitting at a desk, reading books, and writing sermons. The light source came from behind us, over our shoulders, to light up our reading material. Our bookshelves, overflowing with books, lined our walls.

But now our study is our place for producing video content. The light source comes from in front of us to light up our faces. Bookshelves look horrible in the background because they are "visual noise." We replaced our bookshelves with plants, family photos, and fairy lights.

Third, our sermons pivoted to become videos. We had to match our medium. Previously, we could get away with a thirty- to forty-minute monologue because the church hall felt like a classroom (often it *was* a classroom). The medium—preacher at a pulpit with a captive audience sitting in chairs—produced the expectation of a didactic monologue.

We've Become Video Producers

My father can't type. He wasn't expected to. When he was at college, he handwrote his assignments, like everyone did. When he was the chairperson at my church, he handwrote the minutes for the meetings. When he was a doctor, he dictated his reports to a tape recorder, and a secretary typed up his reports on a typewriter. Back in those days, they paid people to type. Typing was a specialized skill that only a few Jedi Knights possessed. You went to typing college to learn how to type.

That all changed in the 1990s with the computer revolution and the arrival of personal computers and word processor programs. Suddenly we were expected to type up assignments, minutes, and reports. No one else was going to do it for us. We were expected to know how to do this for ourselves. Elementary students had to type up their projects. Operating a word processor became a basic life skill.

As a result, many parents and grandparents were left floundering. Many had to ask their children to operate computers and word processors for them. I still remember typing up reports for my father before he was able to upskill and do it for himself.

A similar revolution has happened in the 2010s—with the arrival of easy-to-use video editing programs—and has been accelerated by the COVID-19 pandemic of the 2020s. Suddenly we are expected to be able to produce videos. Last year my eldest son, aged twelve, was required to submit his school geography project not on paper but as a video. This is now a basic skill.

As preachers, we are expected to produce our sermons as videos. Last year, during the COVID-19 pandemic, I told many churches and conferences that I could no longer preach at their event as planned because of travel restrictions. They simply responded by asking me to send my talk to them as a recorded video.

> Video editing programs have done to us what word processors did to our parents and grandparents. Like them, we can get away for a while by asking the nearest teenager (or in many cases, a nine-year-old niece or nephew) to help us out. But sooner or later we will have to upskill and do this for ourselves.

But now that we're a big head on a screen—often a tiny screen!—the expectations are different. This means our sermons need to be shorter. We have to get to the point sooner. The medium sets different expectations, and we need to adjust the shape and speed of our sermons to match.

Fourth, our church services and conferences also pivoted to become videos. Before the pandemic the church service was a physical event that was attended in person. Most people showed up late. The result was that we designed the service as if people would come late. We began with a few songs to a half-full hall. Then we read announcements. We had a time of greeting. Why? Because we were stalling! We were waiting for the latecomers to turn up. The sermon didn't start until thirty minutes after the service started. We preached the sermon as the climactic end of the service.

But now church services and conferences are online. People show up whenever they want, in their pajamas. If they're late, they can rewind. They start the video whenever they want. But here's the thing: they might not want to start the video. They're too busy. Or it's inconvenient. And even if they start the video, if they become disinterested or their children in the room become disinterested, they will log off, sometimes after only a few minutes. This is how this medium works.[7] The result is that we now must design the service as if people will log off. If we think the sermon is the climax of the church service, then it had better come sooner rather than later, before people log off.

The Medium Determines the Form

Have you ever wondered why a pop song is usually three minutes and thirty seconds (3:30) long? Why isn't it ten minutes? Why isn't it twenty-three minutes? Why is it usually 3:30?

There's nothing sacred about 3:30. The simple answer is that this is the length that fits on a 78 rpm phonograph disc. The technology and medium determined the length of the song.

It also determined the form of the song. Most pop songs use this traditional form: verse-verse-chorus-verse-chorus-bridge-chorus-chorus.

There's plenty of time in the 3:30 to build to the big climax of the final two choruses. The listener is not going anywhere. They are listening to the phonograph in their comfy chair. Or they're listening on an FM radio while driving a car.

This has been the way of pop songs from the 1960s to the 2010s. But something changed in the 2020s. TikTok.[8]

People no longer listen to pop music on FM radio. Instead they hear it on TikTok (twelve seconds), in memes (five seconds), in ads (thirty seconds), in club anthems (two and a half minutes), and on streaming services.

The artist now must grab your attention at the start of the song. They also need you to listen all the way to the end of the song, before you've had a chance to log off.

The result is this: the average pop song is now less than three minutes. Many are less than two minutes. The form of the song has also changed. The good stuff has to come first. "Don't bore us; get to the chorus." A typical song is now verse-chorus or simply chorus-chorus-chorus.

The technology and medium determine the length, form, and pace of the song.

It's the same with our preaching. Before COVID-19, when we preached in halls to people sitting in chairs (where it was rude to walk out in the middle of a sermon), our sermons were twenty to forty minutes long. They also had the form point-point-point-application. There's nothing sacred about this formula. It was determined by the medium.

But now our sermons are videos. People listen to us from the tiny screens on their phones. The technology and medium will also determine the length, form, and pace of our sermon.

Our sermons might need to be ten to fifteen minutes long. We say in a sentence what we used to say in a paragraph. We say in five words what used to take us ten words. Our form might also need to change to point-application-application-application. Or simply application. We have to hold them quick, early, and hard in our sermon, before they log off.

HOW TO PREACH TO A CAMERA

When we entered lockdown in March 2020, I—like you—frantically searched online for "how to preach to camera." I found good resources by Glen Scrivener from Speak Life,[9] Karl Faase from Olive Tree Media,[10] and Dominic Steele from the Pastor's Heart,[11] but not much else that was specifically for preachers at that moment.

But at the same time I was clocking up many hours of personal experience in talking to camera. The lockdown opened more doors for my preaching than it closed. Preaching events that were previously impossible were now possible because I could preach to camera from my own study. There was no need for travel or accommodation. Suddenly I was preaching—either livestreamed or recorded—to churches, high school chapels, college groups, seminars, workers, and conferences. In the early stages of lockdown, in a handful of weeks, I spoke at many events in the UK, Europe, Asia, and the USA.[12] The concepts of space and time were blurred. If it was 1:00 p.m. for you in Wheaton or 7:00 p.m. for you in Oxford, then it was 4:00 a.m. for me in my study in Sydney, but *the next day*. I was coming to you from the future!

Within a few months I discovered a repeatable and reliable formula for how to talk to camera. Much of this can be found in *The Post-Covid Playbook*—a short series of videos and pdf files that I created for City Bible Forum. What follows is only a small summary of my findings. For the rest please check out *The Post-Covid Playbook*.[13]

First, when it comes to how to speak to camera, we do everything we can to hold our audience's attention. Our audience is naturally drawn to our eyes if we are looking at them. It's a basic human instinct to look at someone's eyes if they're also looking at us. So we do everything we can to maximize eye contact with our audience. Obviously, this means we look at the camera lens. But this is way harder than it sounds. We ourselves naturally want to look at the faces we see on our laptop screen. Once I taped a fluorescent green paper arrow next to my camera lens to remind me to look at the camera and not the laptop screen. But my eyes then kept looking at the arrow and not the camera lens. There's actually a proverb that says, "Only a fool looks at the arrow and not what it's pointing at"! It made only a fraction-of-an-inch difference, but on the video it was obvious that I was no longer looking directly at the audience.

This, of course, means that it's best if we can speak without notes. I know that this isn't possible for most preachers. I also know that this hot-button issue causes a thermonuclear meltdown at preaching forums. But if ever there was a time to take the plunge, then surely a global pandemic is the time to get out of our comfort zone and preach without notes. I preach without notes because I've told myself, "Hey, if you can't remember what you're going to say, how do you expect your audience to remember?" It also forces me to trim down my sermon to only what is memorable, which increases the signal-to-noise ratio.

We also have to smile. The medium of talking to a camera exaggerates our grumpiness. So we have to compensate by smiling—even slightly more than we think we need to. It reminds me of the time I did radio work. I was told to exaggerate my smile while talking. Even though a radio listener can't see my smile, they can "hear the smile." This means that for video work, we need to smile even more because they can both see and hear our smile.

We also speak with positive energy. I pretend the camera is an empty box and that I need to fill it with energy as I speak. I don't mean that we shout. I mean that we project energy—usually in our tone of voice. In contrast, classroom lecturers read from their notes and often tail off as they finish their sentences, ending more softly than they started. (I'm thinking of my biostatistics lectures at med school!) This is an example of negative energy. It robs the room of energy. But lecturers get away with it because they are essentially dictating while listeners write down their words. But we are now producing video content. We need to project energy to the camera.

It helps if we stand tall when we preach. I prefer standing when I give my talks to camera. If I have to sit, which is rare, then I choose a stool or place the chair on its highest setting. I don't want to slouch. Instead I do the opposite. I repeat this mantra to myself to keep my posture upright: *Head over heart, heart over pelvis.* My shoulders are back and my chest is slightly out, to project energy.

It's also important that we frame ourselves properly. Our head needs to be in the top half or, preferably, one-third of the frame. I want the audience to see at least my chest—even better, to see me from the waist up. This allows us to use our body as part of our body language. This also allows us to use our hands, which are a vital part of our nonverbal communication.

It's interesting that newsreaders are often framed with a headshot. This is because they are largely communicating information and data. In contrast, sports commentators are framed from the waist up. This is because they are communicating emotions, stories, and personalities. Our preaching is probably closer to what the sports commentators are trying to do than what the newsreaders are doing.

Ideally, we should use a different, better camera than the laptop's built-in webcam. This can be our phone's camera (see below for how to do this) or a separate webcam. It should be placed in a proper camera holder and mounted on a tripod. This makes it much easier to make adjustments to the camera angle.

Second, when it comes to what to say to camera, I've learned a lot from watching YouTubers. I may as well learn from them, since that is what we've essentially become! Most YouTubers have several things in common.

They connect relationally with the audience. They care about the audience. We can also do this by thinking of the person we are speaking to and picturing them on the other side of the camera lens that we're looking at. Then we will naturally smile, care, and connect with them.

They hook you very early with a burning question to which you want to know the answer. This might even be the first thing they say. The medium determines the form of the message. We also need to hook our audience as soon as possible.

They have a clear point. They are not merely giving us information. They are arguing for a particular viewpoint. We also need to be clear on what we're trying to say. We're not merely talking about a topic. We've got a point that we want to get across. Our sermon should have a clear direction, and it should always feel like it's moving there.

They are concise. YouTube is a tough and unforgiving medium. The audience usually checks out the length of the video before committing to watching it. If they have to choose between a three-minute video and a twenty-five-minute video, the three-minute video wins every time. Most videos are less than five minutes long.[14]

We also need to be as concise as possible. Right now we're getting away with thirty-minute sermons on video because we have relational capital with our audience: "Oh, there's Pastor Brad preaching. I love Pastor Brad!" But we're going to use up that capital pretty soon. It really has to be that we say in one sentence what used to take us a paragraph to say. Paragraphs don't belong on YouTube.

But the biggest thing I've learned from watching YouTubers is that they really care about what they're saying. When they talk about the topic, they are filled with energy and excitement. They can't wait to talk about it. They really care about their subject. We can follow their lead by crafting a sermon that is so true, so good, so beautiful that we can't wait to deliver it. We are genuinely excited about what we're going to say.

Third, when it comes to filming ourselves, get rid of the bookshelf! I say this as a joke, kind of. There's nothing inherently wrong with a bookshelf as a background, but it's certainly a distraction. We need to do everything we can to increase the signal-to-noise ratio for our viewers. For most of us it will mean exactly that: get rid of the bookshelf. We don't want to distract our audience with visual clutter.

By now we've worked out how to light ourselves well. We want soft lighting from front. A simple fix is to use lamps—covered with cloth or shopping bags—to light up our face. We can also backlight ourselves with some hidden lamps that illuminate us from behind. This helps to contrast us with the background.

We should also have already worked out that the camera needs to be at eye level. The newbie mistake is to have the laptop camera shooting up at us from desk level. This unfortunately distorts our head, making it look like a triangle. It also gives us very large nostrils (and nostril hairs). If we have to use a laptop camera, then we need to place the laptop on a shoebox or some books to elevate it to eye level.

When it comes to sound, the best bang-for-buck investment is to buy an external microphone. It could cost five dollars or fifty dollars, but it will make all the difference. Its sound quality will be far superior to that of the laptop's or camera's built-in microphone. Our audience can put up with poor video quality, but they cannot put up with poor sound quality for long. They eventually fatigue and fade out.

We also need to pay attention to what we're wearing. No more patterns, spots, or stripes because they create weird visual effects. Instead it's best to wear solid colors that contrast us with our background.

TAKING IT TO THE NEXT LEVEL: HOW TO USE OBS AND NDI

If you really want to engage your audience, watch these sample sermons that I preached—to a mix of believers and nonbelievers—to camera from my study or living room.

- "What Would Jesus Say to the Broken?" (recorded): *https://youtu.be/isjt1BFlCOk*
- "What Would Jesus Say to the Afraid?" (livestreamed): *https://youtu.be/e6A0t0stfKM* (starts at 5:08)
- "How Can We Find Joy in a Joyless Year?" (recorded): *https://youtu.be/GJa1oxJxCiM*
- "How Easter Can Give You the Reboot You're Looking For" (recorded): *https://youtu.be/bH7h6oIRoIY*

What do you notice about these videos? I've been able to control the size and shape of both my headshot and the PowerPoint slides. I've been able to change the slides with a clicker. I've also been able to maintain eye contact. And the video quality is better than what you get from a laptop camera. I've achieved all this through two simple but effective tools: OBS and NDI.

How to Use OBS

OBS stands for Open Broadcaster Software. It is a free and open-source software for producing video. This is the secret to producing videos in which you get to control the size and shape of your headshot and PowerPoint slides.

Step 1: Download and Set Up OBS

Download OBS from *https://obsproject.com.*

Go to these YouTube tutorials to set up OBS:

Tech Gumbo
https://youtu.be/DTk99mHDX_I
Right TV (parts 1–3)
https://youtu.be/5pJrHsBLKc8
https://youtu.be/vV6I-IU7oz4
https://youtu.be/BtzDdZTc0mU
Awall
https://youtu.be/hk7W9ECtpZE

Step 2: How to Use PowerPoint Slides with OBS

Watch this short clip: *https://youtu.be/C8f0tPdcC8s.*

Now when you present the slideshow, it won't fill up your whole screen. This way you can continue to see and use both OBS and PowerPoint at the same time.

Step 3: Turn OBS into a Virtual Camera

Watch this clip: *https://youtu.be/bfrknjDzukI.*

Step 4: See What Others Are Doing

For example, I watched this: Nick Nimmin, *https://youtu.be/j2H zbY8E4yQ.*

This is obviously a bit too much for what we're trying to do. But it showed me relevant possibilities to use for my preaching.

How to Use NDI

NDI stands for Network Device Interface. It allows me to convert my phone or tablet into a webcam. This is great news because my phone's camera is far superior in resolution and dynamic range to my laptop's webcam.

Step 1: Download NDI HX to Turn Your Phone into a Webcam

Buy and download NDI HX to turn your phone into a webcam. You can also make an additional purchase and download NDI Capture, which allows you to share the screen of your phone or tablet.

Step 2: Download NDI Virtual Input onto Your Laptop or Computer

Download (free) and install NDI Virtual Input onto your laptop or computer. Now your laptop/computer will detect your phone's camera (if you run NDI HX) and your phone/tablet's screen (if you run NDI Capture).

Step 3: Using NDI as a Video Source for OBS

Watch this tutorial: *https://youtu.be/1OyfzQ-sHRs*.

You'll have to install this plug-in to get NDI to talk to OBS: *https://github.com/Palakis/obs-ndi/releases/tag/4.9.0*

Step 4: See What Others Are Doing

For example, here's Eddie Woo using the following (I reckon) on *www.youtube.com/watch?v=2CaVZyCkcr4*:

1. OBS
2. NDI HX as his webcam (for his face)
3. NDI Capture on his tablet (for the math stuff)

If you watch again my "How Can We Find Joy in a Joyless Year?" *(https://youtu.be/GJa1oxJxCiM)*, I'm using:

1. NDI HX on my iPhone (which converts my iPhone into a webcam)
2. My OBS uses the iPhone webcam as its video source
3. And then I recorded the video from OBS

If you watch again my "What Would Jesus Say to the Broken?" *(https://youtu.be/isjt1BFlCOk)*, I'm using:

1. NDI HX on my iPhone (to convert it into a webcam)
2. OBS for the split screen of my face and the PowerPoint slides
3. Zoom recording for the wider shots of me only (with no slides)

If you watch again my livestreamed "What Would Jesus Say to the Afraid?" *(https://youtu.be/e6A0t0stfKM?t=307)*, I'm using:

1. NDI HX on my iPhone (which converts my iPhone into a webcam)
2. My OBS uses the iPhone webcam as its video source
3. And then I streamed my video from OBS to Zoom (or whatever video conference platform is being used)

Anyway, this is a lot to take in at once. There is a steep learning curve with OBS. But once you've mastered it, you'll never go back to what you were doing before. You will love how you can set up the look and feel of your video to suit you and your presentation style.

CONCLUSION

In Acts 8:1, a great persecution broke out against the church. It forced the apostles to flee to Judea, Samaria, and ultimately the ends of the earth. This was always God's plan—that the apostles take his gospel to Jerusalem, Judea, Samaria, and to the ends of the earth (1:8). Until now, the gospel had stayed largely in Jerusalem. Suddenly the gospel was breaking out from Jerusalem and going to the ends of the earth. But it took a great persecution to be the disruptive force to make it happen.

In 2020, a global pandemic broke out all over the world. It forced preachers into isolation, where they preached to camera from their studies, bedrooms, and closets while wearing pajamas, sweatpants, or (shock!) camouflage cargo shorts. Until now our preaching had stayed largely in our churches, schools, and conference centers. But now our preaching is streamed to all parts of the world. People are listening to us from their studies, bedrooms, and closets. They are probably also wearing pajamas, sweatpants, or camo cargo shorts. But now they're no longer only in our hometown. They might be listening to us from Papua New Guinea, Portugal, or Poland. They might be listening to us today, tomorrow, or next century. Our sermons have become a URL link that people copy, paste, and send to their friends. Our sermons are like the Gideon's Bible that sits in a hotel bedside drawer—at first someone might not click on the link, but maybe at 2:00 a.m. they just might.

My IT friends say that we've had the technology to do this—stream our sermons—for the past decade. But until now it's seemed too hard, and our sermons stayed in-person only. Now our sermons are being beamed all over the world. Our mediums are now YouTube, TikTok, and Twitch. There is no going back. This is the new normal. But it took a global pandemic to make it happen.

APPENDIX 2

The Benefits and Limitations of Expository Preaching

MALCOLM GILL

Several years ago I was asked to preach at a medium-size suburban church in my hometown of Sydney. As is my practice, I went through some standard questions with the inviting church: "What passage or topic would you like me to preach on?" "Who is the audience?" "Is this part of a series or a one-off message?" "How long should I speak?" The church responded with their most important concern: that I preach an expository sermon. This was helpful because that is my bread-and-butter sermon.

When I asked for clarification about which part of the Bible they wanted me to exposit, they told me 1 Kings 18–22. Yes, you read that right. The church wanted me to preach on five chapters of 1 Kings in an expository manner! Given the time constraints, I figured that would give me just enough time to read the passage and conclude with an amen. When I questioned the size of the preaching unit, they explained, "We are committed to expositing the whole Bible every five years, so we need to do larger chunks to get through the Scriptures."

For this church, as with many others, expository preaching is primarily understood as the practice of working consecutively verse by verse, unit by unit, chapter by chapter, book by book through the Bible. This is a healthy and highly beneficial practice. One of the complexities, however, is defining what is meant by expository preaching. Some, like this church, understand it to be preaching through blocks of Scripture, even large ones. Others, however, understand expository preaching to be the careful practice of slowly deliberating over words and phrases, unfolding verses in a protracted manner. Rather than going through the Bible in five years, some spend that long going through one book.[1]

Expository preaching means many things to many people. Almost every preaching book—and most preachers I've encountered—claim to be doing expository preaching, yet my experiences have shown me that there is quite a bit of variation in what that looks like.

So what is expository preaching? The following definitions by Haddon Robinson, Abraham Kuruvilla, and Bryan Chapell prove helpful at this point.

> Expository preaching is the communication of a biblical concept, derived from and transmitted through a historical, grammatical, and literary study of a passage in its context, which the Holy Spirit first applies to the personality and experience of the preacher, then through the preacher, applies to the hearers.[2]

> Biblical preaching, by a leader of the church, in a gathering of Christians for worship, is the communication of the thrust of a pericope of Scripture discerned by theological exegesis, and of its application to that specific body of believers, that they may be conformed to the image of Christ, for the glory of God—all in the power of the Holy Spirit.[3]

> An expository sermon may be defined as a message whose structure and thought are derived from a biblical text, covering its scope, in order to explain how the features and context of the text disclose enduring principles for faithful thinking, living, and worship intended by the Spirit, who inspired the text.[4]

While these definitions emphasize different nuances, they collectively highlight expository preaching's emphases on deriving meaning from careful engagement of the inspired biblical text, explaining the theological and enduring thrust of the text, and seeking contemporary application of the text to both the preacher and their audience. When communicators of the Scriptures employ these skills, they best represent the heart of expository preaching.

THE BENEFITS OF EXPOSITORY PREACHING

As you'll see in the following, there are some very good reasons why one would choose to use this method of preaching. Its popularity as a preaching style isn't arbitrary, after all. Here are four that stand out most to me.

It Values God's Word

One of the most frequent lines of argument for those advocating for expository preaching is the value it places on understanding the Scriptures. Expository preaching seeks to systematically work through a passage, section by section, verse by verse. This is helpful for obvious reasons, not the least of which is that it aims to keep the preacher and listener grounded in the text of the Bible.

To truly exposit the Scriptures requires the discipline of evaluating each unit and seeking to understand the purpose of God in providing each passage. What is God saying to the original author and audience of this passage? Why is the passage structured the way it is? What is being emphasized? How does it fit within the context surrounding it? What are the significant theological ideas that rise to the top in this individual unit? These are some of the questions that the responsible expositor must deal with.

It Points People to the Glory of Christ

Expository preaching is a skill that requires not only a zooming in to look at the text in a specific historical context for a particular purpose but also a zooming out to see how the text fits within the larger framework of Scripture and salvation history. Though made up of many books, the Bible is essentially one story, and the centerpiece of that story is the person and the work of the Lord Jesus Christ. On the road to Emmaus, the resurrected Jesus appeared to two of the disciples. Luke records of Jesus that "beginning with Moses and all the Prophets, he explained to them what was said in all the Scriptures concerning himself" (Luke 24:27). While this verse is not saying that we need to find Jesus in every word or verse in the Old Testament, it is clear that Jesus understood himself and his ministry to be the fulfillment of Old Testament hope. The New Testament consolidates this by providing additional divine insight into the ramifications and significance of Jesus' life, death, and resurrection.

Expository preaching is valuable because it helps the careful student of Scripture understand how passages fit within the framework of the whole Bible. An expositor seeks to make sense of individual pieces of the puzzle by working hard to show how they fit in the larger scheme. The expositor is concerned not only with a unit but also with how that unit contributes to our understanding of God's glory shown in the finished work and person of the Lord Jesus.

It Values Every Part of the Bible

The apostle Paul, in writing to Timothy, declared, "All Scripture is God-breathed and is useful for teaching, rebuking, correcting and training in righteousness, so that the servant of God may be thoroughly equipped for every good work" (2 Tim. 3:16–17). As has been observed by others, the God-breathed Scripture the apostle is referencing is almost certainly the Old Testament. While many of us believe it is God-breathed and is useful, we wrestle a bit with the first word: all.

You see, many of us love parts of the Old Testament—the wise maxims of Proverbs, the poetic songs of the Psalter, the historical narratives of Samuel—but do we really love all of Scripture? Is that unfamiliar prophecy written to an unfamiliar people from the Ancient Near East useful? Does evaluating food or ceremonial laws in Leviticus have benefit? Do the fifteen chapters in Exodus on how to build the tabernacle have value? The answer in the mind of Paul was yes, yes, yes! All of it is "useful for teaching, rebuking, correcting and training in righteousness" (v. 16). Why? So that "the servant of God may be thoroughly equipped for every good work" (v. 17).

Another value of expository preaching is that it takes head-on parts of the Bible that we may be tempted to ignore. If I were to do a series on the Sermon on the Mount (Matthew 5–7), I would naturally run to some parts, such as the Beatitudes, for they are beautiful, rich, profound, and poetic. But I'd rather avoid other passages. I don't know many preachers who would say, "I'd love to do a sermon on forgiving enemies—or even better, on divorce!" But expository preaching requires us to preach what is there. If the passage addresses money, that's where the sermon goes. If it addresses lust, divorce, or anger, we must go there too. In this manner expository preaching sets the agenda as it follows the lead of the text. This has great merit.

It Helps the Listener Develop Skills in Reading the Bible

Several years ago I had the opportunity to serve as a visiting lecturer at a Bible college in Nepal. The institution that invited me was fairly new and was made up of bivocational pastors and gospel workers from across the country. Their twenty-five students were young in their faith, and almost all had been dramatically converted from idolatrous backgrounds. In contrast to the usual questions I received in my teaching in Australia and North America, which were largely about assessment issues, book reports, and exams, the Nepali students' questions were out of my league. They asked, "When you lead four or five people to Christ a week, how do you keep up with discipleship?" "When you go to a non-Christian's house and pray for the healing of someone with cancer in Jesus' name and they are dramatically healed, how do you then transition to share the gospel of Christ?" "When someone gives their life to Christ and are persecuted because they want to get rid of idols from their house, how do you encourage them in their faith?" Here were genuine questions from genuine people in genuine circumstances. While I was not able to answer most of their questions about these issues, there was one thing I could do to help them in their Christian maturity: I introduced them to the skills and basic patterns of reading and understanding the Bible, and I did this via expository preaching.

You see, the big challenge with the Christian communities I was working with in Nepal was not so much an issue of pragmatics, as they were already out serving in many ways. Their bigger need was to develop an understanding of how the Bible fits together. So to support the brothers and sisters in that context, I focused on the habits and processes of reading and studying the Bible in a structured way. I did so by modeling exposition in my teaching and preaching.

Because of low biblical literacy in the country, many of the pastors knew stories from the Scriptures but not really how they were connected. Sermons in this context would loosely stitch one biblical story or verse to another, with little attention given to the original audience, context, or theological issues. As I slowly and methodically exposited consecutive passages, I saw the lights begin to come on for the hearers. Though the purpose of expository preaching—or any preaching, for that matter—is not primarily to model a method, the fact that this style of preaching has certain predictable elements that can be easily reproduced is a wonderful side benefit.

THE LIMITATIONS OF EXPOSITORY PREACHING

For the foregoing reasons, among others, many have rightly heralded expository preaching as a valuable means of communicating God's Word. As with all types of communication, however, there are a few limitations to this method. Here are four that I've seen play out occasionally as I've listened to expository sermons.

It Doesn't Guarantee Biblical or Theological Accuracy

I remember reading, as a seminary student, through D. A. Carson's helpful book *Exegetical Fallacies*, only to discover that I had made most of the mistakes he had written about in the book, even in my preaching![5] The reality is, of course, that no matter how careful we are in our expository approach, there is no guarantee that our exposition of the text will be without error. Who hasn't heard a sermon that is heavy on exegesis of the text but misses the central thrust of the passage?[6] Many of us have heard or given expositions that have presented anachronistic word studies, overplayed historical reconstructions, and ingenious chiasms that, while impressive to the ear, have been wrong. As a seminary teacher once told me, "That's the problem with studying the Bible—it ruins too many good sermons!" No sermon is perfect, because we are all imperfect students.

Any sort of preaching is open to error because, as people, we are all flawed. None of us comes to any passage of Scripture or enters any preaching context without some form of bias or background that influences our sermon. The length of the passage, the constraints of time, the demographic of the audience, and the purpose of the sermon all shape the result. There is more than one correct way to preach a passage. Church history bears witness to this. Chrysostom's sermons on the Psalms are different from John Calvin's, which are different from Charles Spurgeon's, which are different from Martyn Lloyd-Jones's. Each preacher was shaped by context, training, purpose, and personal experience. None of these giants of the faith were infallible. They had different audiences, different styles of communication, different cultural contexts, and different theological shortcomings. If this was true for these historical heavyweights, how much more so for the rest of us!

To suggest that expository preaching, as a method, is a superior model of preaching just because it sticks to the Bible is overly simplistic. Yes, expository preaching focuses on working consecutively through passages, but we should always display an accompanying humility toward the text and an awareness of our own biases and shortcomings.

Expository preaching doesn't guarantee biblical fidelity any more than do other preaching approaches.

It Can Hinder People from Seeing the Big Picture

When I was a young Christian, I attended a church in which we decided in our weekly Bible study to go through the book of Revelation. We were an ambitious group. Every Wednesday night we sought to understand and apply this book to our context. Every week we would delve into a passage and glean from it as much as we could. The elderly gentleman leading the study would break down each phrase and verse, offering up numerous word studies from W. E. Vine's *Expository Dictionary*[7] in between explanations of history, ancient culture, and the odd bit of geography. I would write down as quickly as possible each gold nugget, every word meaning, every nuance. Questions abounded regarding issues of timing, apocalyptic images, and where our contemporary history fit within the pages of Revelation. We were doing serious exposition of the text—or so we thought. In reality, however, if you were to ask me on any given Wednesday during the three years I attended the study where each passage fit, or more important, what was the main thrust of the book, I couldn't have told you. I could see the trees but not the forest. This, of course, can be one of the great dangers of expository preaching.

Expository preaching can tend to zoom so far into a passage that it fails to zoom out and see the larger theological thrust of the passage, the chapter, or even the book. While one may be impressed with someone preaching twelve years through Romans, such a laborious approach may be unhelpful in expressing the larger theme(s) of the book if not showered with regular big-picture review.

Expository preaching that fails to present the larger themes of units, chapters, and books and couch them in the larger framework of Scripture may hinder a holistic understanding of the unity of Scripture. Rather than shining light on the big themes and purposes of the whole, it can easily fall into a reductionism that presents the Bible as a collection of weekly maxims and principles to live by.

It Lends Itself to Particular Styles of Learning

Some might see this limitation as a good thing. If part of the goal of preaching is to exhort a particular audience, then one must communicate in a manner that is appropriate for that group. For many groups, however—particularly those in the majority world—the proposition-based expository approach to preaching is not the culturally familiar method of learning and may be the least helpful.

The shift in educational theory and practice over recent years (which I described in chapter 1) demands that we continue to examine the best ways of communicating. When I think back on my schoolboy days, I remember chalky blackboards, heavy textbooks, and being forced to learn by rote information I would be expected to reproduce on paper at the final exam. My children, however, are receiving an education that is largely interactive, collaborative, and problem based. Shifts in technology, changes in cultural expectation, and new discoveries about learning style have given birth to new ways of expression and a better understanding of how we learn. Just as teachers and administrators have had to adapt to these seismic shifts in the field of education, we also need to take seriously how people learn as we make our way to the pulpit.

The linear nature of learning by proposition and clearly structured outlines suits many of us. But for many in the West under the age of thirty and for those learning and listening in majority world contexts, story, narrative, collaboration, and poetry may be more familiar mediums of teaching. Too firmly holding on to styles we're comfortable with may hinder us from reaching these groups.

It Doesn't Guarantee That God Sets the Agenda

One line sometimes overplayed by many of us in regard to expository preaching is that it lets God set the agenda of the sermon. While it is true that working through a book of the Bible means we must preach what is before us rather than selecting whatever we want to preach, every sermon—including expository ones—involves human decisions:

which book to preach, how large or small a unit to use, whether to preach Mark over six weeks, sixteen weeks, or twenty-six weeks. In preparing sermons, the preacher must consider time restraints, audience, and the series' purpose. To suggest that preaching sequentially through the chapters of a book is following God's agenda is overly simplistic. Every preacher, no matter the preaching style, should approach the sermon with a deep dependence on the Spirit for direction. If sequential exposition of chapters were the only proper way to follow the text, then most of the sermons recorded in the New Testament wouldn't be deemed as following God's agenda. Peter, Stephen, Paul, and the author of Hebrews make use of multiple, nonsequential texts in their sermons.

Over the past 150 years of the church in the West, expository preaching has enjoyed pride of place in many pulpits. Sermons that walk through verses, units, and whole books of Scripture have yielded great fruit, and there is good reason to value this style of preaching. As with all forms of communication, however, it has its shortcomings. For these reasons, among others, it is time to consider other, complementary styles of preaching, such as the topical sermon.

NOTES

Chapter 1: Embracing the Topical Sermon

1. For the benefits and limitations of expository preaching, see appendix 2.
2. Grant Wacker, "How Billy Graham Learned the Art of Preaching," *Christianity Today*, August 27, 2019, https://www.christianitytoday.com/ct /2019/august-web-only/billy-graham-learned-art-of-preaching.html?utm _medium=widgetsocial. Accessed April 3, 2021.
3. Gary Chapman, *The Five Love Languages* (Chicago: Northfield Publishing, 2015).
4. Fred Sanders, *The Deep Things of God: How the Trinity Changes Everything* (Wheaton: Crossway, 2010), 18.
5. It should be noted that expository sermons often begin with the development of an existential need or issue. The major difference between expository and topical sermons, however, is that topical sermons not only raise an issue in the introduction but also use that issue to provide the structure for the remainder of the message.
6. Helmut Thielicke, quoted in *Leadership Journal* 6, no. 1 (1985): 126.
7. Sadly, such preaching is often done under the banner of "faithful preaching." I regularly hear dull, unenthused preaching without life, passion, or relevance. But as long as facts are given, the preaching is considered faithful. I would suggest that if you are boring people with your preaching, you need to find a different ministry.
8. Bryan Chapell, *Christ-Centered Sermons: Models of Redemptive Preaching* (Grand Rapids: Baker Academic, 2013), 55–56.

Chapter 2: How to Approach a Topic

1. I owe my insights to Greg Clarke, formerly from Centre for Public Christianity, Bible Society Australia, thence City Bible Forum, but now with the Australian Institute of Music, who presented the basis of this material in a guest lecture on "Cultural Critique" at a Master of Arts Intensive on "Building Character: The Preacher and Preaching" at Sydney Missionary and Bible College, July

2007. These are my recollections of what Clarke said; unfortunately I can no longer find the handwritten notes that I took during Clarke's lecture.

2. This is my modification of the W-Spectrum, formulated by Warrick Farah and Kyle Meeker, as first described in "The W-Spectrum: Worker Paradigms in Muslim Contexts," *Evangelical Missions Quarterly* 51, no. 4 (October 2015): 366–75, and later appropriated in my book *Evangelism in a Skeptical World: How to Make the Unbelievable News about Jesus More Believable* (Grand Rapids: Zondervan, 2018), 168–70.

Chapter 3: How to Preach to Two Audiences

1. John Dickson, *Hearing Her Voice* (Grand Rapids: Zondervan, 2014), 25.
2. Tim Keller, *Preaching* (London: Hodder & Stoughton, 2015), 51.
3. Bryan Chapell, *Christ-Centered Preaching: Redeeming the Expository Sermon*, 3rd ed. (Grand Rapids: Baker Academic, 2018), 253.
4. Chapell, *Christ-Centered Preaching*, 283.

Chapter 4: How to Address a Topic Theologically

1. This sidebar is a summary and development of ideas explored in chapters 8 and 9 of my previous book, *Evangelism in a Skeptical World*.
2. Don Carson, "Systematic Theology and Biblical Theology," in *New Dictionary of Biblical Theology*, ed. T. Desmond Alexander, Brian S. Rosner, D. A. Carson, and Graeme Goldsworthy (Downers Grove: InterVarsity, 2000), 89–104.
3. David Clark, *To Know and Love God: Method for Theology* (Wheaton: Crossway, 2003), 48–51.
4. I owe these insights to my PhD supervisor, Graham Cole.
5. There is a good discussion about definitions in Julian Baggini and Peter S. Fosl, *The Philosopher's Toolkit: A Compendium of Philosophical Concepts and Methods* (Malden, MA: Blackwell, 2003), 28–31.

    An infamous example of using a definition that is technically correct but not consistent with the audience's expectation of how the word is being used is Bill Clinton's quote, "It depends on what the meaning of the word *is* is."

    See William Safire, "On Language; Alone with 'Alone,' or What 'Is' Is," *www.nytimes.com/1998/10/11/magazine/on-language-alone-with-alone-or -what-is-is.html*. Accessed April 23, 2020.
6. Clayton Christensen, *The Innovator's Dilemma: The Revolutionary Book That Will Change the Way You Do Business* (New York: Harper Business, 2003).
7. Peter Thiel, *Zero to One: Notes on Startups, or How to Build the Future* (London: Virgin, 2014).
8. I owe this insight to Bruce Dipple, my former pastor and a missionary in West Africa with SIM.
9. Ira Glass and Malcolm Gladwell, "Choosing Wrong," *This American Life*,

episode 590 (June 24, 2016), *www.thisamericanlife.org/radio-archives /episode/590/choosing-wrong*.

10. Tom Morris, *If Aristotle Ran General Motors: The New Soul of Business* (New York: Henry Holt, 1998), 33, Kindle.

11. The use of bullet points on a PowerPoint slide is now blamed for the Space Shuttle *Columbia* disaster. Information that communicated the risk of tragedy was lost in the torrent of data on the PowerPoint slide. See James Thomas, "Death by PowerPoint: The Slide That Killed Seven People," *https:// mcdreeamiemusings.com/blog/2019/4/13/gsux1h6bnt8lqjd7w2t2mtvfg81uhx.*

Chapter 5: How to Address a Topic Culturally

1. This and the next chapter borrow but then develop ideas from chapter 5 in my book *Evangelism in a Skeptical World* (Grand Rapids: Zondervan, 2018).

2. I owe this insight to Matthew Kim—that we need CQ (cultural intelligence) in addition to EQ (emotional intelligence) and IQ (informational intelligence). Matthew D. Kim, *Preaching with Cultural Intelligence: Understanding the People Who Hear Our Sermons* (Grand Rapids: Baker, 2017).

3. I am borrowing deeply from Jackson Wu's categories of, definition of, and insights on contextualization—especially that contextualization is more than communication and application; it is also the interpretation of the Bible through a particular culture's lens. See Jackson Wu, *One Gospel for All Nations: A Practical Approach to Biblical Contextualization* (Pasadena: William Carey Library, 2015), Kindle; *Saving God's Face: A Chinese Contextualization of Salvation through Honor and Shame*, EMS Dissertation Series (Pasadena: William Carey International Univ. Press, 2012), 10–68.

4. I owe this insight to David K. Clark, *To Know and Love God: Method for Theology* (Wheaton: Crossway, 2003), 119.

5. For more on the differences between high- and low-context cultures, indirect communication cultures and direct communication cultures, and event- and time-based cultures, see Sarah A. Lanier, *Foreign to Familiar* (Hagerstown: McDougal, 2000).

6. For more on how to speak to concrete-relational learners, see chapter 7 in my book *Evangelism in a Skeptical World* (Grand Rapids: Zondervan, 2018). See also Christine Dillon, *Telling the Gospel through Story: Evangelism That Keeps Hearers Wanting More* (Downers Grove: IVP, 2012).

7. I learned this insight from my PhD supervisor, Graham Cole.

8. Further discussions can be found in Paul G. Hiebert, *Transforming Worldviews: An Anthropological Understanding of How People Change* (Grand Rapids: Baker, 2008), 258–60, 274–76; *Anthropological Reflections on Missiological Issues* (Grand Rapids: Baker, 1994), 71–72; *The Gospel in Human Contexts: Anthropological Explorations for Contemporary Missions* (Grand Rapids: Baker, 2009), 123–25.

9. I owe these categories—"enter" and "challenge"—to Timothy Keller, from his "Contextualization: Wisdom or Compromise?" talk given at Covenant Seminary Connect Conference, 2004.
10. Keller, "Contextualization: Wisdom or Compromise?"
11. The final row of this table is from Paul G. Hiebert, "Critical Contextualization," *International Bulletin of Mission Research* 11, no. 3 (1987): 104–12.

Chapter 6: How to Interpret Culture

1. This chapter borrows but then develops ideas from chapter 5 in my book *Evangelism in a Skeptical World* (Grand Rapids: Zondervan, 2018).
2. Kevin J. Vanhoozer calls them "worlds" of meaning (worldview) and "works" of meaning (texts) in *Everyday Theology: How to Read Cultural Texts and Interpret Trends*, ed. Kevin J. Vanhoozer, Charles A. Anderson, and Michael J. Sleasman (Grand Rapids: Baker, 2007), 26–27.
3. Matthew D. Kim, *Preaching with Cultural Intelligence: Understanding the People Who Hear Our Sermons* (Grand Rapids: Baker, 2017).
4. I believe I got this list from a class on cultural hermeneutics that Kevin J. Vanhoozer taught at Trinity Evangelical Divinity School, Deerfield, Illinois, in 2001.
5. Paul Hiebert's appropriation of Morris Opler's "themes and counterthemes," Emmanuel Todd's demography, and Talcott Parsons' evaluative themes, in Paul G. Hiebert, *Transforming Worldviews: An Anthropological Understanding of How People Change* (Grand Rapids: Baker, 2008), 26–27, 63–64.
6. This is something I write more about in chapters 3, 5, and 6 in *Evangelism in a Skeptical World*.
7. Keller, "Contextualization: Wisdom or Compromise?"
8. I learned this idea—that Jesus is not just the happily ever after but also the far better happily ever after than we dared imagine—from Sam Hilton, a pastor at Hunter Bible Church, Australia. But I've also recently discovered it in a must-watch talk: Andy Crouch, "The Structure of a Story," Echo Conference, *www.youtube.com/watch?v=zmH6seCjDTc*.
9. I heard this advice many years ago in a talk from Timothy Keller.

Chapter 7: How to Address a Topic Pastorally

1. Robert W. Yarbrough, *The Letters to Timothy and Titus* (Grand Rapids: Eerdmans, 2018), 436.

Chapter 8: How to Trace the Topic to Christ

1. Arthur C. Brooks, "Are We Trading Our Happiness for Modern Comforts?" *Atlantic*, October 22, 2020, *www.theatlantic.com/family/archive/2020/10/why-life-has-gotten-more-comfortable-less-happy/616807/*.
2. Robert Waldinger, "What Makes a Good Life? Lessons from the Longest

Study on Happiness," TED, November 2015, *www.ted.com/talks/robert _waldinger_what_makes_a_good_life_lessons_from_the_longest_study_on _happiness.*

Chapter 9: How to Connect with Your Audience

1. Charles Spurgeon, *Lectures to My Students on the Art of Preaching* (Fearn: Christian Focus, 1998), 145.
2. Tim Keller was listed by Baylor University as one of the twelve most influential preachers in the English-speaking world in 2018. See https://www .baylor.edu/truett/index.php?id=951204. Accessed April 4, 2021.
3. Keller identifies the challenge and temptation of those in preaching ministry when he comments, "Preachers today feel under much more pressure to be spectacular than they used to feel. Christians are much less likely to be loyal to a church of a particular place or a particular theological tradition. What they want is to have a great experience on Sunday, and that means they will travel to get to the most gifted preachers. When you put this pressure together with (a) a busy week in which you haven't felt able to prepare well, and (b) the accessibility of so much sermon material through the internet— the temptation to simply re-preach someone else's sermon is very strong." See Tim Keller, "TGC Asks Tim Keller: When Has a Preacher Crossed the Line into Plagiarism in His Sermon?" The Gospel Coalition, December 20, 2010, https://www.thegospelcoalition.org/article/tgc-asks-tim-keller-when -has-a-preacher-crossed-the-line-into-plagiarism-in/. Accessed April 4, 2021.
4. Charles Spurgeon as quoted by Haddon Robinson, "Blending Bible Content and Life Application," in *Mastering Contemporary Preaching*, by Bill Hybels, Stuart Briscoe, and Haddon Robinson (Portland, OR: Multnomah, 1989), 57.
5. Tim Keller, "Dwell Conference Workbook" (unpublished, April 2008), 28–29.
6. Karyn Hobbs, Sonia Clarke, Amuy Rathborne, "The Power of Visual Communication: Showing Your Story to Land the Message," Pricewater houseCoopers, April 2017, https://www.pwc.com.au/the-difference/the -power-of-visual-communication-apr17.pdf. Accessed April 5, 2021.
7. D. L. Nelson, V. S. Reed, and J. R. Walling, "Pictorial Superiority Effect," *Journal of Experimental Psychology: Human Learning and Memory* 2, no. 5 (1976): 523–28.
8. D. M. McBride and B. A. Dosher, "A Comparison of Conscious and Automatic Memory Processes for Picture and Word Stimuli: A Process Dissociation Analysis," *Consciousness and Cognition* 11 (2002): 423–60.

Chapter 10: How to Deliver a Message Worth Hearing

1. Tim Keller, *Preaching* (London: Hodder and Stoughton, 2015), 14.
2. Haddon Robinson, *Biblical Preaching*, 2nd ed. (Grand Rapids, Baker, 2001), 143.
3. For an introduction to this approach, see Eugene Lowry, *The Homiletical Plot:*

The Sermon as Narrative Art Form, expanded ed. (Louisville: Westminster John Knox Press, 2001).

4. David Wenham, "Why I Became an Actor," TED, May 2019, *www.ted.com /talks/david_wenham_why_i_became_an_actor.*

Appendix 1: Topical Preaching and the COVID-19 Pandemic

1. I explored these ideas in work I did with City Bible Forum, called *The Post-Covid Playbook.* You can watch my short, three- to five-minute videos and download the pdf at *bit.ly/postcovidplaybook.*

2. David Brooks, "The First Invasion of America: And the Cultural Earthquake It's Unleashing," *New York Times*, May 21, 2020, *www.nytimes.com/2020 /05/21/opinion/us-coronavirus-history.html*; Christina Zhou, "Why Are Western Countries Being Hit Harder Than East Asian Countries by Coronavirus?" ABC, April 24, 2020, *www.abc.net.au/news/2020–04 –24/coronavirus-response-in-china-south-korea-italy-uk-us-singapore /12158504*; Martin Jacques, "Why East Asia Has Done So Much Better Than the West," World Insight, CGTN, April 22, 2020, *www.martinjacques.com /when-china-rules-the-world/interviews/why-east-asia-has-done-so-much -better-than-the-west/.*

3. David Brooks, "The Pandemic of Fear and Agony: Readers Open Up about Their Mental States," *New York Times*, April 9, 2020, *www.nytimes.com/2020 /04/09/opinion/covid-anxiety.html*; Matthias Pierce et al., "Mental Health before and during the COVID-19 Pandemic: A Longitudinal Probability Sample Survey of the UK Population," *Lancet Psychiatry* 7, no. 10 (Oct. 2020): 883–92, *www.thelancet.com/pdfs/journals/lanpsy/PIIS2215–0366(20)30308–4.pdf.*

4. David Brooks, "Pandemics Kill Compassion, Too: You May Not Like Who You're about to Become," *New York Times*, March 12, 2020, *www.nytimes .com/2020/03/12/opinion/pandemic-coronavirus-compassion.html.*

5. Peter M. Sandman, *Responding to Community Outrage: Strategies for Effective Risk Communication* (American Industrial Hygiene Association, 1993), *http://psandman.com/media/RespondingtoCommunityOutrage.pdf.*

6. From my foggy memory I owe this insight to Craig Springer, Alpha, USA, from his talk at Amplify Outreach Conference 2020, Wheaton, Illinois, and to Ric Thorpe, a church-planting expert in the UK, at a seminar hosted by Alpha, Australia.

7. I credit this observation to Collin Hansen's excellent discussion with Andy Crouch in "What's Next for Our Culture with COVID," in his podcast *Gospelbound*, March 9, 2020, *www.thegospelcoalition.org/podcasts/gospel bound/whats-next-culture-covid.*

8. Nate Sloan and Charlie Harding, "The Culture Warped Pop, For Good," *New York Times*, March 14, 2021, *www.nytimes.com/interactive/2021/03/14 /opinion/pop-music-songwriting.html.*

9. Glen Scrivener, "How to Present to Camera," *Speak Life*, March 30, 2020, *https://youtu.be/UyLeB6VtFVE*.
10. Karl Faase, "7 Hints for Speaking to Camera," *Olive Tree Media, https://vimeo.com/401232380*.
11. Dominic Steele, "What TV Professionals Want Preachers to Know about Communicating through a Camera," *The Pastor's Heart, https://www.the pastorsheart.net/podcast/what-tv-professionals-want*.
12. It was mind-boggling! Here are a few of the organizations that I spoke at: Bain Consulting, Melbourne, Australia; Oxford Inter-Collegiate Christian Union (OICCU), UK; Fellowship of Evangelists in the Universities of Europe (FEUER), all over Europe; Amplify Outreach Conference, Wheaton, IL, USA; Campus Outreach, Bradley University, Peoria, IL, USA; Barnabas, Sydney, Australia; Resource Global, Asia. Shout-out to all of you for taking a chance on the technology and on me to make it all happen.
13. *The Post-Covid Playbook* is available at *bit.ly/postcovidplaybook*.
14. My friends point out counterexamples such as Jordan Peterson or Joe Rogan, whose YouTube videos go longer than one hour. I've often thought about how they can get away with this. I believe it's because these particular counterexamples are playing the culture wars game. They preach to the converted. People watch them to see them score points over the other side. However, that's not the game we're playing. Often I'm preaching to the unconverted. I'm preaching to a disinterested and hostile audience. So I don't have the luxury of time. I need to get their attention quickly and say what I need to say before they've had a chance to disengage and turn away.

Appendix 2: The Benefits and Limitations of Expository Preaching

1. The famed Welsh preacher Martyn Lloyd-Jones is said to have spent more than a decade expositing Paul's letter to the Romans. He preached through the book phrase by phrase, unit by unit.
2. Haddon Robinson, *Biblical Preaching*, 3rd ed. (Grand Rapids: Baker Academic, 2014), 5.
3. Abraham Kuruvilla, *A Vision for Preaching* (Grand Rapids: Baker Academic, 2015), 13.
4. Bryan Chapell, *Christ-Centered Preaching* (Grands Rapids: Baker Academic, 2018), 8–9.
5. D. A. Carson, *Exegetical Fallacies* (Grand Rapids: Baker Academic, 1996).
6. This is highlighted in many of the works by our friend and fellow homiletician Abraham Kuruvilla. See Abraham Kuruvilla, "Time to Kill the Big Idea?" *Journal of the Evangelical Theological Society* 61, no. 4 (2018): 825–46.
7. I would later discover this to be an unreliable source in regard to Greek word studies.